The Top Mediterranean Diet

Cookbook for Beginners 2023

1800 Days Simple, Easy and Amazing Mouthwatering Mediterranean Recipes to Help You Build Healthy Habits | 30-Day Meal Plan

Kadin H. Wehner

Table of Contents

Chapter 5 Beef, Pork, and Lamb

Chapter 6 Poultry

Chapter 7 Beans and Grains

Chapter 8 Vegetables and Sides

Chapter 9 Vegetarian Mains 65

Chapter 10 Pizzas, Wraps, and Sandwiches 73

Chapter 11 Salads 78

Chapter 12 Pasta 85

Chapter 13 Desserts — 91

Chapter 14 Snacks and Appetizers — 98

Chapter 15 Staples, Sauces, Dips, and Dressings — 106

Appendix 1: Measurement Conversion Chart — 111

Appendix 2: The Dirty Dozen and Clean Fifteen — 112

INTRODUCTION

Welcome to the delicious world of the The Top Mediterranean Diet Cookbook for Beginners 2023! Get ready to indulge in mouth-watering dishes that are not only scrumptious but also incredibly healthy. This cookbook is your ultimate guide to cooking up a storm with fresh and vibrant ingredients, inspired by the culinary traditions of the Mediterranean region. Whether you're a seasoned chef or a beginner in the kitchen, this cookbook is perfect for anyone who wants to explore new flavors and enjoy a healthier lifestyle. So, grab your apron and get ready to embark on a culinary journey that will tantalize your taste buds and leave you feeling satisfied and nourished. Bon appétit!

As a writer and avid traveler, I've had the opportunity to explore some of the most beautiful and exotic places on earth. From the bustling streets of Tokyo to the sun-kissed beaches of Bali, I've experienced a world full of vibrant cultures, breathtaking landscapes, and, of course, delicious food.

But no matter where my travels took me, there was one region that always stood out for its incredible cuisine: the Mediterranean. From the fresh seafood of the Greek islands to the fragrant spices of Morocco, the Mediterranean is a culinary paradise that has captured my heart and taste buds.

So, when I returned home from my latest adventure, I knew I had to share my love of Mediterranean cuisine with the world. That's why I wrote this cookbook - to bring the flavors and traditions of this amazing region into your kitchen and onto your plate.

Through my travels, I've learned that food is more than just sustenance; it's a way to connect with people, to learn about their culture and history, and to create memories that last a lifetime. And that's exactly what I hope this cookbook will do for you - inspire you to explore new flavors, try new recipes, and connect with the rich culinary heritage of the Mediterranean.

So, whether you're a seasoned chef or a beginner in the kitchen, I invite you to join me on a culinary journey that will take you from the shores of Greece to the markets of Morocco, and beyond. Let's cook up some delicious memories together!

Brief Overview of the Mediterranean Diet

The Mediterranean diet is a way of eating that is inspired by the traditional dietary patterns of countries surrounding the Mediterranean Sea, such as Greece, Italy, and Spain. It has gained popularity in recent years due to its many health benefits, including reducing the risk of heart disease, stroke, and certain types of cancer.

The Mediterranean diet emphasizes eating whole, unprocessed foods such as fruits, vegetables, whole grains, legumes, nuts, and seeds. Fish and seafood are also important components of this diet, while red meat is consumed in moderation. Olive oil is the primary source of fat, and herbs and spices are used to flavor dishes instead of salt.

In addition to its emphasis on healthy foods, the Mediterranean diet also encourages socializing and enjoying meals with family and friends. It promotes mindful eating and savoring food, rather than rushing through meals or snacking mindlessly.

Overall, the Mediterranean diet is a balanced and sustainable approach to eating that focuses on nourishing the body with wholesome, nutrient-dense foods while also promoting a healthy relationship with food and a sense of community.

Benefits of Following the Mediterranean Diet

The Mediterranean diet is a well-known and highly recommended way of eating that has been associated with numerous health benefits. Here are some of the benefits of following the Mediterranean diet in detail:

1. Reduces the Risk of Heart Disease: The Mediterranean diet is rich in heart-healthy foods such as fruits, vegetables, whole grains, nuts, and olive oil. It also emphasizes lean protein sources such as fish and poultry, while limiting red meat intake. Studies have shown that following the Mediterranean diet can reduce the risk of heart disease by up to 30%.

2. Lowers Blood Pressure: High blood pressure is a major risk factor for heart disease, stroke, and kidney disease. The Mediterranean diet is naturally low in sodium and high in potassium, which helps to lower blood pressure levels.

3. Helps with Weight Loss: The Mediterranean diet is not a strict calorie-restricted diet, but rather a balanced and sustainable approach to eating. It emphasizes whole, nutrient-dense foods that are filling and satisfying, making it easier to maintain a healthy weight over time.

4. Reduces the Risk of Type 2 Diabetes: The Mediterranean diet is rich in fiber, which helps to regulate blood sugar levels and prevent insulin resistance. Studies have shown that following the Mediterranean diet can reduce the risk of developing type 2 diabetes by up to 50%.

5. Improves Brain Health: The Mediterranean diet is rich in antioxidants, healthy fats, and anti-inflammatory compounds, all of which are important for brain health. Studies have shown that following the Mediterranean diet can improve cognitive function, reduce the risk of Alzheimer's disease, and slow down age-related cognitive decline.

6. Promotes Longevity: The Mediterranean diet is associated with a longer lifespan and a reduced risk of premature death. Studies have shown that following the Mediterranean diet can increase life expectancy by up to 10 years.

In summary, the Mediterranean diet is a healthy and sustainable way of eating that can improve overall health and reduce the risk of chronic diseases. It emphasizes whole, nutrient-dense foods, promotes a healthy relationship with food, and encourages socializing and enjoying meals with family and friends.

Importance of a Balanced and Nutritious Diet

A balanced and nutritious diet is essential for maintaining good health and preventing chronic diseases. Here are some of the reasons why a balanced and nutritious diet is important in detail:

1. Provides Essential Nutrients: A balanced and nutritious diet provides the body with all the essential nutrients it needs to function properly, including vitamins, minerals, protein, carbohydrates, and healthy fats. These nutrients are necessary for maintaining strong bones, healthy skin, a robust immune system, and optimal organ function.

2. Reduces the Risk of Chronic Diseases: A balanced and nutritious diet can help reduce the risk of chronic diseases such as heart disease, stroke, type 2 diabetes, and certain types of cancer. This is because a diet rich in fruits, vegetables, whole grains, lean protein sources, and healthy fats can help lower blood pressure, reduce inflammation, and improve insulin sensitivity.

3. Promotes Healthy Weight Management: A balanced and nutritious diet can help maintain a healthy weight by providing the body with nutrient-dense foods that are filling and satisfying. Eating a variety of foods from different food groups can also help prevent overeating and promote portion control.

4. Boosts Energy Levels: A balanced and nutritious diet can provide the body with sustained energy throughout the day. Foods that are high in fiber, protein, and healthy fats can help regulate blood sugar levels and prevent energy crashes.

5. Improves Mental Health: A balanced and nutritious diet can also have a positive impact on mental health. Studies have shown that diets high in fruits, vegetables, whole grains, and omega-3 fatty acids can help reduce symptoms of depression and anxiety.

In summary, a balanced and nutritious diet is important for overall health and well-being. It provides the body with essential nutrients, reduces the risk of chronic diseases, promotes healthy weight management, boosts energy levels, and improves mental health. By making small changes to your diet and incorporating more nutrient-dense foods, you can reap the many benefits of a balanced and nutritious diet.

Chapter 1 Basics of the Mediterranean Diet

Key Food Groups and Their Nutritional Benefits

The Mediterranean diet is a healthy and balanced way of eating that emphasizes whole, nutrient-dense foods. Here are some key food groups in the Mediterranean diet and their nutritional benefits:

1. Fruits and Vegetables: Fruits and vegetables are an important part of the Mediterranean diet. They are rich in vitamins, minerals, antioxidants, and fiber, which can help reduce the risk of chronic diseases such as heart disease, stroke, and cancer. Eating a variety of colorful fruits and vegetables can also help improve digestion, boost immunity, and promote healthy skin.

2. Whole Grains: Whole grains such as brown rice, quinoa, and whole wheat pasta are a staple in the Mediterranean diet. They are high in fiber, vitamins, and minerals, and can help regulate blood sugar levels and reduce the risk of heart disease and type 2 diabetes. Eating whole grains can also help you feel fuller for longer and prevent overeating.

3. Legumes: Legumes such as lentils, chickpeas, and beans are a great source of plant-based protein, fiber, and complex carbohydrates. They are also low in fat and can help reduce the risk of heart disease, lower cholesterol levels, and improve digestive health.

4. Nuts and Seeds: Nuts and seeds such as almonds, walnuts, and chia seeds are a great source of healthy fats, protein, and fiber. They can help reduce inflammation, lower cholesterol levels, and improve brain function. Eating nuts and seeds in moderation can also help with weight management, as they are filling and satisfying.

5. Fish and Seafood: Fish and seafood are an important source of lean protein in the Mediterranean diet. They are also rich in omega-3 fatty acids, which can help reduce inflammation, lower blood pressure, and improve heart health. Eating fish and seafood at least twice a week can help reduce the risk of chronic diseases and promote overall health.

6. Olive Oil: Olive oil is a primary source of fat in the Mediterranean diet. It is rich in monounsaturated fats, which can help reduce inflammation, lower cholesterol levels, and improve heart health. Using olive oil instead of other types of oils or butter can also help with weight management.

In summary, the key food groups in the Mediterranean diet are fruits and vegetables, whole grains, legumes, nuts and seeds, fish and seafood, and olive oil. These foods are nutrient-dense and provide a wide range of health benefits, including reducing the risk of chronic diseases and promoting overall health and well-being.

Portion Sizes and Recommended Daily Intake

Here are some general guidelines for portion sizes and recommended daily intake based on the Mediterranean diet:

1. Fruits and Vegetables: Aim for at least 5 servings of fruits and vegetables per day. A serving size is typically 1 cup of raw or cooked vegetables or 1 medium-sized fruit.

2. Whole Grains: Aim for 3-4 servings of whole grains per day. A serving size is typically 1/2 cup of cooked grains or 1 slice of whole grain bread.

3. Legumes: Aim for 2-3 servings of legumes per week. A serving size is typically 1/2 cup of cooked legumes.

4. Nuts and Seeds: Aim for a handful (about 1/4 cup) of nuts and seeds per day.

5. Fish and Seafood: Aim for at least 2 servings of fish and seafood per week. A serving size is typically 3-4 ounces.

6. Olive Oil: Aim for 2-3 tablespoons of olive oil per day.

7. Dairy: Aim for 2-3 servings of dairy products per day. A serving size is typically 1 cup of milk or yogurt or 1.5 ounces of cheese.

8. Poultry, Eggs, and Red Meat: These should be consumed in moderation. A serving size of poultry or red meat is typically 3-4 ounces, while a serving size of eggs is 1-2 eggs.

9. Sweets and Desserts: These should be consumed in moderation. Try to limit your intake of processed sweets and desserts and opt for natural sweeteners such as honey or fresh fruit instead.

It's important to note that these are general guidelines and individual needs may vary depending on factors such as age, gender, activity level, and overall health status. It's also important to pay attention to portion sizes and listen to your body's hunger and fullness cues.

In summary, following the Mediterranean diet involves eating a variety of whole, nutrient-dense foods in moderation. Paying attention to portion sizes and recommended daily intake can help ensure that you are getting all the nutrients you need while maintaining a healthy weight and reducing the risk of chronic diseases.

Chapter 2 Getting Started with the Mediterranean Diet

Essential Kitchen Tools and Equipment

The Mediterranean diet emphasizes whole, nutrient-dense foods that are often prepared using simple cooking methods. Here are some essential kitchen tools and equipment for the Mediterranean diet:

1. Chef's Knife: A good quality chef's knife is essential for preparing fruits, vegetables, and meats for Mediterranean dishes.

2. Cutting Board: A sturdy cutting board is necessary for chopping and slicing ingredients for Mediterranean recipes.

3. Grater: A grater can be used to grate cheese, vegetables, and citrus zest for Mediterranean dishes.

4. Garlic Press: A garlic press is a handy tool for crushing garlic cloves quickly and easily.

5. Blender or Food Processor: A blender or food processor can be used to make sauces, dips, and smoothies using Mediterranean ingredients such as tomatoes, herbs, and nuts.

6. Salad Spinner: A salad spinner can help wash and dry greens quickly and efficiently for Mediterranean salads.

7. Baking Sheet: A baking sheet is useful for roasting vegetables and fish in the oven.

8. Non-Stick Skillet: A non-stick skillet is ideal for sautéing vegetables, cooking eggs, and searing fish for Mediterranean recipes.

9. Dutch Oven: A Dutch oven is a versatile piece of cookware that can be used for making stews, soups, and casseroles with Mediterranean ingredients such as legumes and whole grains.

10. Citrus Juicer: A citrus juicer can be used to extract juice from lemons, limes, and oranges for use in Mediterranean recipes.

In summary, these essential kitchen tools and equipment can help you prepare healthy and delicious Mediterranean meals at home. By investing in quality tools and equipment, you can make meal prep easier and more efficient while enjoying the many health benefits of the Mediterranean diet.

Meal Planning and Grocery Shopping Tips

Meal planning and grocery shopping are important aspects of following the Mediterranean diet. Here are some tips to help you plan and shop for healthy and delicious Mediterranean meals:

1. Plan Your Meals: Take some time each week to plan your meals and snacks for the upcoming week. This will help you stay on track with your healthy eating goals and avoid impulse purchases at the grocery store.

2. Make a Grocery List: Once you have planned your meals, make a grocery list of the ingredients you will need. This will help you stay organized at the store and avoid forgetting any important items.

3. Shop the Perimeter of the Store: When you arrive at the grocery store, start by shopping the perimeter of the store where fresh produce, meats, and dairy products are typically located. These whole, nutrient-dense foods are the foundation of the Mediterranean diet.

4. Choose Whole Foods: Focus on choosing whole, minimally processed foods such as fruits, vegetables, whole grains, legumes, nuts, and seeds. Avoid packaged and processed foods that are high in added sugars, salt, and unhealthy fats.

5. Buy Seasonal Produce: Choosing seasonal produce can help you save money and enjoy the freshest and most flavorful fruits and vegetables.

6. Stock Up on Staples: Keep your pantry stocked with Mediterranean staples such as olive oil, canned tomatoes, legumes, and whole grains so that you always have healthy options on hand.

7. Try New Recipes: Experiment with new Mediterranean recipes to keep your meals interesting and varied. Look for recipes that use seasonal ingredients and focus on whole, nutrient-dense foods.

8. Shop with a Full Stomach: Shopping on an empty stomach can lead to impulse purchases and unhealthy food choices. Eat a healthy snack or meal before heading to the store to help you make better choices.

In summary, meal planning and grocery shopping are important components of following the Mediterranean diet. By planning ahead, making a grocery list, and focusing on whole, nutrient-dense foods, you can enjoy healthy and delicious Mediterranean meals at home.

Incorporating Physical Activity into Your Lifestyle

Incorporating physical activity into your lifestyle is an important part of maintaining a healthy and balanced Mediterranean diet. Here are some tips to help you get started:

1. Start Slowly: If you're new to exercise, start slowly and gradually increase the intensity and duration of your workouts over time. This will help prevent injury and ensure that you enjoy the process.

2. Find Activities You Enjoy: Choose activities that you enjoy such as walking, swimming, cycling, or dancing. This will help you stay motivated and make exercise feel less like a chore.

3. Make it a Habit: Schedule regular workouts into your weekly routine and treat them as non-negotiable appointments with yourself. This will help you establish a consistent exercise habit.

4. Mix It Up: Vary your workouts to prevent boredom and challenge different muscle groups. Try incorporating strength training, cardio, and flexibility exercises into your routine.

5. Get Outside: Take advantage of the great outdoors by going for a hike, bike ride, or swim in the ocean. Fresh air and sunshine can do wonders for your mood and overall health.

6. Involve Friends and Family: Exercise with friends and family members to make it more fun and social. Join a group fitness class or organize a weekend hike with friends.

7. Stay Active Throughout the Day: Look for ways to stay active throughout the day, such as taking the stairs instead of the elevator, going for a walk during your lunch break, or doing a quick workout at home before work.

In summary, incorporating physical activity into your lifestyle is an important part of maintaining a healthy and balanced Mediterranean diet. By starting slowly, finding activities you enjoy, making it a habit, mixing it up, getting outside, involving friends and family, and staying active throughout the day, you can establish a sustainable exercise routine that supports your overall health and well-being.

Tips for Dining Out

Dining out can be a challenge when you're trying to follow a Mediterranean diet, but with a little planning and preparation, it's possible to make healthy choices while still enjoying the experience. Here are some tips for dining out:

1. Research the Restaurant: Before you go out to eat, research the restaurant online to see if they have a menu that includes Mediterranean-style dishes. Look for dishes that include whole grains, vegetables, lean proteins, and healthy fats.

2. Ask for Modifications: Don't be afraid to ask your server to modify your dish to fit your dietary needs. For example, you can ask for grilled chicken instead of fried, or request that your salad dressing be served on the side.

3. Choose Grilled or Baked Options: When ordering meat or fish, choose grilled or baked options instead of fried. This will help reduce the amount of unhealthy fats in your meal.

4. Start with a Salad: Starting your meal with a salad is a great way to fill up on nutrient-dense vegetables and fiber before moving on to the main course.

5. Share Dishes: Consider sharing dishes with your dining companions to help control portion sizes and avoid overeating.

6. Limit Alcohol Consumption: Alcohol can add unnecessary calories and disrupt your healthy eating goals. Consider limiting your alcohol consumption or choosing lower-calorie options such as wine or light beer.

7. Practice Mindful Eating: Take your time when eating and practice mindful eating by savoring each bite and paying attention to your body's hunger and fullness cues.

In summary, dining out can be challenging when following a Mediterranean diet, but with a little planning and preparation, it's possible to make healthy choices while still enjoying the experience. By researching the restaurant, asking for modifications, choosing grilled or baked options, starting with a salad, sharing dishes, limiting alcohol consumption, and practicing mindful eating, you can enjoy a delicious and nutritious meal while still sticking to your healthy eating goals.

Get Started

Making long-term dietary changes can be challenging, but it's important to remember that the benefits are worth it. By making healthier food choices, you can improve your overall health and reduce your risk of developing chronic diseases such as heart disease, diabetes, and certain types of cancer.

To help you make lasting changes, start by setting realistic goals. Instead of trying to overhaul your entire diet overnight, focus on making small changes that you can stick with over time. For example, try swapping out sugary drinks for water or reducing your portion sizes.

It's also important to find healthy foods that you enjoy. Experiment with different recipes and flavors to find meals that are both nutritious and delicious. And don't be afraid to ask for support from friends and family members. Having a support system can make all the difference when it comes to sticking to your dietary goals.

Remember, making long-term dietary changes is a journey, not a destination. Be patient with yourself and celebrate your successes along the way. With time and commitment, you can create a healthier lifestyle that will benefit you for years to come.

30-Day Meal Plan

DAYS	BREAKFAST	LUNCH	DINNER	SNACK/DESSERT
1	Butternut Squash and Ricotta Frittata	Quinoa Salad in Endive Boats	Crustless Spanakopita	Savory Lentil Dip
2	Tortilla Española (Spanish Omelet)	White Beans with Kale	Grilled Eggplant Stacks	Spiced Maple Nuts
3	Breakfast Panini with Eggs, Olives, and Tomatoes	Two-Bean Bulgur Chili	Cheese Stuffed Zucchini	Garlic-Mint Yogurt Dip
4	Kagianas	Quinoa Salad with Chicken, Chickpeas, and Spinach	Three-Cheese Zucchini Boats	Tirokafteri (Spicy Feta and Yogurt Dip)
5	Quinoa Porridge with Apricots	Barley Salad with Lemon-Tahini Dressing	Pesto Spinach Flatbread	Baked Eggplant Baba Ganoush
6	Breakfast Hash	Domatorizo (Greek Tomato Rice)	Cauliflower Rice-Stuffed Peppers	Mediterranean Trail Mix
7	Strawberry Collagen Smoothie	Garbanzo and Pita No-Bake Casserole	Vegetable Burgers	Black Bean Corn Dip
8	Veggie Hash with Eggs	White Bean Cassoulet	Stuffed Pepper Stew	Cheesy Dates
9	Oatmeal with Apple and Cardamom	Herbed Polenta	Root Vegetable Soup with Garlic Aioli	Bravas-Style Potatoes
10	Spanish Tortilla with Potatoes and Peppers	Cilantro Lime Rice	Cheesy Cauliflower Pizza Crust	Asiago Shishito Pepper
11	Marinara Eggs with Parsley	Broccoli Crust Pizza	Traditional Greek Salad	Smoky Baba Ghanoush
12	Summer Day Fruit Salad	Spinach-Artichoke Stuffed Mushrooms	Beets with Goat Cheese and Chermoula	Roasted Chickpeas
13	Heart-Healthy Hazelnut-Collagen Shake	Fava Bean Purée with Chicory	Beets with Goat Cheese and Chermoula	Roasted Mushrooms with Garlic
14	C+C Overnight Oats	Zucchini Lasagna	Tricolor Tomato Summer Salad	Cream Cheese Wontons
15	Tiropita (Greek Cheese Pie)	Stuffed Portobellos	Double-Apple Spinach Salad	Vegetable Pot Stickers
16	Feta and Herb Frittata	Tortellini in Red Pepper Sauce	Easy Greek Salad	Strawberry Ricotta Parfaits
17	Broccoli-Mushroom Frittata	Pistachio Mint Pesto Pasta	Riviera Tuna Salad	Minty Cantaloupe Granita
18	Smoky Sausage Patties	Tangy Asparagus and Broccoli	Endive with Shrimp	Banana Cream Pie Parfaits

DAYS	BREAKFAST	LUNCH	DINNER	SNACK/DESSERT
19	Spinach and Feta Egg Bake	Broccoli-Cheese Fritters	Sicilian Salad	Chocolate Pudding
20	Spinach Pie	Crispy Tofu	Spanish Potato Salad	Greek Yogurt Ricotta Mousse
21	Baked Ricotta with Pears	Mediterranean Quinoa and Garbanzo Salad	Tomato Rice	Blueberry Pomegranate Granita
22	Herb & Cheese Fritters	No-Mayo Florence Tuna Salad	White Beans with Garlic and Tomatoes	Roasted Honey-Cinnamon Apples
23	Greek Yogurt and Berries	Israeli Salad with Nuts and Seeds	White Bean and Barley Soup	Olive Oil Greek Yogurt Brownies
24	Gluten-Free Granola Cereal	Pistachio Quinoa Salad with Pomegranate Citrus Vinaigrette	Greek Chickpeas with Coriander and Sage	Spiced Baked Pears with Mascarpone
25	Kagianas	Italian Tuna and Olive Salad	Rice and Lentils	Strawberry Panna Cotta
26	Breakfast Hash	Roasted Broccoli Panzanella Salad	Garlic Shrimp with Quinoa	Cretan Cheese Pancakes
27	Veggie Hash with Eggs	French Lentil Salad with Parsley and Mint	Lentils with Cilantro and Lime	S'mores
28	Marinara Eggs with Parsley	Blackened Cajun Chicken Tenders	Moroccan Date Pilaf	Lemon Coconut Cake
29	Summer Day Fruit Salad	One-Pot Pork Loin Dinner	Fava Beans with Ground Meat	Grilled Peaches with Greek Yogurt
30	C+C Overnight Oats	Cod Gratin	No-Stir Polenta with Arugula, Figs, and Blue Cheese	Lemon Fool

Chapter 3 Breakfasts

Butternut Squash and Ricotta Frittata

Prep time: 10 minutes | Cook time: 33 minutes |
Serves 2 to 3

1 cup cubed (½-inch) butternut squash (5½ ounces / 156 g)
2 tablespoons olive oil
Kosher salt and freshly ground black pepper, to taste
4 fresh sage leaves, thinly sliced
6 large eggs, lightly beaten
½ cup ricotta cheese
Cayenne pepper

1. In a bowl, toss the squash with the olive oil and season with salt and black pepper until evenly coated. Sprinkle the sage on the bottom of a cake pan and place the squash on top. Place the pan in the air fryer and bake at 400ºF (204ºC) for 10 minutes. Stir to incorporate the sage, then cook until the squash is tender and lightly caramelized at the edges, about 3 minutes more. 2. Pour the eggs over the squash, dollop the ricotta all over, and sprinkle with cayenne. Bake at 300ºF (149ºC) until the eggs are set and the frittata is golden brown on top, about 20 minutes. Remove the pan from the air fryer and cut the frittata into wedges to serve.

Per Serving:
calories: 289 | fat: 22g | protein: 18g | carbs: 5g | fiber: 1g | sodium: 184mg

Tortilla Española (Spanish Omelet)

Prep time: 10 minutes | Cook time: 40 minutes |
Serves 4

1½ pounds (680 g) Yukon gold potatoes, scrubbed and thinly sliced
3 tablespoons olive oil, divided
1 teaspoon kosher salt, divided
1 sweet white onion, thinly sliced
3 cloves garlic, minced
8 eggs
½ teaspoon ground black pepper

1. Preheat the oven to 350°F(180°C). Line 2 baking sheets with parchment paper. 2. In a large bowl, toss the potatoes with 1 tablespoon of the oil and ½ teaspoon of the salt until well coated. Spread over the 2 baking sheets in a single layer. Roast the potatoes, rotating the baking sheets halfway through cooking, until tender but not browned, about 15 minutes. Using a spatula, remove the potatoes from the baking sheets and let cool until warm. 3. Meanwhile, in a medium skillet over medium-low heat, cook the onion in 1 tablespoon of the oil, stirring, until soft and golden, about 10 minutes. Add the garlic and cook until fragrant, about 2 minutes. Transfer the onion and garlic to a plate and let cool until warm. 4. In a large bowl, beat the eggs, pepper, and the remaining ½ teaspoon salt vigorously until the yolks and whites are completely combined and slightly frothy. Stir in the potatoes and onion and garlic and combine well, being careful not to break too many potatoes. 5. In the same skillet over medium-high heat, warm the remaining 1 tablespoon oil until shimmering, swirling to cover the whole surface. Pour in the egg mixture and spread the contents evenly. Cook for 1 minute and reduce the heat to medium-low. Cook until the edges of the egg are set and the center is slightly wet, about 8 minutes. Using a spatula, nudge the omelet to make sure it moves freely in the skillet. 6. Place a rimless plate, the size of the skillet, over the omelet. Place one hand over the plate and, in a swift motion, flip the omelet onto the plate. Slide the omelet back into the skillet, cooked side up. Cook until completely set, a toothpick inserted into the middle comes out clean, about 6 minutes. 7. Transfer to a serving plate and let cool for 5 minutes. Serve warm or room temperature.

Per Serving:
calories: 376 | fat: 19g | protein: 15g | carbs: 37g | fiber: 5g | sodium: 724mg

Kagianas

Prep time: 5 minutes | Cook time: 10 minutes |
Serves 2

2 teaspoons extra virgin olive oil
2 tablespoons finely chopped onion (any variety)
¼ teaspoon fine sea salt, divided
1 medium tomato (any variety), chopped
2 eggs
1 ounce (28 g) crumbled feta
½ teaspoon dried oregano
1 teaspoon chopped fresh mint
Pinch of freshly ground black pepper for serving

1. Heat the olive oil in a small pan placed over medium heat. When the oil begins to shimmer, add the onions along with ⅛ teaspoon sea salt. Sauté for about 3 minutes or until the onions are soft. 2. Add the tomatoes, stir, then reduce the heat to low and simmer for 8 minutes or until the mixture thickens. 3. While the tomatoes are cooking, beat the eggs in a small bowl. 4. When the tomatoes have thickened, pour the eggs into the pan and increase the heat to medium. Continue cooking, using a spatula to stir the eggs and tomatoes continuously, for 2–3 minutes or until the eggs are set. Remove the pan from the heat. 5. Add the feta, oregano, and mint, and stir to combine. 6. Transfer to a plate. Top with a pinch of black pepper and the remaining ⅛ teaspoon sea salt. Serve promptly.

Per Serving:
calories: 156 | fat: 12g | protein: 8g | carbs: 4g | fiber: 1g | sodium: 487mg

Veggie Hash with Eggs

Prep time: 20 minutes | Cook time: 6¼ hours |
Serves 2

Nonstick cooking spray
1 onion, chopped
2 garlic cloves, minced
1 red bell pepper, chopped
1 yellow summer squash, chopped
2 carrots, chopped
2 Yukon Gold potatoes, peeled and chopped
2 large tomatoes, seeded and
chopped
¼ cup vegetable broth
½ teaspoon salt
⅛ teaspoon freshly ground black pepper
½ teaspoon dried thyme leaves
3 or 4 eggs
½ teaspoon ground sweet paprika

1. Spray the slow cooker with the nonstick cooking spray. 2. In the slow cooker, combine all the ingredients except the eggs and paprika, and stir. 3. Cover and cook on low for 6 hours. 4. Uncover and make 1 indentation in the vegetable mixture for each egg. Break 1 egg into a small cup and slip the egg into an indentation. Repeat with the remaining eggs. Sprinkle with the paprika. 5. Cover and cook on low for 10 to 15 minutes, or until the eggs are just set, and serve.

Per Serving:

calories: 381 | fat: 8g | protein: 17g | carbs: 64g | fiber: 12g | sodium: 747mg

Sunny-Side Up Baked Eggs with Swiss Chard, Feta, and Basil

Prep time: 15 minutes | Cook time: 10 to 15 minutes | Serves 4

1 tablespoon extra-virgin olive oil, divided
½ red onion, diced
½ teaspoon kosher salt
¼ teaspoon nutmeg
⅛ teaspoon freshly ground
black pepper
4 cups Swiss chard, chopped
¼ cup crumbled feta cheese
4 large eggs
¼ cup fresh basil, chopped or cut into ribbons

1. Preheat the oven to 375°F (190°C). Place 4 ramekins on a half sheet pan or in a baking dish and grease lightly with olive oil. 2. Heat the remaining olive oil in a large skillet or sauté pan over medium heat. Add the onion, salt, nutmeg, and pepper and sauté until translucent, about 3 minutes. Add the chard and cook, stirring, until wilted, about 2 minutes. 3. Split the mixture among the 4 ramekins. Add 1 tablespoon feta cheese to each ramekin. Crack 1 egg on top of the mixture in each ramekin. Bake for 10 to 12 minutes, or until the egg white is set. 4. Allow to cool for 1 to 2 minutes, then carefully transfer the eggs from the ramekins to a plate with a fork or spatula. Garnish with the basil.

Per Serving:

calories: 140 | fat: 10g | protein: 9g | carbs: 4g | fiber: 4g | sodium: 370mg

Summer Day Fruit Salad

Prep time: 5 minutes | Cook time: 0 minutes | Serves 8

2 cups cubed honeydew melon
2 cups cubed cantaloupe
2 cups red seedless grapes
1 cup sliced fresh strawberries
1 cup fresh blueberries
Zest and juice of 1 large lime
½ cup unsweetened toasted coconut flakes
¼ cup honey
¼ teaspoon sea salt
½ cup extra-virgin olive oil

1. Combine all of the fruits, the lime zest, and the coconut flakes in a large bowl and stir well to blend. Set aside. 2. In a blender, combine the lime juice, honey, and salt and blend on low. Once the honey is incorporated, slowly add the olive oil and blend until opaque. 3. Pour the dressing over the fruit and mix well. Cover and refrigerate for at least 4 hours before serving, stirring a few times to distribute the dressing.

Per Serving:

calories: 249 | fat: 15g | protein: 1g | carbs: 30g | fiber: 3g | sodium: 104mg

Marinara Eggs with Parsley

Prep time: 5 minutes |Cook time: 15 minutes|
Serves: 6

1 tablespoon extra-virgin olive oil
1 cup chopped onion (about ½ medium onion)
2 garlic cloves, minced (about 1 teaspoon)
2 (14½-ounce / 411-g) cans Italian diced tomatoes,
undrained, no salt added
6 large eggs
½ cup chopped fresh flat-leaf (Italian) parsley
Crusty Italian bread and grated Parmesan or Romano cheese, for serving (optional)

1. In a large skillet over medium-high heat, heat the oil. Add the onion and cook for 5 minutes, stirring occasionally. Add the garlic and cook for 1 minute. 2. Pour the tomatoes with their juices over the onion mixture and cook until bubbling, 2 to 3 minutes. While waiting for the tomato mixture to bubble, crack one egg into a small custard cup or coffee mug. 3. When the tomato mixture bubbles, lower the heat to medium. Then use a large spoon to make six indentations in the tomato mixture. Gently pour the first cracked egg into one indentation and repeat, cracking the remaining eggs, one at a time, into the custard cup and pouring one into each indentation. Cover the skillet and cook for 6 to 7 minutes, or until the eggs are done to your liking (about 6 minutes for soft-cooked, 7 minutes for harder cooked). 4. Top with the parsley, and serve with the bread and grated cheese, if desired.

Per Serving:

calories: 127 | fat: 7g | protein: 8g | carbs: 8g | fiber: 2g | sodium: 82mg

Spinach Pie

Prep time: 10 minutes | Cook time: 25 minutes |

Serves 8

Nonstick cooking spray	¼ teaspoon ground nutmeg
2 tablespoons extra-virgin olive oil	4 large eggs, divided
1 onion, chopped	1 cup grated Parmesan cheese, divided
1 pound (454 g) frozen spinach, thawed	2 puff pastry doughs, (organic, if available), at room temperature
¼ teaspoon garlic salt	
¼ teaspoon freshly ground black pepper	4 hard-boiled eggs, halved

1. Preheat the oven to 350°F(180ºC). Spray a baking sheet with nonstick cooking spray and set aside. 2. Heat a large sauté pan or skillet over medium-high heat. Put in the oil and onion and cook for about 5 minutes, until translucent. 3. Squeeze the excess water from the spinach, then add to the pan and cook, uncovered, so that any excess water from the spinach can evaporate. Add the garlic salt, pepper, and nutmeg. Remove from heat and set aside to cool. 4. In a small bowl, crack 3 eggs and mix well. Add the eggs and ½ cup Parmesan cheese to the cooled spinach mix. 5. On the prepared baking sheet, roll out the pastry dough. Layer the spinach mix on top of dough, leaving 2 inches around each edge. 6. Once the spinach is spread onto the pastry dough, place hard-boiled egg halves evenly throughout the pie, then cover with the second pastry dough. Pinch the edges closed. 7. Crack the remaining egg in a small bowl and mix well. Brush the egg wash over the pastry dough. 8. Bake for 15 to 20 minutes, until golden brown and warmed through.

Per Serving:

calories: 417 | fat: 28g | protein: 17g | carbs: 25g | fiber: 3g | sodium: 490mg

Quickie Honey Nut Granola

Prep time: 10 minutes |Cook time: 20 minutes|

Serves: 6

2½ cups regular rolled oats	½ cup chopped dried apricots
⅓ cup coarsely chopped almonds	2 tablespoons ground flaxseed
⅛ teaspoon kosher or sea salt	¼ cup honey
½ teaspoon ground cinnamon	¼ cup extra-virgin olive oil
	2 teaspoons vanilla extract

1. Preheat the oven to 325°F(165ºC). Line a large, rimmed baking sheet with parchment paper. 2. In a large skillet, combine the oats, almonds, salt, and cinnamon. Turn the heat to medium-high and cook, stirring often, to toast, about 6 minutes. 3. While the oat mixture is toasting, in a microwave-safe bowl, combine the apricots, flaxseed, honey, and oil. Microwave on high for about 1 minute, or until very hot and just beginning to bubble. (Or heat these ingredients in a small saucepan over medium heat for about 3 minutes.) 4. Stir the vanilla into the honey mixture, then pour it over the oat mixture in the skillet. Stir well. 5. Spread out the granola on the prepared baking sheet. Bake for 15 minutes, until lightly browned. Remove from the oven and cool completely. 6. Break the granola into small pieces, and store in an airtight container in the refrigerator for up to 2 weeks (if it lasts that long!).

Per Serving:

calories: 449 | fat: 17g | protein: 13g | carbs: 64g | fiber: 9g | sodium: 56mg

Baked Ricotta with Pears

Prep time: 5 minutes |Cook time: 25 minutes|

Serves: 4

Nonstick cooking spray	1 tablespoon sugar
1 (16-ounce / 454-g) container whole-milk ricotta cheese	1 teaspoon vanilla extract
2 large eggs	¼ teaspoon ground nutmeg
¼ cup white whole-wheat flour or whole-wheat pastry flour	1 pear, cored and diced
	2 tablespoons water
	1 tablespoon honey

1. Preheat the oven to 400°F(205ºC). Spray four 6-ounce ramekins with nonstick cooking spray. 2. In a large bowl, beat together the ricotta, eggs, flour, sugar, vanilla, and nutmeg. Spoon into the ramekins. Bake for 22 to 25 minutes, or until the ricotta is just about set. Remove from the oven and cool slightly on racks. 3. While the ricotta is baking, in a small saucepan over medium heat, simmer the pear in the water for 10 minutes, until slightly softened. Remove from the heat, and stir in the honey. 4. Serve the ricotta ramekins topped with the warmed pear.

Per Serving:

calories: 306 | fat: 17g | protein: 17g | carbs: 21g | fiber: 1g | sodium: 131mg

Grilled Halloumi with Whole-Wheat Pita Bread

Prep time: 5 minutes | Cook time: 10 minutes |

Serves 4

2 teaspoons olive oil	1 Persian cucumber, thinly sliced
8 (½-inch-thick) slices of halloumi cheese	1 large tomato, sliced
4 whole-wheat pita rounds	½ cup pitted Kalamata olives

1. Brush a bit of olive oil on a grill pan and heat it over medium-high heat. 2. Brush the cheese slices all over with olive oil. Add the cheese slices in a single layer and cook until grill marks appear on the bottom, about 3 minutes. Flip the slices over and grill until grill marks appear on the second side, about 2 to 3 minutes more. 3. While the cheese is cooking, heat the pita bread, either in a skillet or in a toaster. 4. Serve the cheese inside of the pita pockets with the sliced cucumber, tomato, and olives.

Per Serving:

calories: 358 | fat: 24g | protein: 17g | carbs: 21g | fiber: 4g | sodium: 612mg

Breakfast Hash

Prep time: 10 minutes | Cook time: 30 minutes | Serves 6

Oil, for spraying
3 medium russet potatoes, diced
½ yellow onion, diced
1 green bell pepper, seeded and diced
2 tablespoons olive oil
2 teaspoons granulated garlic
1 teaspoon salt
½ teaspoon freshly ground black pepper

1. Line the air fryer basket with parchment and spray lightly with oil. 2. In a large bowl, mix together the potatoes, onion, bell pepper, and olive oil. 3. Add the garlic, salt, and black pepper and stir until evenly coated. 4. Transfer the mixture to the prepared basket. 5. Air fry at 400ºF (204ºC) for 20 to 30 minutes, shaking or stirring every 10 minutes, until browned and crispy. If you spray the potatoes with a little oil each time you stir, they will get even crispier.

Per Serving:
calories: 133 | fat: 5g | protein: 3g | carbs: 21g | fiber: 2g | sodium: 395mg

Quinoa Porridge with Apricots

Prep time: 10 minutes | Cook time: 12 minutes | Serves 4

1½ cups quinoa, rinsed and drained
1 cup chopped dried apricots
2½ cups water
1 cup almond milk
1 tablespoon rose water
½ teaspoon cardamom
¼ teaspoon salt

1. Place all ingredients in the Instant Pot®. Stir to combine. Close lid, set steam release to Sealing, press the Rice button, and set time to 12 minutes. When the timer beeps, let pressure release naturally, about 20 minutes. 2. Press the Cancel button, open lid, and fluff quinoa with a fork. Serve warm.

Per Serving:
calories: 197 | fat: 2g | protein: 3g | carbs: 44g | fiber: 4g | sodium: 293mg

Strawberry Collagen Smoothie

Prep time: 5 minutes | Cook time: 0 minutes | Serves 1

3 ounces (85 g) fresh or frozen strawberries
¾ cup unsweetened almond milk
¼ cup coconut cream or goat's cream
1 large egg
1 tablespoon chia seeds or flax meal
2 tablespoons grass-fed collagen powder
¼ teaspoon vanilla powder or 1 teaspoon unsweetened vanilla extract

Zest from ½ lemon
1 tablespoon macadamia oil
Optional: ice cubes, to taste

1. Place all of the ingredients in a blender and pulse until smooth and frothy. Serve immediately.

Per Serving:
calories: 515 | fat: 42g | protein: 10g | carbs: 30g | fiber: 4g | sodium: 202mg

Heart-Healthy Hazelnut-Collagen Shake

Prep time: 5 minutes | Cook time: 0 minutes | Serves 1

1½ cups unsweetened almond milk
2 tablespoons hazelnut butter
2 tablespoons grass-fed collagen powder
½–1 teaspoon cinnamon
⅛ teaspoon LoSalt or pink Himalayan salt
⅛ teaspoon sugar-free almond extract
1 tablespoon macadamia oil or hazelnut oil

1. Place all of the ingredients in a blender and pulse until smooth and frothy. Serve immediately.

Per Serving:
calories: 507 | fat: 41g | protein: 3g | carbs: 35g | fiber: 12g | sodium: 569mg

Mediterranean Fruit Bulgur Breakfast Bowl

Prep time: 5 minutes |Cook time: 15 minutes| Serves: 6

1½ cups uncooked bulgur
2 cups 2% milk
1 cup water
½ teaspoon ground cinnamon
2 cups frozen (or fresh, pitted) dark sweet cherries
8 dried (or fresh) figs, chopped
½ cup chopped almonds
¼ cup loosely packed fresh mint, chopped
Warm 2% milk, for serving (optional)

1. In a medium saucepan, combine the bulgur, milk, water, and cinnamon. Stir once, then bring just to a boil. Cover, reduce the heat to medium-low, and simmer for 10 minutes or until the liquid is absorbed. 2. Turn off the heat, but keep the pan on the stove, and stir in the frozen cherries (no need to thaw), figs, and almonds. Stir well, cover for 1 minute, and let the hot bulgur thaw the cherries and partially hydrate the figs. Stir in the mint. 3. Scoop into serving bowls. Serve with warm milk, if desired. You can also serve it chilled.

Per Serving:
calories: 273 | fat: 7g | protein: 10g | carbs: 48g | fiber: 8g | sodium: 46mg

Broccoli-Mushroom Frittata

Prep time: 10 minutes | Cook time: 20 minutes |
Serves 2

1 tablespoon olive oil
1½ cups broccoli florets, finely chopped
½ cup sliced brown mushrooms
¼ cup finely chopped onion

½ teaspoon salt
¼ teaspoon freshly ground black pepper
6 eggs
¼ cup Parmesan cheese

1. In a nonstick cake pan, combine the olive oil, broccoli, mushrooms, onion, salt, and pepper. Stir until the vegetables are thoroughly coated with oil. Place the cake pan in the air fryer basket and set the air fryer to 400°F (204°C). Air fry for 5 minutes until the vegetables soften. 2. Meanwhile, in a medium bowl, whisk the eggs and Parmesan until thoroughly combined. Pour the egg mixture into the pan and shake gently to distribute the vegetables. Air fry for another 15 minutes until the eggs are set. 3. Remove from the air fryer and let sit for 5 minutes to cool slightly. Use a silicone spatula to gently lift the frittata onto a plate before serving.

Per Serving:
calories: 329 | fat: 23g | protein: 24g | carbs: 6g | fiber: 0g | sodium: 793mg

Feta and Herb Frittata

Prep time : 10 minutes | Cook time: 30 minutes |
Serves 6

¼ cup olive oil, divided
1 medium onion, halved and thinly sliced
1 clove garlic, minced
8 sheets phyllo dough
8 eggs
¼ cup chopped fresh basil, plus additional for garnish

¼ cup chopped flat-leaf parsley, plus additional for garnish
1 teaspoon salt
½ teaspoon freshly ground black pepper
4 ounces (113 g) crumbled feta cheese

1. Preheat the oven to 400°F(205°C). 2. Heat 2 tablespoons of the olive oil in a medium skillet over medium-high heat. Add the onions and cook, stirring frequently, until softened, about 5 minutes. Add the garlic and cook, stirring, for 1 minute more. Remove from the heat and set aside to cool. 3. While the onion mixture is cooling, make the crust. Place a damp towel on the counter and cover with a sheet of parchment paper. Lay the phyllo sheets in a stack on top of the parchment and cover with a second sheet of parchment and then a second damp towel. 4. Brush some of the remaining olive oil in a 9-by-9-inch baking dish or a 9-inch pie dish. Layer the softened phyllo sheets in the prepared dish, brushing each with some of the olive oil before adding the next phyllo sheet. 5. Next, make the filling. In a large bowl, whisk the eggs with the onion mixture, basil, parsley, salt, and pepper. Add the feta cheese and mix well. Pour the egg mixture into the prepared crust, folding any excess phyllo inside the baking dish. 6. Bake in the preheated oven for about 25 to 30 minutes, until the crust is golden brown and the egg

filling is completely set in the center. Cut into rectangles or wedges and serve garnished with basil and parsley.

Per Serving:
calories: 298 | fat: 20g | protein: 12g | carbs: 17g | fiber: 1g | sodium: 769mg

Smoky Sausage Patties

Prep time: 30 minutes | Cook time: 9 minutes |
Serves 8

1 pound (454 g) ground pork
1 tablespoon coconut aminos
2 teaspoons liquid smoke
1 teaspoon dried sage
1 teaspoon sea salt

½ teaspoon fennel seeds
½ teaspoon dried thyme
½ teaspoon freshly ground black pepper
¼ teaspoon cayenne pepper

1. In a large bowl, combine the pork, coconut aminos, liquid smoke, sage, salt, fennel seeds, thyme, black pepper, and cayenne pepper. Work the meat with your hands until the seasonings are fully incorporated. 2. Shape the mixture into 8 equal-size patties. Using your thumb, make a dent in the center of each patty. Place the patties on a plate and cover with plastic wrap. Refrigerate the patties for at least 30 minutes. 3. Working in batches if necessary, place the patties in a single layer in the air fryer, being careful not to overcrowd them. 4. Set the air fryer to 400°F (204°C) and air fry for 5 minutes. Flip and cook for about 4 minutes more.

Per Serving:
calories: 70 | fat: 2g | protein: 12g | carbs: 0g | fiber: 0g | sodium: 329mg

Oatmeal with Apple and Cardamom

Prep time: 10 minutes | Cook time: 7 minutes |
Serves 4

1 tablespoon light olive oil
1 large Granny Smith, Honeycrisp, or Pink Lady apple, peeled, cored, and diced
½ teaspoon ground cardamom

1 cup steel-cut oats
3 cups water
¼ cup maple syrup
½ teaspoon salt

1. Press the Sauté button on the Instant Pot® and heat oil. Add apple and cardamom and cook until apple is just softened, about 2 minutes. Press the Cancel button. 2. Add oats, water, maple syrup, and salt to pot, and stir well. Close lid, set steam release to Sealing, press the Manual button, and set time to 5 minutes. 3. When the timer beeps, let pressure release naturally for 10 minutes, then quick-release the remaining pressure until the float valve drops. Press the Cancel button, open lid, and stir well. Serve hot.

Per Serving:
calories: 249 | fat: 6g | protein: 6g | carbs: 48g | fiber: 5g | sodium: 298mg

Spinach and Feta Egg Bake

Avocado oil spray
⅓ cup diced red onion
1 cup frozen chopped spinach, thawed and drained
4 large eggs
¼ cup heavy (whipping) cream

Sea salt and freshly ground black pepper, to taste
¼ teaspoon cayenne pepper
½ cup crumbled feta cheese
¼ cup shredded Parmesan cheese

1. Spray a deep pan with oil. Put the onion in the pan, and place the pan in the air fryer basket. Set the air fryer to 350ºF (177ºC) and bake for 7 minutes. 2. Sprinkle the spinach over the onion. 3. In a medium bowl, beat the eggs, heavy cream, salt, black pepper, and cayenne. Pour this mixture over the vegetables. 4. Top with the feta and Parmesan cheese. Bake for 16 to 18 minutes, until the eggs are set and lightly brown.

Per Serving:
calories: 366 | fat: 26g | protein: 25g | carbs: 8g | fiber: 3g | sodium: 520mg

Herb & Cheese Fritters

3 medium zucchini
8 ounces (227 g) frozen spinach, thawed and squeezed dry (weight excludes water squeezed out)
4 large eggs
½ teaspoon salt
¼ teaspoon black pepper
3 tablespoons flax meal or

coconut flour
¼ cup grated Pecorino Romano
2 cloves garlic, minced
¼ cup chopped fresh herbs, such as parsley, basil, oregano, mint, chives, and/or thyme
¼ cup extra-virgin avocado oil or ghee

1. Grate the zucchini and place in a bowl lined with cheesecloth. Set aside for 5 minutes, then twist the cheesecloth around the zucchini and squeeze out as much liquid as you can. You should end up with about 13 ounces (370 g) of drained zucchini. 2. In a mixing bowl, combine the zucchini, spinach, eggs, salt, and pepper. Add the flax meal and Pecorino and stir again. Add the garlic and herbs and mix through. 3. Heat a large pan greased with 1 tablespoon of ghee over medium heat. Once hot, use a ¼-cup measuring cup to make the fritters (about 57 g/2 ounces each). Place in the hot pan and shape with a spatula. Cook in batches for 3 to 4 minutes per side, until crisp and golden. Grease the pan between each batch until all the ghee has been used. 4. Eat warm or cold, as a breakfast, side, or snack. Store in the fridge for up to 4 days or freeze for up to 3 months.

Per Serving:
calories: 239 | fat: 20g | protein: 10g | carbs: 8g | fiber: 3g | sodium: 426mg

Spanish Tortilla with Potatoes and Peppers

½ cup olive oil, plus 2 tablespoons, divided
2 pounds (907 g) baking potatoes, peeled and cut into ¼-inch slices
2 onions, thinly sliced

1 roasted red pepper, drained and cut into strips
6 eggs
2 teaspoons salt
1 teaspoon freshly ground black pepper

1. In a large skillet over medium heat, heat ½ cup of the olive oil. Add the potatoes and cook, stirring occasionally, until the potatoes are tender, about 20 minutes. Remove the potatoes from the pan with a slotted spoon and discard the remaining oil. 2. In a medium skillet over medium heat, heat the remaining 2 tablespoons of olive oil. Add the onions and cook, stirring frequently, until softened and golden brown, about 10 minutes. Remove the onions from the pan with a slotted spoon, leaving the oil in the pan, and add them to the potatoes. Add the pepper slices to the potatoes as well. 3. In a large bowl, whisk together the eggs, salt, and pepper. Add the cooked vegetables to the egg mixture and gently toss to combine. 4. Heat the medium skillet over low heat. Add the egg-vegetable mixture to the pan and cook for about 10 minutes, until the bottom is lightly browned. Use a spatula to loosen the tortilla and transfer the whole thing to a large plate, sliding it out of the pan so that the browned side is on the bottom. Invert the skillet over the tortilla and then lift the plate to flip it back into the skillet with the browned side on top. Return to the stove and continue to cook over low heat until the tortilla is fully set in the center, about 5 more minutes. 5. Serve the tortilla warm or at room temperature.

Per Serving:
calories: 370 | fat: 26g | protein: 9g | carbs: 29g | fiber: 5g | sodium: 876mg

C+C Overnight Oats

½ cup vanilla, unsweetened almond milk (not Silk brand)
½ cup rolled oats
2 tablespoons sliced almonds
2 tablespoons simple sugar

liquid sweetener
1 teaspoon chia seeds
¼ teaspoon ground cardamom
¼ teaspoon ground cinnamon

1. In a mason jar, combine the almond milk, oats, almonds, liquid sweetener, chia seeds, cardamom, and cinnamon and shake well. Store in the refrigerator for 8 to 24 hours, then serve cold or heated.

Per Serving:
calories: 131 | fat: 6g | protein: 5g | carbs: 17g | fiber: 4g | sodium: 45mg

Breakfast Panini with Eggs, Olives, and Tomatoes

Prep time: 5 minutes | Cook time: 0 minutes | Serves 4

1 (12-ounce / 340-g) round whole-wheat pagnotta foggiana or other round, crusty bread
2 tablespoons olive oil
½ cup sliced pitted cured olives, such as Kalamata
8 hard-boiled eggs, peeled and sliced into rounds
2 medium tomatoes, thinly sliced into rounds
12 large leaves fresh basil

1. Split the bread horizontally and brush the cut sides with the olive oil. 2. Arrange the sliced olives on the bottom half of the bread in a single layer. Top with a layer of the egg slices, then the tomato slices, and finally the basil leaves. Cut the sandwich into quarters and serve immediately.

Per Serving:

calories: 427 | fat: 21g | protein: 23g | carbs: 39g | fiber: 7g | sodium: 674mg

Flax, Date, and Walnut Steel-Cut Oats

Prep time: 5 minutes | Cook time: 5 minutes | Serves 4

1 tablespoon light olive oil
1 cup steel-cut oats
3 cups water
⅓ cup chopped pitted dates
¼ cup ground flax
¼ teaspoon salt
½ cup toasted chopped walnuts

1. Place oil, oats, water, dates, flax, and salt in the Instant Pot® and stir well. Close lid, set steam release to Sealing, press the Manual button, and set time to 5 minutes. 2. When the timer beeps, let pressure release naturally for 10 minutes, then quick-release the remaining pressure until the float valve drops. Press the Cancel button, open lid, and stir in walnuts. Serve hot.

Per Serving:

calories: 322 | fat: 18g | protein: 10g | carbs: 42g | fiber: 8g | sodium: 150mg

Tiropita (Greek Cheese Pie)

Prep time: 15 minutes | Cook time: 45 minutes | Serves 12

1 tablespoon extra virgin olive oil plus 3 tablespoons for brushing
1 pound (454 g) crumbled feta
8 ounces (227g) ricotta cheese
2 tablespoons chopped fresh mint, or 1 tablespoon dried mint
2 tablespoons chopped fresh dill, or 1 tablespoon dried dill
¼ teaspoon freshly ground black pepper
3 eggs
12 phyllo sheets, defrosted
1 teaspoon white sesame seeds

1. Preheat the oven to 350°F (180 C). Brush a 9 × 13-inch (23 × 33cm) casserole dish with olive oil. 2. Combine the feta and ricotta in a large bowl, using a fork to mash the ingredients together. Add the mint, dill, and black pepper, and mix well. In a small bowl, beat the eggs and then add them to the cheese mixture along with 1 tablespoon olive oil. Mix well. 3. Carefully place 1 phyllo sheet in the bottom of the prepared dish. (Keep the rest of the dough covered with a damp towel.) Brush the sheet with olive oil, then place a second phyllo sheet on top of the first and brush with olive oil. Repeat until you have 6 layers of phyllo. 4. Spread the cheese mixture evenly over the phyllo and then fold the excess phyllo edges in and over the mixture. Cover the mixture with 6 more phyllo sheets, repeating the process by placing a single phyllo sheet in the pan and brushing it with olive oil. Roll the excess phyllo in to form an edge around the pie. 5. Brush the top phyllo layer with olive oil and then use a sharp knife to score it into 12 pieces, being careful to cut only through the first 3–4 layers of the phyllo dough. Sprinkle the sesame seeds and a bit of water over the top of the pie. 6. Place the pie on the middle rack of the oven. Bake for 40 minutes or until the phyllo turns a deep golden color. Carefully lift one side of the pie to ensure the bottom crust is baked. If it's baked, move the pan to the bottom rack and bake for an additional 5 minutes. 7. Remove the pie from the oven and set aside to cool for 15 minutes. Use a sharp knife to cut the pie into 12 pieces. Store covered in the refrigerator for up to 3 days.

Per Serving:

calories: 230 | fat: 15g | protein: 11g | carbs: 13g | fiber: 1g | sodium: 510mg

Harissa Shakshuka with Bell Peppers and Tomatoes

Prep time: 10 minutes | Cook time: 20 minutes | Serves 4

1½ tablespoons extra-virgin olive oil
2 tablespoons harissa
1 tablespoon tomato paste
½ onion, diced
1 bell pepper, seeded and diced
3 garlic cloves, minced
1 (28-ounce / 794-g) can no-salt-added diced tomatoes
½ teaspoon kosher salt
4 large eggs
2 to 3 tablespoons fresh basil, chopped or cut into ribbons

1. Preheat the oven to 375°F (190ºC). 2. Heat the olive oil in a 12-inch cast-iron pan or ovenproof skillet over medium heat. Add the harissa, tomato paste, onion, and bell pepper; sauté for 3 to 4 minutes. Add the garlic and cook until fragrant, about 30 seconds. Add the diced tomatoes and salt and simmer for about 10 minutes. 3. Make 4 wells in the sauce and gently break 1 egg into each. Transfer to the oven and bake until the whites are cooked and the yolks are set, 10 to 12 minutes. 4. Allow to cool for 3 to 5 minutes, garnish with the basil, and carefully spoon onto plates.

Per Serving:

calories: 190 | fat: 10g | protein: 9g | carbs: 15g | fiber: 4g | sodium: 255mg

Gluten-Free Granola Cereal

Prep time: 7 minutes | Cook time: 30 minutes | Makes 3½ cups

Oil, for spraying
1½ cups gluten-free rolled oats
½ cup chopped walnuts
½ cup chopped almonds
½ cup pumpkin seeds

¼ cup maple syrup or honey
1 tablespoon toasted sesame oil or vegetable oil
1 teaspoon ground cinnamon
½ teaspoon salt
½ cup dried cranberries

1. Preheat the air fryer to 250°F (121°C). Line the air fryer basket with parchment and spray lightly with oil. (Do not skip the step of lining the basket; the parchment will keep the granola from falling through the holes.) 2. In a large bowl, mix together the oats, walnuts, almonds, pumpkin seeds, maple syrup, sesame oil, cinnamon, and salt. 3. Spread the mixture in an even layer in the prepared basket. 4. Cook for 30 minutes, stirring every 10 minutes. 5. Transfer the granola to a bowl, add the dried cranberries, and toss to combine. 6. Let cool to room temperature before storing in an airtight container.

Per Serving:

calories: 322 | fat: 17g | protein: 11g | carbs: 35g | fiber: 6g | sodium: 170mg

Greek Yogurt and Berries

Prep time: 5 minutes | Cook time: 30 minutes | Serves 4

4 cups plain full-fat Greek yogurt
1 cup granola
½ cup blackberries
2 bananas, sliced and frozen

1 teaspoon chia seeds, for topping
1 teaspoon chopped fresh mint leaves, for topping
4 teaspoons honey, for topping (optional)

1. Evenly divide the yogurt among four bowls. Top with the granola, blackberries, bananas, chia seeds, mint, and honey (if desired), dividing evenly among the bowls. Serve.

Per Serving:

calories: 283 | fat: 9g | protein: 12g | carbs: 42g | fiber: 5g | sodium: 115mg

Chapter 4 Fish and Seafood

Cod Gratin

Prep time: 10 minutes | Cook time: 22 minutes | Serves 4

½ cup olive oil, divided
1 pound (454 g) fresh cod
1 cup black olives, pitted and chopped
4 leeks, trimmed and sliced
1 cup whole-wheat breadcrumbs
¾ cup low-salt chicken stock
Sea salt and freshly ground pepper, to taste

1. Preheat the oven to 350ºF (180ºC). 2. Brush 4 gratin dishes with the olive oil. 3. Place the cod on a baking dish, and bake for 5–7 minutes. Cool and cut into 1-inch pieces. 4. Heat the remaining olive oil in a large skillet. 5. Add the olives and leeks, and cook over medium-low heat until the leeks are tender. 6. Add the breadcrumbs and chicken stock, stirring to mix. 7. Gently fold in the pieces of cod. Divide the mixture between the 4 gratin dishes, and drizzle with olive oil. 8. Season with sea salt and freshly ground pepper. Bake for 15 minutes or until warmed through.

Per Serving:
calories: 538 | fat: 33g | protein: 26g | carbs: 35g | fiber: 4g | sodium: 538mg

Escabeche

Prep time: 10 minutes | Cook time: 20 minutes | Serves 4

1 pound (454 g) wild-caught Spanish mackerel fillets, cut into four pieces
1 teaspoon salt
½ teaspoon freshly ground black pepper
8 tablespoons extra-virgin olive oil, divided
1 bunch asparagus, trimmed
and cut into 2-inch pieces
1 (13¾-ounce / 390-g) can artichoke hearts, drained and quartered
4 large garlic cloves, peeled and crushed
2 bay leaves
¼ cup red wine vinegar
½ teaspoon smoked paprika

1. Sprinkle the fillets with salt and pepper and let sit at room temperature for 5 minutes. 2. In a large skillet, heat 2 tablespoons olive oil over medium-high heat. Add the fish, skin-side up, and cook 5 minutes. Flip and cook 5 minutes on the other side, until browned and cooked through. Transfer to a serving dish, pour the cooking oil over the fish, and cover to keep warm. 3. Heat the remaining 6 tablespoons olive oil in the same skillet over medium heat. Add the asparagus, artichokes, garlic, and bay leaves and sauté until the vegetables are tender, 6 to 8 minutes. 4. Using a slotted spoon, top the fish with the cooked vegetables, reserving the oil in the skillet. Add the vinegar and paprika to the oil and whisk to combine well. Pour the vinaigrette over the fish and vegetables and let sit at room temperature for at least 15 minutes, or marinate in the refrigerator up to 24 hours for a deeper flavor. Remove the bay leaf before serving.

Per Serving:
calories: 459 | fat: 34g | protein: 26g | carbs: 13g | fiber: 6g | sodium: 597mg

Grilled Halibut Steaks with Romesco Sauce

Prep time: 20 minutes | Cook time: 10 minutes | Serves 2

For the Romesco Sauce:
½ cup jarred roasted piquillo peppers
2 tablespoons sun-dried tomatoes in olive oil with herbs
2 small garlic cloves
¼ cup raw, unsalted almonds
2 tablespoons red wine vinegar
Pinch salt
¼ teaspoon smoked paprika (or
more to taste)
¼ cup olive oil
1 to 2 tablespoons water
For the Halibut:
2 (5-ounce / 142-g) halibut steaks
1 tablespoon olive oil
Salt
Freshly ground black pepper

Make the Romesco Sauce: 1. Combine the piquillo peppers, sun-dried tomatoes, garlic, almonds, vinegar, salt, and paprika in a food processor or a blender and blend until mostly smooth. While the mixture is blending, drizzle in the olive oil. 2. Taste and adjust seasonings. If you prefer a smoother sauce, add water, 1 tablespoon at a time, until sauce reaches your desired consistency. Make the Salmon: 1. Heat the grill to medium-high and oil the grill grates. 2. Brush the fish with olive oil, and season with salt and pepper. 3. When the grill is hot, grill the fish for about 5 minutes per side, or until it's opaque and flakes easily. Serve topped with a few tablespoons of the romesco sauce. 4. Store any remaining sauce in an airtight container in the refrigerator for up to a week.

Per Serving:
calories: 264 | fat: 13g | protein: 31g | carbs: 3g | fiber: 1g | sodium: 109mg

Pistachio-Crusted Whitefish

Prep time: 10 minutes | Cook time: 20 minutes |

Serves 2

¼ cup shelled pistachios
1 tablespoon fresh parsley
1 tablespoon grated Parmesan cheese
1 tablespoon panko bread crumbs

2 tablespoons olive oil
¼ teaspoon salt
10 ounces (283 g) skinless whitefish (1 large piece or 2 smaller ones)

1. Preheat the oven to 350°F(180°C) and set the rack to the middle position. Line a sheet pan with foil or parchment paper. 2. Combine all of the ingredients except the fish in a mini food processor, and pulse until the nuts are finely ground. Alternatively, you can mince the nuts with a chef's knife and combine the ingredients by hand in a small bowl. 3. Place the fish on the sheet pan. Spread the nut mixture evenly over the fish and pat it down lightly. 4. Bake the fish for 20 to 30 minutes, depending on the thickness, until it flakes easily with a fork.

Per Serving:

calories: 267 | fat: 18g | protein: 28g | carbs: 1g | fiber: 0g | sodium: 85mg

Red Snapper with Peppers and Potatoes

Prep time: 15 minutes | Cook time: 4 to 6 hours |

Serves 4

1 pound (454 g) red potatoes, chopped
1 green bell pepper, seeded and sliced
1 red bell pepper, seeded and sliced
½ onion, sliced
1 (15 ounces / 425 g) can no-salt-added diced tomatoes
⅓ cup whole Kalamata olives, pitted

5 garlic cloves, minced
1 teaspoon dried thyme
1 teaspoon dried rosemary
Juice of 1 lemon
Sea salt
Freshly ground black pepper
1½ to 2 pounds (680 to 907 g) fresh red snapper fillets
2 lemons, thinly sliced
¼ cup chopped fresh parsley

1. In a slow cooker, combine the potatoes, green and red bell peppers, onion, tomatoes, olives, garlic, thyme, rosemary, and lemon juice. Season with salt and black pepper. Stir to mix well. 2. Nestle the snapper into the vegetable mixture in a single layer, cutting it into pieces to fit if needed. Top it with lemon slices. 3. Cover the cooker and cook for 4 to 6 hours on Low heat, or until the potatoes are tender. 4. Garnish with fresh parsley for serving.

Per Serving:

calories: 350 | fat: 5g | protein: 45g | carbs: 41g | fiber: 8g | sodium: 241mg

Cod Stew with Olives

Prep time: 20 minutes | Cook time: 15 minutes |

Serves 4

3 tablespoons olive oil
1 medium onion, peeled and diced
1 stalk celery, diced
1 medium carrot, peeled and chopped
2 cloves garlic, peeled and minced
1 tablespoon chopped fresh oregano
½ teaspoon ground fennel

1 sprig fresh thyme
1 (14½-ounce / 411-g) can diced tomatoes
1½ cups vegetable broth
1 pound (454 g) cod fillets, cut into 1" pieces
⅓ cup sliced green olives
¼ teaspoon ground black pepper
2 tablespoons chopped fresh dill

1. Press the Sauté button on the Instant Pot® and heat oil. Add onion, celery, and carrot. Cook until vegetables are soft, about 6 minutes. Add garlic, oregano, fennel, and thyme. Cook for 30 seconds, then add tomatoes and vegetable broth. Stir well. Press the Cancel button. 2. Close lid, set steam release to Sealing, press the Manual button, and set time to 3 minutes. 3. When the timer beeps, quick-release the pressure until the float valve drops and open lid. Press the Cancel button, then press the Sauté button and add fish, olives, and pepper. Cook until fish is opaque, 3–5 minutes. Sprinkle with dill and serve hot.

Per Serving:

calories: 200 | fat: 16g | protein: 7g | carbs: 14g | fiber: 3g | sodium: 379mg

Crispy Fish Sticks

Prep time: 15 minutes | Cook time: 10 minutes |

Serves 4

1 ounce (28 g) pork rinds, finely ground
¼ cup blanched finely ground almond flour
½ teaspoon Old Bay seasoning

1 tablespoon coconut oil
1 large egg
1 pound (454 g) cod fillet, cut into ¾-inch strips

1. Place ground pork rinds, almond flour, Old Bay seasoning, and coconut oil into a large bowl and mix together. In a medium bowl, whisk egg. 2. Dip each fish stick into the egg and then gently press into the flour mixture, coating as fully and evenly as possible. Place fish sticks into the air fryer basket. 3. Adjust the temperature to 400ºF (204ºC) and air fry for 10 minutes or until golden. 4. Serve immediately.

Per Serving:

calories: 223 | fat: 14g | protein: 21g | carbs: 2g | fiber: 1g | sodium: 390mg

Spicy Trout over Sautéed Mediterranean Salad

Prep time: 10 minutes | Cook time: 30 minutes | Serves 4

2 pounds (907 g) rainbow trout fillets (about 6 fillets)
Salt
Ground white pepper
1 tablespoon extra-virgin olive oil
1 pound (454 g) asparagus
4 medium golden potatoes, thinly sliced
1 scallion, thinly sliced, green and white parts separated
1 garlic clove, finely minced
1 large carrot, thinly sliced
2 Roma tomatoes, chopped
8 pitted kalamata olives, chopped
¼ cup ground cumin
2 tablespoons dried parsley
2 tablespoons paprika
1 tablespoon vegetable bouillon seasoning
½ cup dry white wine

1. Lightly season the fish with salt and white pepper and set aside. 2. In a large sauté pan or skillet, heat the oil over medium heat. Add and stir in the asparagus, potatoes, the white part of the scallions, and garlic to the hot oil. Cook and stir for 5 minutes, until fragrant. Add the carrot, tomatoes, and olives; continue to cook for 5 to 7 minutes, until the carrots are slightly tender. 3. Sprinkle the cumin, parsley, paprika, and vegetable bouillon seasoning over the pan. Season with salt. Stir to incorporate. Put the trout on top of the vegetables and add the wine to cover the vegetables. 4. Reduce the heat to low, cover, and cook for 5 to 7 minutes, until the fish flakes easily with a fork and juices run clear. Top with scallion greens and serve.

Per Serving:
calories: 493 | fat: 19g | protein: 40g | carbs: 41g | fiber: 7g | sodium: 736mg

Garlicky Broiled Sardines

Prep time: 5 minutes | Cook time: 3 minutes | Serves 4

4 (3¼-ounce / 92-g) cans sardines (about 16 sardines), packed in water or olive oil
2 tablespoons extra-virgin olive oil (if sardines are packed in water)
4 garlic cloves, minced
½ teaspoon red pepper flakes
½ teaspoon salt
¼ teaspoon freshly ground black pepper

1. Preheat the broiler. Line a baking dish with aluminum foil. Arrange the sardines in a single layer on the foil. 2. Combine the olive oil (if using), garlic, and red pepper flakes in a small bowl and spoon over each sardine. Season with salt and pepper. 3. Broil just until sizzling, 2 to 3 minutes. 4. To serve, place 4 sardines on each plate and top with any remaining garlic mixture that has collected in the baking dish.

Per Serving:
calories: 197 | fat: 11g | protein: 23g | carbs: 1g | fiber: 0g | sodium: 574mg

Salmon Cakes with Bell Pepper and Lemon Yogurt

Prep time: 15 minutes | Cook time: 15 minutes | Serves 4

¼ cup whole-wheat bread crumbs
¼ cup mayonnaise
1 large egg, beaten
1 tablespoon chives, chopped
1 tablespoon fresh parsley, chopped
Zest of 1 lemon
¾ teaspoon kosher salt, divided
¼ teaspoon freshly ground
black pepper
2 (5 to 6-ounce / 142 to 170-g) cans no-salt boneless/skinless salmon, drained and finely flaked
½ bell pepper, diced small
2 tablespoons extra-virgin olive oil, divided
1 cup plain Greek yogurt
Juice of 1 lemon

1. In a large bowl, combine the bread crumbs, mayonnaise, egg, chives, parsley, lemon zest, ½ teaspoon of the salt, and black pepper and mix well. Add the salmon and the bell pepper and stir gently until well combined. Shape the mixture into 8 patties. 2. Heat 1 tablespoon of the olive oil in a large skillet over medium-high heat. Cook half the cakes until the bottoms are golden brown, 4 to 5 minutes. Adjust the heat to medium if the bottoms start to burn. Flip the cakes and cook until golden brown, an additional 4 to 5 minutes. Repeat with the remaining 1 tablespoon olive oil and the rest of the cakes. 3. In a small bowl, combine the yogurt, lemon juice, and the remaining ¼ teaspoon salt and mix well. Serve with the salmon cakes.

Per Serving:
calories: 330 | fat: 23g | protein: 21g | carbs: 9g | fiber: 1g | sodium: 385mg

Honey-Balsamic Salmon

Prep time: 5 minutes | Cook time: 8 minutes | Serves 2

Oil, for spraying
2 (6-ounce / 170-g) salmon fillets
¼ cup balsamic vinegar
2 tablespoons honey
2 teaspoons red pepper flakes
2 teaspoons olive oil
½ teaspoon salt
¼ teaspoon freshly ground black pepper

1. Line the air fryer basket with parchment and spray lightly with oil. 2. Place the salmon in the prepared basket. 3. In a small bowl, whisk together the balsamic vinegar, honey, red pepper flakes, olive oil, salt, and black pepper. Brush the mixture over the salmon. 4. Roast at 390ºF (199ºC) for 7 to 8 minutes, or until the internal temperature reaches 145ºF (63ºC). Serve immediately.

Per Serving:
calories: 353 | fat: 12g | protein: 35g | carbs: 24g | fiber: 1g | sodium: 590mg

Seared Scallops with Braised Dandelion Greens

Prep time: 5 minutes | Cook time: 15 minutes | Serves 4

3 tablespoons olive oil, divided
2 cloves garlic, thinly sliced
1 pound (454 g) dandelion greens
1 cup low-sodium chicken broth or water
½ teaspoon kosher salt, divided
¼ teaspoon ground black pepper, divided
1 cup chopped fresh mint
1 cup chopped fresh flat-leaf parsley
1 pound (454 g) scallops, muscle tabs removed
Lemon wedges, for serving

1. In a large skillet over medium-high heat, warm 1 tablespoon of the oil. Cook the garlic until softened, about 2 minutes. Add the dandelion greens and broth or water and bring to a boil. Cover and cook until the greens are wilted, 2 minutes. Season with ¼ teaspoon of the salt and ⅛ teaspoon of the pepper. Cover and cook until the greens are tender, 5 to 10 minutes. Stir in the mint and parsley. 2. Meanwhile, pat the scallops dry and season with the remaining ¼ teaspoon salt and the remaining ⅛ teaspoon pepper. In a large nonstick skillet over medium heat, warm 1 tablespoon of the oil. Add the scallops in a single layer and cook without disturbing until browned, 1 to 2 minutes. Add the remaining 1 tablespoon oil to the skillet, flip the scallops, and cook until browned on the other side, 1 to 2 minutes. Serve the scallops over the braised greens and with the lemon wedges.

Per Serving:
calories: 235 | fat: 12g | protein: 18g | carbs: 17g | fiber: 5g | sodium: 850mg

Halibut in Parchment with Zucchini, Shallots, and Herbs

Prep time: 15 minutes | Cook time: 15 minutes | Serves 4

½ cup zucchini, diced small
1 shallot, minced
4 (5-ounce / 142-g) halibut fillets (about 1 inch thick)
4 teaspoons extra-virgin olive oil
¼ teaspoon kosher salt
⅛ teaspoon freshly ground black pepper
1 lemon, sliced into ⅛-inch-thick rounds
8 sprigs of thyme

1. Preheat the oven to 450ºF (235ºC). Combine the zucchini and shallots in a medium bowl. 2. Cut 4 (15-by-24-inch) pieces of parchment paper. Fold each sheet in half horizontally. Draw a large half heart on one side of each folded sheet, with the fold along the center of the heart. Cut out the heart, open the parchment, and lay it flat. 3. Place a fillet near the center of each parchment heart. Drizzle 1 teaspoon olive oil on each fillet. Sprinkle with salt and pepper. Top each fillet with lemon slices and 2 sprigs of thyme. Sprinkle each fillet with one-quarter of the zucchini and shallot mixture.

Fold the parchment over. 4. Starting at the top, fold the edges of the parchment over, and continue all the way around to make a packet. Twist the end tightly to secure. 5. Arrange the 4 packets on a baking sheet. Bake for about 15 minutes. Place on plates; cut open. Serve immediately.

Per Serving:
calories: 190 | fat: 7g | protein: 27g | carbs: 5g | fiber: 1g | sodium: 170mg

Asian Swordfish

Prep time: 10 minutes | Cook time: 6 to 11 minutes | Serves 4

4 (4-ounce / 113-g) swordfish steaks
½ teaspoon toasted sesame oil
1 jalapeño pepper, finely minced
2 garlic cloves, grated
1 tablespoon grated fresh ginger
½ teaspoon Chinese five-spice powder
⅛ teaspoon freshly ground black pepper
2 tablespoons freshly squeezed lemon juice

1. Place the swordfish steaks on a work surface and drizzle with the sesame oil. 2. In a small bowl, mix the jalapeño, garlic, ginger, five-spice powder, pepper, and lemon juice. Rub this mixture into the fish and let it stand for 10 minutes. 3. Roast the swordfish in the air fryer at 380ºF (193ºC) for 6 to 11 minutes, or until the swordfish reaches an internal temperature of at least 140ºF (60ºC) on a meat thermometer. Serve immediately.

Per Serving:
calories: 175 | fat: 8g | protein: 22g | carbs: 2g | fiber: 0g | sodium: 93mg

Chilean Sea Bass with Olive Relish

Prep time: 10 minutes | Cook time: 10 minutes | Serves 2

Olive oil spray
2 (6-ounce / 170-g) Chilean sea bass fillets or other firm-fleshed white fish
3 tablespoons extra-virgin olive oil
½ teaspoon ground cumin
½ teaspoon kosher salt
½ teaspoon black pepper
⅓ cup pitted green olives, diced
¼ cup finely diced onion
1 teaspoon chopped capers

1. Spray the air fryer basket with the olive oil spray. Drizzle the fillets with the olive oil and sprinkle with the cumin, salt, and pepper. Place the fish in the air fryer basket. Set the air fryer to 325ºF (163ºC) for 10 minutes, or until the fish flakes easily with a fork. 2. Meanwhile, in a small bowl, stir together the olives, onion, and capers. 3. Serve the fish topped with the relish.

Per Serving:
calories: 379 | fat: 26g | protein: 32g | carbs: 3g | fiber: 1g | sodium: 581mg

Sage-Stuffed Whole Trout with Roasted Vegetables

Prep time: 10 minutes | Cook time: 35 minutes | Serves 4

2 red bell peppers, seeded and cut into 1-inch-wide strips
1 (15 ounces / 425 g) can artichoke hearts, drained and cut into quarters
1 large red onion, halved through the stem and cut into 1-inch-wide wedges
4 cloves garlic, halved
3 tablespoons olive oil, divided
1½ teaspoons salt, divided
¾ teaspoon freshly ground black pepper, divided
2 whole rainbow trout, cleaned with head on
3 cups sage leaves
Juice of ½ lemon

1. Preheat the oven to 475°F (245°C). 2. In a large baking dish, toss the bell peppers, artichoke hearts, onion, and garlic with 2 tablespoons of the olive oil. Sprinkle with 1 teaspoon of salt and ½ teaspoon of pepper. Roast the vegetables in the preheated oven for 20 minutes. Reduce the heat to 375°F (190°C). 3. While the vegetables are roasting, prepare the fish. Brush the fish inside and out with the remaining 1 tablespoon of olive oil and season with the remaining ½ teaspoon of salt and ¼ teaspoon of pepper. Stuff each fish with half of the sage leaves. 4. Remove the vegetables from the oven and place the fish on top. Put back in the oven and bake at 375°F (190°C) for about 15 minutes more, until the fish is cooked through. Remove from the oven, squeeze the lemon juice over the fish, and let rest for 5 minutes. 5. To serve, halve the fish. Spoon roasted vegetables onto 4 serving plates and serve half a fish alongside each, topped with some of the sage leaves.

Per Serving:

calories: 349 | fat: 16g | protein: 24g | carbs: 34g | fiber: 17g | sodium: 879mg

Italian Halibut with Grapes and Olive Oil

Prep time: 15 minutes | Cook time: 20 minutes | Serves 4

¼ cup extra-virgin olive oil
4 boneless halibut fillets, 4 ounces (113 g) each
4 cloves garlic, roughly chopped
1 small red chile pepper, finely chopped
2 cups seedless green grapes
A handful of fresh basil leaves, roughly torn
½ teaspoon unrefined sea salt or salt
Freshly ground black pepper

1. Heat the olive oil in a large, heavy-bottomed skillet over medium-high heat. Add the halibut, followed by the garlic, chile pepper, grapes, basil, and the salt and pepper. Pour in 1¾ cups of water, turn the heat down to medium-low, cover, and cook the fish

until opaque, or for 7 minutes on each side. 2. Remove the fish from the pan and place on a large serving dish. Raise the heat, cook the sauce for 30 seconds to concentrate the flavors slightly. Taste and adjust salt and pepper. Pour sauce over the fish.

Per Serving:

calories: 389 | fat: 29g | protein: 17g | carbs: 15g | fiber: 1g | sodium: 384mg

Salmon Fritters with Zucchini

Prep time: 15 minutes | Cook time: 12 minutes | Serves 4

2 tablespoons almond flour
1 zucchini, grated
1 egg, beaten
6 ounces (170 g) salmon fillet,
diced
1 teaspoon avocado oil
½ teaspoon ground black pepper

1. Mix almond flour with zucchini, egg, salmon, and ground black pepper. 2. Then make the fritters from the salmon mixture. 3. Sprinkle the air fryer basket with avocado oil and put the fritters inside. 4. Cook the fritters at 375°F (191°C) for 6 minutes per side.

Per Serving:

calories: 102 | fat: 4g | protein: 11g | carbs: 4g | fiber: 1g | sodium: 52mg

Halibut Fillets with Vegetables

Prep time: 20 minutes | Cook time: 5 minutes | Serves 2

1 cup chopped broccoli
1 large potato, peeled and diced
1 large carrot, peeled and grated
1 small zucchini, trimmed and grated
4 ounces (113 g) mushrooms, sliced
¼ teaspoon dried thyme
¼ teaspoon grated lemon zest
1 (½-pound / 227-g) halibut fillet
½ cup white wine
½ cup lemon juice
1 teaspoon dried parsley
¼ teaspoon salt
¼ teaspoon ground black pepper
⅛ teaspoon ground nutmeg

1. Place the rack and steamer basket in the Instant Pot®. Place broccoli, potato, carrot, zucchini, and mushrooms in layers in the basket. Sprinkle thyme and lemon zest over vegetables. 2. Place fish over vegetables. Pour wine and lemon juice over fish. Sprinkle parsley, salt, and pepper over the fish and vegetables. 3. Close lid, set steam release to Sealing, press the Manual button, and set time to 5 minutes. When the timer beeps, quick-release the pressure until the float valve drops and open lid. Divide fish and vegetables between two plates. Sprinkle nutmeg over each serving.

Per Serving:

calories: 278 | fat: 3g | protein: 31g | carbs: 23g | fiber: 5g | sodium: 409mg

Tuscan Tuna and Zucchini Burgers

Prep time: 10 minutes |Cook time: 10 minutes|

Serves: 4

3 slices whole-wheat sandwich bread, toasted
2 (5-ounce / 142-g) cans tuna in olive oil, drained
1 cup shredded zucchini (about ¾ small zucchini)
1 large egg, lightly beaten
¼ cup diced red bell pepper (about ¼ pepper)

1 tablespoon dried oregano
1 teaspoon lemon zest
¼ teaspoon freshly ground black pepper
¼ teaspoon kosher or sea salt
1 tablespoon extra-virgin olive oil
Salad greens or 4 whole-wheat rolls, for serving (optional)

1. Crumble the toast into bread crumbs using your fingers (or use a knife to cut into ¼-inch cubes) until you have 1 cup of loosely packed crumbs. Pour the crumbs into a large bowl. Add the tuna, zucchini, egg, bell pepper, oregano, lemon zest, black pepper, and salt. Mix well with a fork. With your hands, form the mixture into four (½-cup-size) patties. Place on a plate, and press each patty flat to about ¾-inch thick. 2. In a large skillet over medium-high heat, heat the oil until it's very hot, about 2 minutes. Add the patties to the hot oil, then turn the heat down to medium. Cook the patties for 5 minutes, flip with a spatula, and cook for an additional 5 minutes. Enjoy as is or serve on salad greens or whole-wheat rolls.

Per Serving:

calories: 255 | fat: 11g | protein: 26g | carbs: 12g | fiber: 2g | sodium: 570mg

Roasted Branzino with Lemon and Herbs

Prep time: 10 minutes | Cook time: 20 minutes |

Serves 2

1 to 1½ pounds (454 to 680 g) branzino, scaled and gutted
Salt
Freshly ground black pepper
1 tablespoon olive oil

1 lemon, sliced
3 garlic cloves, minced
¼ cup chopped fresh herbs (any mixture of oregano, thyme, parsley, and rosemary)

1. Preheat the oven to 425ºF (220ºC) and set the rack to the middle position. 2. Lay the cleaned fish in a baking dish and make 4 to 5 slits in it, about 1½ inches apart. 3. Season the inside of the branzino with salt and pepper and drizzle with olive oil. 4. Fill the cavity of the fish with lemon slices. Sprinkle the chopped garlic and herbs over the lemon and close the fish. 5. Roast the fish for 15 to 20 minutes, or until the flesh is opaque and it flakes apart easily. 6. Before eating, open the fish, remove the lemon slices, and carefully pull out the bone.

Per Serving:

calories: 287 | fat: 12g | protein: 42g | carbs: 2g | fiber: 0g | sodium: 151mg

Balsamic-Glazed Black Pepper Salmon

Prep time: 5 minutes | Cook time: 8 minutes | Serves 4

½ cup balsamic vinegar
1 tablespoon honey
4 (8-ounce / 227-g) salmon fillets

Sea salt and freshly ground pepper, to taste
1 tablespoon olive oil

1. Heat a cast-iron skillet over medium-high heat. Mix the vinegar and honey in a small bowl. 2. Season the salmon fillets with the sea salt and freshly ground pepper; brush with the honey-balsamic glaze. 3. Add olive oil to the skillet, and sear the salmon fillets, cooking for 3 to 4 minutes on each side until lightly browned and medium rare in the center. 4. Let sit for 5 minutes before serving.

Per Serving:

calories: 478 | fat: 17g | protein: 65g | carbs: 10g | fiber: 0g | sodium: 246mg

Lime Lobster Tails

Prep time: 10 minutes | Cook time: 6 minutes |

Serves 4

4 lobster tails, peeled
2 tablespoons lime juice

½ teaspoon dried basil
½ teaspoon coconut oil, melted

1. Mix lobster tails with lime juice, dried basil, and coconut oil. 2. Put the lobster tails in the air fryer and cook at 380ºF (193ºC) for 6 minutes.

Per Serving:

calories: 123 | fat: 2g | protein: 25g | carbs: 1g | fiber: 0g | sodium: 635mg

Fried Fresh Sardines

Prep time: 5 minutes | Cook time: 5 minutes | Serves 4

Avocado oil
1½ pounds (680 g) whole fresh sardines, scales removed
1 teaspoon salt

1 teaspoon freshly ground black pepper
2 cups flour

1. Preheat a deep skillet over medium heat. Pour in enough oil so there is about 1 inch of it in the pan. 2. Season the fish with the salt and pepper. 3. Dredge the fish in the flour so it is completely covered. 4. Slowly drop in 1 fish at a time, making sure not to overcrowd the pan. 5. Cook for about 3 minutes on each side or just until the fish begins to brown on all sides. Serve warm.

Per Serving:

calories: 581 | fat: 20g | protein: 48g | carbs: 48g | fiber: 2g | sodium: 583mg

Creole Crayfish

Prep time: 10 minutes | Cook time: 3 to 4 hours | Serves 2

1½ cups diced celery
1 large yellow onion, chopped
2 small bell peppers, any colors, chopped
1 (8-ounce / 227-g) can tomato sauce
1 (28-ounce / 794-g) can whole tomatoes, broken up, with the

juice
1 clove garlic, minced
½ teaspoon sea salt
¼ teaspoon black pepper
6 drops hot pepper sauce (like tabasco)
1 pound (454 g) precooked crayfish meat

1. Place the celery, onion, and bell peppers in the slow cooker. Add the tomato sauce, tomatoes, and garlic. Sprinkle with the salt and pepper and add the hot sauce. 2. Cover and cook on high for 3 to 4 hours or on low for 6 to 8 hours. 3. About 30 minutes before the cooking time is completed, add the crayfish. 4. Serve hot.

Per Serving:
calories: 334 | fat: 4g | protein: 43g | carbs: 34g | fiber: 13g | sodium: 659mg

Crushed Marcona Almond Swordfish

Prep time: 25 minutes | Cook time: 15 minutes | Serves 4

½ cup almond flour
¼ cup crushed Marcona almonds
½ to 1 teaspoon salt, divided
2 pounds (907 g) Swordfish, preferably 1 inch thick
1 large egg, beaten (optional)
¼ cup pure apple cider
¼ cup extra-virgin olive oil, plus more for frying
3 to 4 sprigs flat-leaf parsley,

chopped
1 lemon, juiced
1 tablespoon Spanish paprika
5 medium baby portobello mushrooms, chopped (optional)
4 or 5 chopped scallions, both green and white parts
3 to 4 garlic cloves, peeled
¼ cup chopped pitted kalamata olives

1. On a dinner plate, spread the flour and crushed Marcona almonds and mix in the salt. Alternately, pour the flour, almonds, and ¼ teaspoon of salt into a large plastic food storage bag. Add the fish and coat it with the flour mixture. If a thicker coat is desired, repeat this step after dipping the fish in the egg (if using). 2. In a measuring cup, combine the apple cider, ¼ cup of olive oil, parsley, lemon juice, paprika, and ¼ teaspoon of salt. Mix well and set aside. 3. In a large, heavy-bottom sauté pan or skillet, pour the olive oil to a depth of ⅛ inch and heat on medium heat. Once the oil is hot, add the fish and brown for 3 to 5 minutes, then turn the fish over and add the mushrooms (If using), scallions, garlic, and olives. Cook for an additional 3 minutes. Once the other side of the fish is brown, remove the fish from the pan and set aside. 4. Pour the cider mixture into the skillet and mix well with the vegetables. Put the fried fish into the skillet on top of the mixture and cook with sauce on medium-low heat for 10 minutes, until the fish flakes easily with a fork. Carefully remove the fish from the pan and plate. Spoon the sauce over the fish. Serve with white rice or home-fried potatoes.

Per Serving:
calories: 620 | fat: 37g | protein: 63g | carbs: 10g | fiber: 5g | sodium: 644mg

Wild Cod Oreganata

Prep time: 10 minutes | Cook time: 20 minutes | Serves 2

10 ounces (283 g) wild cod (1 large piece or 2 smaller ones)
⅓ cup panko bread crumbs
1 tablespoon dried oregano
Zest of 1 lemon
½ teaspoon salt
Pinch freshly ground black

pepper
1 tablespoon olive oil
2 tablespoons freshly squeezed lemon juice
2 tablespoons white wine
1 tablespoon minced fresh parsley

1. Preheat the oven to 350°F(180°C). Place the cod in a baking dish and pat it dry with a paper towel. 2. In a small bowl, combine the panko, oregano, lemon zest, salt, pepper, and olive oil and mix well. Pat the panko mixture onto the fish. 3. Combine the lemon juice and wine in a small bowl and pour it around the fish. 4. Bake the fish for 20 minutes, or until it flakes apart easily and reaches an internal temperature of 145°F(63°C). 5. Garnish with fresh minced parsley.

Per Serving:
calories: 203 | fat: 8g | protein: 23g | carbs: 9g | fiber: 2g | sodium: 149mg

Grilled Bluefish

Prep time: 10 minutes | Cook time: 8 minutes | Serves 4

1 cup olive oil
½ cup white wine
¼ cup fresh basil leaves, chopped
Juice and zest of 2 lemons or oranges
2–3 garlic cloves, minced

1 teaspoon ground cumin
1 teaspoon thyme
2 pinches cayenne pepper
4 bluefish or fish fillets
Sea salt and freshly ground pepper, to taste

1. Combine all the ingredients except the fish in a plastic bag or shallow bowl. 2. Divide marinade in half, reserving half in the refrigerator and placing the fish in the other half of the marinade. 3. Refrigerate for at least 1 hour. Heat the grill to medium-high. 4. Brush the grates with olive oil, and grill the fish for 6–8 minutes, turning halfway through the cooking time. 5. Season with sea salt and freshly ground pepper, to taste. Warm the reserved marinade and serve with the fish.

Per Serving:
calories: 713 | fat: 61g | protein: 31g | carbs: 7g | fiber: 0g | sodium: 93mg

Citrus Mediterranean Salmon with Lemon Caper Sauce

Prep time: 15 minutes | Cook time: 22 minutes | Serves 2

2 tablespoons fresh lemon juice
⅓ cup orange juice
1 tablespoon extra virgin olive oil
⅛ teaspoon freshly ground black pepper
2 (6-ounce / 170-g) salmon fillets
Lemon Caper Sauce:
2 tablespoons extra virgin olive oil

1 tablespoon finely chopped red onion
1 garlic clove, minced
2 tablespoons fresh lemon juice
5 ounces (142) dry white wine
2 tablespoons capers, rinsed
⅛ teaspoon freshly ground black pepper

1. Preheat the oven to 350°F (180°C). 2. In a small bowl, combine the lemon juice, orange juice, olive oil, and black pepper. Whisk until blended, then pour the mixture into a zipper-lock bag. Place the fillets in the bag, shake gently, and transfer the salmon to the refrigerator to marinate for 10 minutes. 3. When the salmon is done marinating, transfer the fillets and marinade to a medium baking dish. Bake for 10–15 minutes or until the salmon is cooked through and the internal temperature reaches 165°F (74°C). Remove the salmon from the oven and cover loosely with foil. Set aside to rest. 4. While the salmon is resting, make the lemon caper sauce by heating the olive oil in a medium pan over medium heat. When the olive oil begins to shimmer, add the onions and sauté for 3 minutes, stirring frequently, then add the garlic and sauté for another 30 seconds. 5. Add the lemon juice and wine. Bring the mixture to a boil and cook until the sauce becomes thick, about 2–3 minutes, then remove the pan from the heat. Add the capers and black pepper, and stir. 6. Transfer the fillets to 2 plates, and spoon 1½ tablespoons of the sauce over each fillet. Store covered in the refrigerator for up to 3 days.

Per Serving:
calories: 485 | fat: 28g | protein: 36g | carbs: 11g | fiber: 1g | sodium: 331mg

Simple Poached Turbot

Prep time: 10 minutes | Cook time: 50 minutes | Serves 4

1 cup vegetable or chicken stock
½ cup dry white wine
1 yellow onion, sliced
1 lemon, sliced

4 sprigs fresh dill
½ teaspoon sea salt
4 (6-ounce / 170-g) turbot fillets

1. Combine the stock and wine in the slow cooker. Cover and heat on high for 20 to 30 minutes. 2. Add the onion, lemon, dill, salt, and turbot to the slow cooker. Cover and cook on high for about 20 minutes, until the turbot is opaque and cooked through according to taste. Serve hot.

Per Serving:
calories: 210 | fat: 5g | protein: 29g | carbs: 6g | fiber: 1g | sodium: 565mg

Chapter 5 Beef, Pork, and Lamb

Greek Lamb Burgers

Prep time: 10 minutes | Cook time: 10 minutes |
Serves 4

1 pound (454 g) ground lamb
½ teaspoon salt
½ teaspoon freshly ground
black pepper

4 tablespoons feta cheese,
crumbled
Buns, toppings, and tzatziki, for
serving (optional)

1. Preheat a grill, grill pan, or lightly oiled skillet to high heat. 2. In a large bowl, using your hands, combine the lamb with the salt and pepper. 3. Divide the meat into 4 portions. Divide each portion in half to make a top and a bottom. Flatten each half into a 3-inch circle. Make a dent in the center of one of the halves and place 1 tablespoon of the feta cheese in the center. Place the second half of the patty on top of the feta cheese and press down to close the 2 halves together, making it resemble a round burger. 4. Cook the stuffed patty for 3 minutes on each side, for medium-well. Serve on a bun with your favorite toppings and tzatziki sauce, if desired.

Per Serving:
calories: 345 | fat: 29g | protein: 20g | carbs: 1g | fiber: 0g | sodium: 462mg

Stewed Pork with Greens

Prep time: 10 minutes | Cook time: 1 hour 40
minutes | Serves 3

¾ teaspoon fine sea salt, divided
½ teaspoon freshly ground
black pepper, divided
1¼ pounds (567g) pork
shoulder, trimmed and cut into
1½-inch chunks
6 tablespoons extra virgin olive
oil, divided
1 bay leaf
3 allspice berries
2 tablespoons dry red wine

1 medium onion (any variety),
chopped
2 spring onions, sliced (white
parts only)
1 leek, sliced (white parts only)
¼ cup chopped fresh dill
1 pound (454 g) Swiss chard,
roughly chopped
3 tablespoons fresh lemon juice
plus more for serving

1. Sprinkle ¼ teaspoon of the sea salt and ¼ teaspoon of the black pepper over the pork. Rub the seasonings into the meat. 2. Add 1 tablespoon of the olive oil to a heavy pan over medium-high heat. Add the bay leaf and allspice berries, then add the meat and brown for 2–3 minutes per side. 3. Add the red wine and let it bubble, then use a wooden spatula to scrape the browned bits from the pan. Continue simmering until the liquid has evaporated, about 3 minutes, then transfer the meat and juices to a plate. Set aside. 4. Heat 4 tablespoons of the olive oil in a large pot placed over medium heat. Add the onion, spring onions, and leeks, and sauté until soft, about 5 minutes, then add the dill and sauté for 1–2 minutes more. 5. Add the meat and juices to the pot and sprinkle another ¼ teaspoon sea salt and ¼ teaspoon black pepper over the meat. Add just enough hot water to cover the meat halfway (start with less water), then cover and reduce the heat to low. Simmer for about 1 hour or until the meat is tender. 6. Remove the lid and add the chard and lemon juice. Use tongs to toss the chard and mix well. Continue simmering for about 5 minutes, then drizzle in the last tablespoon of olive oil and mix again. Cover and simmer for another 20 minutes, mixing occasionally, until the greens are wilted, then remove the pot from the heat. 7. Let stand covered for 10 minutes, then add a squeeze of lemon before serving. Allow to cool completely before covering and storing in the refrigerator for up to 2 days.

Per Serving:
calories: 565 | fat: 38g | protein: 39g | carbs: 15g | fiber: 4g | sodium: 592mg

Beef Kofta

Prep time: 10 minutes | Cook time: 20 minutes |
Serves 4

Olive oil cooking spray
½ onion, roughly chopped
1-inch piece ginger, peeled
2 garlic cloves, peeled
⅓ cup fresh parsley
⅓ cup fresh mint
1 pound (454 g) ground beef
1 tablespoon ground cumin

1 tablespoon ground coriander
1 teaspoon ground cinnamon
¾ teaspoon kosher salt
½ teaspoon ground sumac
¼ teaspoon ground cloves
¼ teaspoon freshly ground
black pepper

1. Preheat the oven to 400ºF (205ºC). Grease a 12-cup muffin tin with olive oil cooking spray. 2. In a food processor, add the onion, ginger, garlic, parsley, and mint; process until minced. 3. Place the onion mixture in a large bowl. Add the beef, cumin, coriander, cinnamon, salt, sumac, cloves, and black pepper and mix together thoroughly with your hands. 4. Divide the beef mixture into 12 balls and place each one in a cup of the prepared muffin tin. Bake for 20 minutes.

Per Serving:
calories: 225 | fat: 12g | protein: g24 | carbs: 5g | fiber: 2g | sodium: 290mg

Greek-Style Ground Beef Pita Sandwiches

Prep timePrep Time: 15 minutes | Cook Time: 10 minutes | Serves 2

For the beef
1 tablespoon olive oil
½ medium onion, minced
2 garlic cloves, minced
6 ounces (170 g) lean ground beef
1 teaspoon dried oregano
For the yogurt sauce
⅓ cup plain Greek yogurt
1 ounce (28 g) crumbled feta cheese (about 3 tablespoons)
1 tablespoon minced fresh

parsley
1 tablespoon minced scallion
1 tablespoon freshly squeezed lemon juice
Pinch salt
For the sandwiches
2 large Greek-style pitas
½ cup cherry tomatoes, halved
1 cup diced cucumber
Salt
Freshly ground black pepper

Make the beef Heat the olive oil in a sauté pan over medium high-heat. Add the onion, garlic, and ground beef and sauté for 7 minutes, breaking up the meat well. When the meat is no longer pink, drain off any fat and stir in the oregano. Turn off the heat. Make the yogurt sauce In a small bowl, combine the yogurt, feta, parsley, scallion, lemon juice, and salt. To assemble the sandwiches 1. Warm the pitas in the microwave for 20 seconds each. 2. To serve, spread some of the yogurt sauce over each warm pita. Top with the ground beef, cherry tomatoes, and diced cucumber. Season with salt and pepper. Add additional yogurt sauce if desired.

Per Serving:
calories: 541 | fat: 21g | protein: 29g | carbs: 57g | fiber: 4g | sodium: 694mg

Stuffed Pork Loin with Sun-Dried Tomato and Goat Cheese

Prep time: 15 minutes | Cook time: 30 to 40 minutes | Serves 6

1 to 1½ pounds (454 to 680 g) pork tenderloin
1 cup crumbled goat cheese
4 ounces (113 g) frozen spinach, thawed and well drained
2 tablespoons chopped sun-dried tomatoes
2 tablespoons extra-virgin olive

oil (or seasoned oil marinade from sun-dried tomatoes), plus ¼ cup, divided
½ teaspoon salt
½ teaspoon freshly ground black pepper
Zucchini noodles or sautéed greens, for serving

1. Preheat the oven to 350°F(180°C). Cut cooking twine into eight (6-inch) pieces. 2. Cut the pork tenderloin in half lengthwise, leaving about an inch border, being careful to not cut all the way through to the other side. Open the tenderloin like a book to form a large rectangle. Place it between two pieces of parchment paper or plastic wrap and pound to about ¼-inch thickness with a meat mallet, rolling pin, or the back of a heavy spoon. 3. In a small bowl, combine the goat cheese, spinach, sun-dried tomatoes, 2 tablespoons olive oil, salt, and pepper and mix to incorporate well. 4. Spread the filling over the surface of the pork, leaving a 1-inch border from one long edge and both short edges. To roll, start from the long edge with filling and roll towards the opposite edge. Tie cooking twine around the pork to secure it closed, evenly spacing each of the eight pieces of twine along the length of the roll. 5. In a Dutch oven or large oven-safe skillet, heat ¼ cup olive oil over medium-high heat. Add the pork and brown on all sides. Remove from the heat, cover, and bake until the pork is cooked through, 45 to 75 minutes, depending on the thickness of the pork. Remove from the oven and let rest for 10 minutes at room temperature. 6. To serve, remove the twine and discard. Slice the pork into medallions and serve over zucchini noodles or sautéed greens, spooning the cooking oil and any bits of filling that fell out during cooking over top.

Per Serving:
calories: 270 | fat: 20g | protein: 20g | carbs: 2g | fiber: 1g | sodium: 392mg

One-Pot Pork Loin Dinner

Prep time: 35 minutes | Cook time: 28 minutes | Serves 6

1 tablespoon olive oil
1 small onion, peeled and diced
1 pound (454 g) boneless pork loin, cut into 1" pieces
½ teaspoon salt
¼ teaspoon ground black pepper
½ cup white wine
1 cup low-sodium chicken broth
1 large rutabaga, peeled and diced
1 large turnip, peeled and diced

4 small Yukon Gold or red potatoes, quartered
4 medium carrots, peeled and diced
1 stalk celery, finely diced
½ cup sliced leeks, white part only
½ teaspoon mild curry powder
¼ teaspoon dried thyme
2 teaspoons dried parsley
3 tablespoons lemon juice
2 large Granny Smith apples, peeled, cored, and diced

1. Press the Sauté button on the Instant Pot® and heat oil. Add onion and cook until tender, about 3 minutes. Add pork and season with salt and pepper. Cook until pork begins to brown, about 5 minutes. Add wine, broth, rutabaga, and turnip and stir well. Add potatoes, carrots, celery, leeks, curry powder, thyme, parsley, and lemon juice to the pot. Stir to combine. Press the Cancel button. 2. Close lid, set steam release to Sealing, press the Manual button, and set time to 15 minutes. When the timer beeps, let pressure release naturally, about 25 minutes. Press the Cancel button. 3. Open lid and add diced apples. Press the Sauté button and simmer for 5 minutes or until apples are tender. Serve immediately in large bowls.

Per Serving:
calories: 271 | fat: 4g | protein: 14g | carbs: 30g | fiber: 5g | sodium: 316mg

Balsamic Beef and Vegetable Stew

Prep time: 30 minutes | Cook time: 54 minutes |

Serves 8

1 pound (454 g) beef stew meat, cut into 1" pieces	minced
	4 sprigs thyme
2 tablespoons all-purpose flour	2 tablespoons chopped fresh
¼ teaspoon salt	oregano
¼ teaspoon ground black pepper	2 bay leaves
	¼ cup balsamic vinegar
2 tablespoons olive oil, divided	1½ cups beef broth
2 medium carrots, peeled and sliced	1 (14½-ounce / 411-g) can diced tomatoes, drained
2 stalks celery, sliced	1 medium russet potato, cut into
1 medium onion, peeled and chopped	1" pieces
	1 (6-ounce / 170-g) can large
8 ounces (227 g) whole crimini mushrooms, quartered	black olives, drained and quartered
3 cloves garlic, peeled and	¼ cup chopped fresh parsley

1. In a medium bowl, add beef, flour, salt, and pepper. Toss meat with seasoned flour until thoroughly coated. Set aside. 2. Press the Sauté button on the Instant Pot® and heat 1 tablespoon oil. Place half of the beef pieces in a single layer, leaving space between each piece to prevent steaming, and brown well on all sides, about 3 minutes per side. Transfer beef to a medium bowl and repeat with remaining 1 tablespoon oil and beef. 3. Add carrots, celery, and onion to the pot. Cook until tender, about 8 minutes. Add mushrooms, garlic, thyme, oregano, and bay leaves. Stir well. 4. Slowly add balsamic vinegar and beef broth, scraping bottom of pot well to release any brown bits. Add tomatoes, potato, and browned beef along with any juices. Press the Cancel button. 5. Close lid, set steam release to Sealing, press the Stew button, and set time to 40 minutes. When the timer beeps, quick-release the pressure until the float valve drops, open lid, and stir well. Remove and discard thyme and bay leaves. Stir in olives and parsley. Serve immediately.

Per Serving:
calories: 332| fat: 17g | protein: 16g | carbs: 15g | fiber: 5g | sodium: 404mg

Mediterranean Chimichurri Skirt Steak

Prep time: 10 minutes | Cook time: 15 minutes |

Serves 4

¾ cup fresh mint	4 garlic cloves, peeled
¾ cup fresh parsley	½ teaspoon red pepper flakes
⅔ cup extra-virgin olive oil	½ teaspoon kosher salt
⅓ cup lemon juice	1 to 1½ pounds (454 to 680 g)
Zest of 1 lemon	skirt steak, cut in half if longer
2 tablespoons dried oregano	than grill pan

1. In a food processor or blender, add the mint, parsley, olive oil, lemon juice, lemon zest, oregano, garlic, red pepper flakes, and

salt. Process until the mixture reaches your desired consistency—anywhere from a slightly chunky to smooth purée. Remove a half cup of the chimichurri mixture and set aside. 2. Pour the remaining chimichurri mixture into a medium bowl or zip-top bag and add the steak. Mix together well and marinate for at least 30 minutes, and up to 8 hours in the refrigerator. 3. In a grill pan over medium-high heat, add the steak and cook 4 minutes on each side (for medium rare). Cook an additional 1 to 2 minutes per side for medium. 4. Place the steak on a cutting board, tent with foil to keep it warm, and let it rest for 10 minutes. Thinly slice the steak crosswise against the grain and serve with the reserved sauce.

Per Serving:
calories: 460 | fat: 38g | protein: 28g | carbs: 5g | fiber: 2g | sodium: 241mg

Savoy Cabbage Rolls

Prep time: 10 minutes | Cook time: 16 minutes |

Serves 10

1 medium head savoy cabbage	1 tablespoon olive oil
3 cups water, divided	2 tablespoons minced fresh
½ pound (227 g) ground beef	mint
1 cup long-grain rice	1 teaspoon dried tarragon
1 small red bell pepper, seeded and minced	1 teaspoon salt
	½ teaspoon ground black
1 medium onion, peeled and diced	pepper
	2 tablespoons lemon juice
1 cup beef broth	

1. Remove the large outer leaves from cabbage and set aside. Remove remaining cabbage leaves and place them in the Instant Pot®. Pour in 1 cup water. 2. Close lid, set steam release to Sealing, press the Steam button, and set time to 1 minute. Press the Adjust button to change the pressure to Low. When the timer beeps, quick-release the pressure until the float valve drops and then open lid. Press the Cancel button. Drain cabbage leaves in a colander and then move them to a kitchen towel. 3. In a medium mixing bowl, add ground beef, rice, bell pepper, onion, broth, olive oil, mint, tarragon, salt, and black pepper. Stir to combine. 4. Place the large uncooked cabbage leaves on the bottom of the Instant Pot®. 5. Remove the stem running down the center of each steamed cabbage leaf and tear each leaf in half lengthwise. Place 1 tablespoon ground beef mixture in the center of each cabbage piece. Loosely fold the sides of the leaf over the filling and then fold the top and bottom of the leaf over the folded sides. As you complete them, place each stuffed cabbage leaf in the pot. 6. Pour remaining 2 cups water and lemon juice over the stuffed cabbage rolls. Close lid, set steam release to Sealing, press the Manual button, and set time to 15 minutes. When the timer beeps, let pressure release naturally for 10 minutes. Quick-release any remaining pressure until the float valve drops and then open lid. 7. Carefully move stuffed cabbage rolls to a serving platter. Serve warm.

Per Serving:
calories: 117 | fat: 3g | protein: 6g | carbs: 15g | fiber: 0g | sodium: 337mg

Parmesan-Crusted Pork Chops

Prep time: 5 minutes | Cook time: 12 minutes |

Serves 4

1 large egg
½ cup grated Parmesan cheese
4 (4-ounce / 113-g) boneless
pork chops
½ teaspoon salt
¼ teaspoon ground black
pepper

1. Whisk egg in a medium bowl and place Parmesan in a separate medium bowl. 2. Sprinkle pork chops on both sides with salt and pepper. Dip each pork chop into egg, then press both sides into Parmesan. 3. Place pork chops into ungreased air fryer basket. Adjust the temperature to 400°F (204°C) and air fry for 12 minutes, turning chops halfway through cooking. Pork chops will be golden and have an internal temperature of at least 145°F (63°C) when done. Serve warm.

Per Serving:

calories: 218 | fat: 9g | protein: 32g | carbs: 1g | fiber: 0g | sodium: 372mg

Rack of Lamb with Pistachio Crust

Prep time: 10 minutes | Cook time: 19 minutes |

Serves 2

½ cup finely chopped pistachios
3 tablespoons panko bread
crumbs
1 teaspoon chopped fresh
rosemary
2 teaspoons chopped fresh
oregano
Salt and freshly ground black
pepper, to taste
1 tablespoon olive oil
1 rack of lamb, bones trimmed
of fat and frenched
1 tablespoon Dijon mustard

1. Preheat the air fryer to 380°F (193°C). 2. Combine the pistachios, bread crumbs, rosemary, oregano, salt and pepper in a small bowl. (This is a good job for your food processor if you have one.) Drizzle in the olive oil and stir to combine. 3. Season the rack of lamb with salt and pepper on all sides and transfer it to the air fryer basket with the fat side facing up. Air fry the lamb for 12 minutes. Remove the lamb from the air fryer and brush the fat side of the lamb rack with the Dijon mustard. Coat the rack with the pistachio mixture, pressing the bread crumbs onto the lamb with your hands and rolling the bottom of the rack in any of the crumbs that fall off. 4. Return the rack of lamb to the air fryer and air fry for another 3 to 7 minutes or until an instant read thermometer reads 140°F (60°C) for medium. Add or subtract a couple of minutes for lamb that is more or less well cooked. (Your time will vary depending on how big the rack of lamb is.) 5. Let the lamb rest for at least 5 minutes. Then, slice into chops and serve.

Per Serving:

calories: 716 | fat: 45g | protein: 64g | carbs: 17g | fiber: 5g | sodium: 344mg

Beef Stew with Red Wine

Prep time: 15 minutes | Cook time: 46 minutes |

Serves 8

1 pound (454 g) beef stew meat,
cut into 1" pieces
2 tablespoons all-purpose flour
¼ teaspoon salt
¼ teaspoon ground black
pepper
2 tablespoons olive oil, divided
1 pound (454 g) whole crimini
mushrooms
2 cloves garlic, peeled and
minced
4 sprigs thyme
2 bay leaves
8 ounces (227 g) baby carrots
8 ounces (227 g) frozen pearl
onions, thawed
1 cup red wine
½ cup beef broth
¼ cup chopped fresh parsley

1. In a medium bowl, toss beef with flour, salt, and pepper until thoroughly coated. Set aside. 2. Press the Sauté button on the Instant Pot® and heat 1 tablespoon oil. Add half of the beef pieces in a single layer, leaving space between each piece to prevent steaming, and brown well on all sides, about 3 minutes per side. Transfer beef to a medium bowl and repeat with remaining 1 tablespoon oil and beef. Press the Cancel button. 3. Add mushrooms, garlic, thyme, bay leaves, carrots, onions, wine, and broth to the Instant Pot®. Stir well. Close lid, set steam release to Sealing, press the Stew button, and set time to 40 minutes. When the timer beeps, quick-release the pressure until the float valve drops, open lid, and stir well. Remove and discard thyme and bay leaves. Sprinkle with parsley and serve hot.

Per Serving:

calories: 206 | fat: 13g | protein: 12g | carbs: 6g | fiber: 1g | sodium: 186mg

Mediterranean Pork with Olives

Prep time: 10 minutes | Cook time: 6 to 8 hours |

Serves 4

1 small onion, sliced
4 thick-cut, bone-in pork chops
1 cup low-sodium chicken
broth
Juice of 1 lemon
2 garlic cloves, minced
1 teaspoon sea salt
1 teaspoon dried oregano
1 teaspoon dried parsley
½ teaspoon freshly ground
black pepper
2 cups whole green olives,
pitted
1 pint cherry tomatoes

1. Put the onion in a slow cooker and arrange the pork chops on top. 2. In a small bowl, whisk together the chicken broth, lemon juice, garlic, salt, oregano, parsley, and pepper. Pour the sauce over the pork chops. Top with the olives and tomatoes. 3. Cover the cooker and cook for 6 to 8 hours on Low heat.

Per Serving:

calories: 339 | fat: 14g | protein: 42g | carbs: 6g | fiber: 4g | sodium: 708mg

Beef and Wild Mushroom Stew

Prep time: 15 minutes | Cook time: 1 hour 15 minutes | Serves 8

2 pounds (907 g) fresh porcini or morel mushrooms
⅓ cup olive oil
2 pounds (907 g) lean, boneless beef, cut into 2-inch cubes
2 medium onions, finely chopped
1 clove garlic, minced
1 cup dry white wine
1 teaspoon thyme, minced
Sea salt and freshly ground pepper, to taste

1. Wash the mushrooms carefully by soaking them in cold water and swirling them around. 2. Trim away any soft parts of the mushrooms. 3. Heat the olive oil in a heavy stew pot over medium-high heat. Brown the meat evenly on all sides, and set aside on a plate. 4. Add the onions, garlic, and mushrooms to the olive oil, and cook for 5–8 minutes, or until the onions are tender, stirring frequently. 5. Add the remaining ingredients and return the browned meat to the pot. Cover and bring to a boil, then reduce heat to low and simmer. Simmer for 1 hour, or until the meat is tender and flavorful. 6. Season with sea salt and freshly ground pepper to taste.

Per Serving:
calories: 343 | fat: 22g | protein: 26g | carbs: 9g | fiber: 2g | sodium: 93mg

Lamb Kofte with Yogurt Sauce

Prep time: 30 minutes | Cook time: 15 minutes | Serves 4

1 pound (454 g) ground lamb
½ cup finely chopped fresh mint, plus 2 tablespoons
¼ cup almond or coconut flour
¼ cup finely chopped red onion
¼ cup toasted pine nuts
2 teaspoons ground cumin
1½ teaspoons salt, divided
1 teaspoon ground cinnamon
1 teaspoon ground ginger
½ teaspoon ground nutmeg
½ teaspoon freshly ground black pepper
1 cup plain whole-milk Greek yogurt
2 tablespoons extra-virgin olive oil
Zest and juice of 1 lime

1. Heat the oven broiler to the low setting. You can also bake these at high heat (450 to 475°F/ 235 to 245ºC) if you happen to have a very hot broiler. Submerge four wooden skewers in water and let soak at least 10 minutes to prevent them from burning. 2. In a large bowl, combine the lamb, ½ cup mint, almond flour, red onion, pine nuts, cumin, 1 teaspoon salt, cinnamon, ginger, nutmeg, and pepper and, using your hands, incorporate all the ingredients together well. 3. Form the mixture into 12 egg-shaped patties and let sit for 10 minutes. 4. Remove the skewers from the water, thread 3 patties onto each skewer, and place on a broiling pan or wire rack on top of a baking sheet lined with aluminum foil. Broil on the top rack until golden and cooked through, 8 to 12 minutes, flipping once halfway through cooking. 5. While the meat cooks, in a small bowl, combine the yogurt, olive oil, remaining 2 tablespoons chopped mint, remaining ½ teaspoon salt, and lime zest and juice and whisk to combine well. Keep cool until ready to use. 6. Serve the skewers with yogurt sauce.

Per Serving:
calories: 420 | fat: 32g | protein: 28g | carbs: 8g | fiber: 2g | sodium: 875mg

Herbed Lamb Meatballs

Prep time: 10 minutes | Cook time: 6 to 8 hours | Serves 4

1 (28-ounce / 794-g) can no-salt-added diced tomatoes
2 garlic cloves, minced, divided
1 pound (454 g) raw ground lamb
1 small onion, finely diced, or 1 tablespoon dried onion flakes
1 large egg
2 tablespoons bread crumbs
1 teaspoon dried basil
1 teaspoon dried oregano
1 teaspoon dried rosemary
1 teaspoon dried thyme
1 teaspoon sea salt
½ teaspoon freshly ground black pepper

1. In a slow cooker, combine the tomatoes and 1 clove of garlic. Stir to mix well. 2. In a large bowl, mix together the ground lamb, onion, egg, bread crumbs, basil, oregano, rosemary, thyme, salt, pepper, and the remaining 1 garlic clove until all of the ingredients are well-blended. Shape the meat mixture into 10 to 12 (2½-inch) meatballs. Put the meatballs in the slow cooker. 3. Cover the cooker and cook for 6 to 8 hours on Low heat.

Per Serving:
calories: 406 | fat: 28g | protein: 23g | carbs: 16g | fiber: 5g | sodium: 815mg

Pork and Cannellini Bean Stew

Prep time: 15 minutes | Cook time: 1 hour | Serves 6

1 cup dried cannellini beans
¼ cup olive oil
1 medium onion, diced
2 pounds (907 g) pork roast, cut into 1-inch chunks
3 cups water
1 (8-ounce/ 227-g) can tomato paste
¼ cup flat-leaf parsley, chopped
½ teaspoon dried thyme
Sea salt and freshly ground pepper, to taste

1. Rinse and sort the beans. 2. Cover beans with water, and allow to soak overnight. Heat the olive oil in a large stew pot. 3. Add the onion, stirring occasionally, until golden brown. 4. Add the pork chunks and cook 5 to 8 minutes, stirring frequently, until the pork is browned. Drain and rinse the beans, and add to the pot. 5. Add the water, and bring to a boil. Reduce heat and simmer for 45 minutes, until beans are tender. 6. Add the tomato paste, parsley, and thyme, and simmer an additional 15 minutes, or until the sauce thickens slightly. Season to taste.

Per Serving:
calories: 373 | fat: 16g | protein: 39g | carbs: 19g | fiber: 4g | sodium: 107mg

Braised Pork with Broccoli Rabe and Sage

Prep time: 15 minutes | Cook time: 50 minutes |

Serves 4

1½ pounds (680 g) boneless pork butt roast, trimmed and cut into 2-inch pieces
½ teaspoon table salt
½ teaspoon pepper
1 tablespoon extra-virgin olive oil
2 tablespoons minced fresh sage, divided

5 garlic cloves, peeled and smashed
1 tablespoon all-purpose flour
¼ cup chicken broth
¼ cup dry white wine
1 pound (454 g) broccoli rabe, trimmed and cut into 1-inch pieces
½ teaspoon grated orange zest

1. Pat pork dry with paper towels and sprinkle with salt and pepper. Using highest sauté function, heat oil in Instant Pot for 5 minutes (or until just smoking). Brown pork on all sides, 6 to 8 minutes; transfer to plate. 2. Add 1 tablespoon sage, garlic, and flour to fat left in pot and cook, using highest sauté function, until fragrant, about 1 minute. Stir in broth and wine, scraping up any browned bits. Return pork to pot along with any accumulated juices. Lock lid in place and close pressure release valve. Select high pressure cook function and cook for 30 minutes. 3. Turn off Instant Pot and let pressure release naturally for 15 minutes. Quick-release any remaining pressure, then carefully remove lid, allowing steam to escape away from you. Transfer pork to serving dish, tent with aluminum foil, and let rest while preparing broccoli rabe. 4. Whisk sauce until smooth and bring to simmer using highest sauté function. Stir in broccoli rabe and cook, partially covered, until tender and bright green, about 3 minutes. Stir in orange zest and remaining 1 tablespoon sage. Serve pork with broccoli rabe mixture.

Per Serving:

calories: 340 | fat: 16g | protein: 37g | carbs: 7g | fiber: 3g | sodium: 490mg

Greek Meatball Soup

Prep time: 20 minutes | Cook time: 45 minutes |

Serves 5

1 pound (454 g) ground beef
⅓ cup orzo
4 large eggs
1 onion, finely chopped
2 garlic cloves, minced
2 tablespoons finely chopped

fresh Italian parsley
Sea salt
Freshly ground black pepper
½ cup all-purpose flour
5 to 6 cups chicken broth
Juice of 2 lemons

1. In a large bowl, combine the ground beef, orzo, 1 egg, the onion, garlic, and parsley and stir until well mixed. Season with salt and pepper and mix again. 2. Place the flour in a small bowl. 3. Roll the meat mixture into a ball about the size of a golf ball and dredge it in the flour to coat, shaking off any excess. Place the meatball in a stockpot and repeat with the remaining meat mixture. 4. Pour enough broth into the pot to cover the meatballs by about 1 inch. Bring the broth to a boil over high heat. Reduce the heat to low, cover, and simmer for 30 to 45 minutes, until the meatballs are cooked through. 5. While the meatballs are simmering, in a small bowl, whisk the 3 remaining eggs until frothy. Add the lemon juice and whisk well. 6. When the meatballs are cooked, while whisking continuously, slowly pour 1½ cups of the hot broth into the egg mixture. Pour the egg mixture back into the pot and mix well. Bring back to a simmer, then remove from the heat and serve.

Per Serving:

calories: 297 | fat: 9g | protein: 27g | carbs: 28g | fiber: 1g | sodium: 155mg

Braised Pork Loin with Port and Dried Plums

Prep time: 20 minutes | Cook time: 6 hours 25

minutes | Serves 10

1 (3¼-pound / 1.5-kg)boneless pork loin roast, trimmed
1½ teaspoons black pepper
1 teaspoon sea salt
1 teaspoon dry mustard
1 teaspoon dried sage
½ teaspoon dried thyme
1 tablespoon olive oil
2 large yellow onions, sliced
1 cup finely chopped leek, white and light green parts,

rinsed
1 large carrot, finely chopped
½ cup port or other sweet red wine
⅔ cup chicken stock
1 cup pitted dried plums (about 20)
2 bay leaves
2 tablespoons cornstarch
2 tablespoons water

1. Cut the pork roast in half crosswise. 2. Combine the pepper, salt, dry mustard, sage, and thyme in a small bowl. Rub the seasoning mixture over the surface of the roast halves. 3. Heat a Dutch oven over medium-high heat. Add the olive oil to pan and swirl to coat. Add the pork and brown on all sides, about 4 minutes. Place the pork in the slow cooker. 4. Add the onions, leek, and carrot to the Dutch oven, and sauté for 5 minutes or until vegetables are golden. 5. Stir in the wine and stock, and cook for about 1 minute, scraping the bottom of the pan with a wooden spoon to loosen up the flavorful browned bits. 6. Pour the wine-vegetable mixture over the pork in slow cooker. Add the plums and bay leaves. 7. Cover and cook on high for 1 hour. Reduce the heat to low, and cook for 5 to 6 hours, or until the pork is tender. 8. Remove the pork from the slow cooker, set aside on a platter, and keep warm. Increase the heat to high. 9. Combine the cornstarch and 2 tablespoons water in a small bowl. Whisk to combine, and then whisk into the cooking liquid in the slow cooker. 10. Cook, uncovered, for 15 minutes or until the sauce is thick, stirring frequently. 11. Discard the bay leaves. Slice the pork, and serve hot with the sauce.

Per Serving:

calories: 269 | fat: 8g | protein: 37g | carbs: 9g | fiber: 1g | sodium: 329mg

Easy Honey-Garlic Pork Chops

Prep time: 15 minutes | Cook time: 25 minutes | Serves 4

4 pork chops, boneless or bone-in

¼ teaspoon salt

⅛ teaspoon freshly ground black pepper

3 tablespoons extra-virgin olive oil

5 tablespoons low-sodium chicken broth, divided

6 garlic cloves, minced

¼ cup honey

2 tablespoons apple cider vinegar

1. Season the pork chops with salt and pepper and set aside. 2. In a large sauté pan or skillet, heat the oil over medium-high heat. Add the pork chops and sear for 5 minutes on each side, or until golden brown. 3. Once the searing is complete, move the pork to a dish and reduce the skillet heat from medium-high to medium. Add 3 tablespoons of chicken broth to the pan; this will loosen the bits and flavors from the bottom of the skillet. 4. Once the broth has evaporated, add the garlic to the skillet and cook for 15 to 20 seconds, until fragrant. Add the honey, vinegar, and the remaining 2 tablespoons of broth. Bring the heat back up to medium-high and continue to cook for 3 to 4 minutes. 5. Stir periodically; the sauce is ready once it's thickened slightly. Add the pork chops back into the pan, cover them with the sauce, and cook for 2 minutes. Serve.

Per Serving:

calories: 302 | fat: 16g | protein: 22g | carbs: 19g | fiber: 0g | sodium: 753mg

Beef and Mushroom Stroganoff

Prep time: 15 minutes | Cook time: 31 minutes | Serves 6

2 tablespoons olive oil

1 medium onion, peeled and chopped

2 cloves garlic, peeled and minced

1 pound (454 g) beef stew meat, cut into 1" pieces

3 tablespoons all-purpose flour

¼ teaspoon salt

¼ teaspoon ground black pepper

2 cups beef broth

1 pound (454 g) sliced button mushrooms

1 pound (454 g) wide egg noodles

½ cup low-fat plain Greek yogurt

1. Press the Sauté button on the Instant Pot® and heat oil. Add onion and cook until soft, about 5 minutes. Add garlic and cook until fragrant, about 30 seconds. 2. Combine beef, flour, salt, and pepper in a medium bowl and toss to coat beef completely. Add beef to the pot and cook, stirring often, until browned, about 10 minutes. Stir in beef broth and scrape any brown bits from bottom of pot. Stir in mushrooms and press the Cancel button. 3. Close lid, set steam release to Sealing, press the Manual button, and set time to 10 minutes. When the timer beeps, quick-release the pressure until the float valve drops, open lid, and stir well. Press the Cancel button. 4. Add noodles and stir, making sure noodles are submerged in liquid. Close lid, set steam release to Sealing, press the Manual button, and set time to 5 minutes. 5. When the timer beeps, quick-release the pressure until the float valve drops. Open lid and stir well. Press the Cancel button and cool for 5 minutes, then stir in yogurt. Serve hot.

Per Serving:

calories: 446 | fat: 13g | protein: 19g | carbs: 63g | fiber: 4g | sodium: 721mg

Pork and Beef Egg Rolls

Prep time: 30 minutes | Cook time: 7 to 8 minutes per batch | Makes 8 egg rolls

¼ pound (113 g) very lean ground beef

¼ pound (113 g) lean ground pork

1 tablespoon soy sauce

1 teaspoon olive oil

½ cup grated carrots

2 green onions, chopped

2 cups grated Napa cabbage

¼ cup chopped water chestnuts

¼ teaspoon salt

¼ teaspoon garlic powder

¼ teaspoon black pepper

1 egg

1 tablespoon water

8 egg roll wraps

Oil for misting or cooking spray

1. In a large skillet, brown beef and pork with soy sauce. Remove cooked meat from skillet, drain, and set aside. 2. Pour off any excess grease from skillet. Add olive oil, carrots, and onions. Sauté until barely tender, about 1 minute. 3. Stir in cabbage, cover, and cook for 1 minute or just until cabbage slightly wilts. Remove from heat. 4. In a large bowl, combine the cooked meats and vegetables, water chestnuts, salt, garlic powder, and pepper. Stir well. If needed, add more salt to taste. 5. Beat together egg and water in a small bowl. 6. Fill egg roll wrappers, using about ¼ cup of filling for each wrap. Roll up and brush all over with egg wash to seal. Spray very lightly with olive oil or cooking spray. 7. Place 4 egg rolls in air fryer basket and air fry at 390ºF (199ºC) for 4 minutes. Turn over and cook 3 to 4 more minutes, until golden brown and crispy. 8. Repeat to cook remaining egg rolls.

Per Serving:

calories: 176 | fat: 5g | protein: 11g | carbs: 22g | fiber: 2g | sodium: 339mg

Indian Mint and Chile Kebabs

Prep time: 30 minutes | Cook time: 15 minutes | Serves 4

1 pound (454 g) ground lamb
½ cup finely minced onion
¼ cup chopped fresh mint
¼ cup chopped fresh cilantro
1 tablespoon minced garlic

½ teaspoon ground turmeric
½ teaspoon cayenne pepper
¼ teaspoon ground cardamom
¼ teaspoon ground cinnamon
1 teaspoon kosher salt

1. In the bowl of a stand mixer fitted with the paddle attachment, combine the lamb, onion, mint, cilantro, garlic, turmeric, cayenne, cardamom, cinnamon, and salt. Mix on low speed until you have a sticky mess of spiced meat. If you have time, let the mixture stand at room temperature for 30 minutes (or cover and refrigerate for up to a day or two, until you're ready to make the kebabs). 2. Divide the meat into eight equal portions. Form each into a long sausage shape. Place the kebabs in a single layer in the air fryer basket. Set the air fryer to 350°F (177°C) for 10 minutes. Increase the air fryer temperature to 400°F (204°C) and cook for 3 to 4 minutes more to brown the kebabs. Use a meat thermometer to ensure the kebabs have reached an internal temperature of 160°F / 71°C (medium).

Per Serving:

calories: 231 | fat: 14g | protein: 23g | carbs: 3g | fiber: 1g | sodium: 648mg

Ground Lamb with Lentils and Pomegranate Seeds

Prep time: 15 minutes | Cook time: 15 minutes | Serves 4

1 tablespoon extra-virgin olive oil
½ pound (227 g) ground lamb
1 teaspoon red pepper flakes
½ teaspoon ground cumin
½ teaspoon kosher salt
¼ teaspoon freshly ground black pepper
2 garlic cloves, minced

2 cups cooked, drained lentils
1 hothouse or English cucumber, diced
⅓ cup fresh mint, chopped
⅓ cup fresh parsley, chopped
Zest of 1 lemon
1 cup plain Greek yogurt
½ cup pomegranate seeds

1. Heat the olive oil in a large skillet or sauté pan over medium-high heat. Add the lamb and season with the red pepper flakes, cumin, salt, and black pepper. Cook the lamb without stirring until the bottom is brown and crispy, about 5 minutes. Stir and cook for another 5 minutes. Using a spatula, break up the lamb into smaller pieces. Add the garlic and cook, stirring occasionally, for 1 minute. Transfer the lamb mixture to a medium bowl. 2. Add the lentils to the skillet and cook, stirring occasionally, until brown and crisp, about 5 minutes. Return the lamb to the skillet, mix, and warm through, about 3 minutes. Transfer to the large bowl. Add the cucumber, mint, parsley, and lemon zest, mixing together gently. 3. Spoon the yogurt into 4 bowls and top each with some of the lamb mixture. Garnish with the pomegranate seeds.

Per Serving:

calories: 370 | fat: 18g | protein: 24g | carbs: 30g | fiber: 10g | sodium: 197mg

Chapter 6 Poultry

Blackened Cajun Chicken Tenders

Prep time: 10 minutes | Cook time: 17 minutes |
Serves 4

2 teaspoons paprika
1 teaspoon chili powder
½ teaspoon garlic powder
½ teaspoon dried thyme
¼ teaspoon onion powder
⅛ teaspoon ground cayenne

pepper
2 tablespoons coconut oil
1 pound (454 g) boneless,
skinless chicken tenders
¼ cup full-fat ranch dressing

1. In a small bowl, combine all seasonings. 2. Drizzle oil over chicken tenders and then generously coat each tender in the spice mixture. Place tenders into the air fryer basket. 3. Adjust the temperature to 375ºF (191ºC) and air fry for 17 minutes. 4. Tenders will be 165ºF (74ºC) internally when fully cooked. Serve with ranch dressing for dipping.

Per Serving:
calories: 266 | fat: 17g | protein: 26g | carbs: 2g | fiber: 1g | sodium: 207mg

Curried Chicken and Lentil Salad

Prep time: 15 minutes | Cook time: 13 minutes |
Serves 8

1 teaspoon olive oil
2 pounds (907 g) boneless,
skinless chicken breasts, cut
into ½" pieces
1 cup dried lentils, rinsed and
drained
2 cups water
2½ teaspoons curry powder,
divided
2 small Golden Delicious
apples, divided

1 teaspoon lemon juice
2 cups halved seedless grapes
1 cup roasted salted cashews
2 stalks celery, diced
½ small red onion, peeled and
diced
¾ cup plain low-fat yogurt
¼ cup mayonnaise
11 ounces (312 g) baby salad
greens

1. Press the Sauté button on the Instant Pot® and heat oil. Add chicken and cook for 5 minutes or until browned. Stir in lentils, water, and 1 teaspoon curry powder. Halve one of the apples; core and dice 1 half and add it to the pot. Coat the cut side of the other half of the apple with lemon juice to prevent it from turning brown and set aside. Press the Cancel button. 2. Close lid, set steam release to Sealing, press the Manual button, and set time to 8 minutes. When the timer beeps, let pressure release naturally, about 20 minutes. Open lid. 3. Transfer the contents of the Instant Pot® to a large bowl and set aside to cool. 4. Dice reserved apple half, and core and dice remaining apple. Add to chicken and lentil mixture along with grapes, cashews, celery, and red onion. 5. In a small bowl, mix together yogurt, mayonnaise, and remaining 1½ teaspoons curry powder. Drizzle over chicken and lentil mixture, and stir to combine. Serve over salad greens.

Per Serving:
calories: 404 | fat: 18g | protein: 41g | carbs: 21g | fiber: 3g | sodium: 177mg

Chicken and Shrimp Paella

Prep time: 20 minutes | Cook time: 40 minutes |
Serves 6

3 tablespoons olive oil
1 onion, chopped (about 2 cups)
5 garlic cloves, minced
1 pound (454 g) chicken
breasts, cut into 1-inch pieces
1 cup Arborio rice
1 teaspoon ground cumin
1 teaspoon smoked paprika
½ teaspoon ground turmeric
1½ cups low-sodium chicken
broth
1 (14½-ounce / 411-g) can

diced tomatoes, with their
juices
Zest and juice of 1 lemon
½ teaspoon salt
1 cup thawed frozen peas
1 medium zucchini, cut into
cubes (about 2 cups)
8 ounces (227 g) uncooked
shrimp, thawed, peeled, and
deveined
2 tablespoons chopped fresh
parsley

1. In a large saucepan, heat 2 tablespoons of the olive oil over medium heat. Add the onion and cook, occasionally stirring, for 5 minutes, or until softened. Add the garlic, chicken, rice, and remaining 1 tablespoon olive oil. Stir until the rice is coated with the oil. 2. Add the cumin, smoked paprika, turmeric, broth, tomatoes with their juices, lemon zest, lemon juice, and salt. Spread the rice mixture evenly in the pan. Bring to a boil. Reduce the heat to medium-low, cover, and cook for 25 minutes—do not stir. 3. Remove the lid and stir in the peas and zucchini. Add the shrimp, nestling them into the rice. Cover and cook for 8 to 10 minutes. Remove from the heat and let stand for 10 minutes. 4. Top with the parsley and serve.

Per Serving:
calories: 310 | fat: 18g | protein: 26g | carbs: 18g | fiber: 7g | sodium: 314mg

Gingery Quinoa Chicken

Prep time: 15 minutes | Cook time: 6 to 8 hours |
Serves 2

1 teaspoon extra-virgin olive oil
½ cup quinoa
½ cup low-sodium chicken broth
½ cup coconut milk
1 teaspoon minced fresh ginger
1 teaspoon minced garlic

Zest of 1 lime
½ teaspoon ground coriander
2 bone-in, skinless chicken thighs
⅛ teaspoon sea salt
Freshly ground black pepper
Juice of 1 lime, for garnish

1. Grease the inside of the slow cooker with the olive oil. 2. Put the quinoa, broth, coconut milk, ginger, garlic, zest, and coriander in the crock. Stir thoroughly. 3. Season the chicken thighs with the salt and a few grinds of the black pepper. Place them on top of the quinoa. 4. Cover and cook for 6 to 8 hours, until the quinoa has absorbed all the liquid and the chicken is cooked through. 5. Drizzle each portion with lime juice just before serving.

Per Serving:
calories: 571 | fat: 27g | protein: 47g | carbs: 36g | fiber: 5g | sodium: 369mg

Roast Chicken

Prep time: 20 minutes | Cook time: 55 minutes |
Serves 4

¼ cup white wine
2 tablespoons olive oil, divided
1 tablespoon Dijon mustard
1 garlic clove, minced
1 teaspoon dried rosemary
Juice and zest of 1 lemon
Sea salt and freshly ground pepper, to taste

1 large roasting chicken, giblets removed
3 large carrots, peeled and cut into chunks
1 fennel bulb, peeled and cut into ½-inch cubes
2 celery stalks, cut into chunks

1. Preheat the oven to 400ºF (205ºC). 2. Combine the white wine, 1 tablespoon of olive oil, mustard, garlic, rosemary, lemon juice and zest, sea salt, and freshly ground pepper in a small bowl. 3. Place the chicken in a shallow roasting pan on a roasting rack. 4. Rub the entire chicken, including the cavity, with the wine and mustard mixture. 5. Place the chicken in the oven and roast for 15 minutes. 6. Toss the vegetables with the remaining tablespoon of olive oil, and place around the chicken. 7. Turn the heat down to 375ºF (190ºC). 8. Roast an additional 40–60 minutes, basting the chicken every 15 minutes with the drippings in the bottom of the pan. 9. Cook chicken until internal temperature reaches 180ºF (82ºC) in between the thigh and the body of the chicken. When you remove the instant-read thermometer, the juices should run clear. 10. Let the chicken rest for at least 10–15 minutes before serving.

Per Serving:
calories: 387 | fat: 14g | protein: 50g | carbs: 12g | fiber: 4g | sodium: 306mg

Greek Turkey Burger

Prep time: 10 minutes | Cook time: 10 minutes |
Serves 4

1 pound (454 g) ground turkey
1 medium zucchini, grated
¼ cup whole-wheat bread crumbs
¼ cup red onion, minced
¼ cup crumbled feta cheese
1 large egg, beaten
1 garlic clove, minced

1 tablespoon fresh oregano, chopped
1 teaspoon kosher salt
¼ teaspoon freshly ground black pepper
1 tablespoon extra-virgin olive oil

1. In a large bowl, combine the turkey, zucchini, bread crumbs, onion, feta cheese, egg, garlic, oregano, salt, and black pepper, and mix well. Shape into 4 equal patties. 2. Heat the olive oil in a large nonstick grill pan or skillet over medium-high heat. Add the burgers to the pan and reduce the heat to medium. Cook on one side for 5 minutes, then flip and cook the other side for 5 minutes more.

Per Serving:
calories: 285 | fat: 16g | protein: 26g | carbs: 9g | fiber: 2g | sodium: 465mg

Tex-Mex Chicken Roll-Ups

Prep time: 10 minutes | Cook time: 14 to 17 minutes
| Serves 8

2 pounds (907 g) boneless, skinless chicken breasts or thighs
1 teaspoon chili powder
½ teaspoon smoked paprika
½ teaspoon ground cumin
Sea salt and freshly ground

black pepper, to taste
6 ounces (170 g) Monterey Jack cheese, shredded
4 ounces (113 g) canned diced green chiles
Avocado oil spray

1. Place the chicken in a large zip-top bag or between two pieces of plastic wrap. Using a meat mallet or heavy skillet, pound the chicken until it is about ¼ inch thick. 2. In a small bowl, combine the chili powder, smoked paprika, cumin, and salt and pepper to taste. Sprinkle both sides of the chicken with the seasonings. 3. Sprinkle the chicken with the Monterey Jack cheese, then the diced green chiles. 4. Roll up each piece of chicken from the long side, tucking in the ends as you go. Secure the roll-up with a toothpick. 5. Set the air fryer to 350ºF (177ºC). Spray the outside of the chicken with avocado oil. Place the chicken in a single layer in the basket, working in batches if necessary, and roast for 7 minutes. Flip and cook for another 7 to 10 minutes, until an instant-read thermometer reads 160ºF (71ºC). 6. Remove the chicken from the air fryer and allow it to rest for about 5 minutes before serving.

Per Serving:
calories: 220 | fat: 10g | protein: 31g | carbs: 1g | fiber: 0g | sodium: 355mg

Spice-Rubbed Chicken Thighs

Prep time: 10 minutes | Cook time: 25 minutes |
Serves 4

4 (4-ounce / 113-g) bone-in, skin-on chicken thighs	2 teaspoons chili powder
½ teaspoon salt	1 teaspoon paprika
½ teaspoon garlic powder	1 teaspoon ground cumin
	1 small lime, halved

1. Pat chicken thighs dry and sprinkle with salt, garlic powder, chili powder, paprika, and cumin. 2. Squeeze juice from ½ lime over thighs. Place thighs into ungreased air fryer basket. Adjust the temperature to 380ºF (193ºC) and roast for 25 minutes, turning thighs halfway through cooking. Thighs will be crispy and browned with an internal temperature of at least 165ºF (74ºC) when done. 3. Transfer thighs to a large serving plate and drizzle with remaining lime juice. Serve warm.

Per Serving:
calories: 151 | fat: 5g | protein: 23g | carbs: 3g | fiber: 1g | sodium: 439mg

Chicken Korma

Prep time: 20 minutes | Cook time: 3 to 4 hours |
Serves 6

Marinade:	3 cloves
1 tablespoon coriander seeds, ground	3 green cardamom pods
1 teaspoon salt	1-inch piece cassia bark
6 whole black peppercorns	1 to 3 dried red chiles
1-inch piece fresh ginger, roughly chopped	2 onions, minced
3 garlic cloves, roughly chopped	⅓ cup creamed coconut
12 boneless chicken thighs, skinned and chopped into chunks	2 heaped tablespoons ground almonds
1 cup Greek yogurt	1 teaspoon ground white poppy seeds
1 heaped teaspoon gram flour	Pinch of saffron
1 teaspoon turmeric	2 tablespoons milk
Korma:	1 teaspoon garam masala
1 tablespoon ghee or vegetable oil	Handful fresh coriander leaves, finely chopped
	1 tablespoon chopped toasted almonds
	Squeeze of lemon juice

Make the Marinade: 1. Place the coriander seeds, salt, and peppercorns into a mortar and pestle and crush, or grind them in a spice grinder. Then add the roughly chopped ginger and garlic, and pound (or grind) to create an aromatic paste. 2. Place the chicken in a large bowl and add the yogurt, gram flour, turmeric, and spice paste. Stir thoroughly, cover, and leave to marinate for an hour, or longer if possible, in the refrigerator. Make the Korma: 3. Heat the slow cooker to high and add the oil. Add the cloves, cardamom pods, cassia bark, and the dried red chiles, and toast until fragrant, about 1 minute. 4. Add the minced onions, and then add the marinated chicken. Cover and cook for 2 hours on low, or for 1 hour on high. 5. Pour in the creamed coconut, ground almonds, and poppy seeds, then stir. Cover and cook on low for 2 more hours. 6. Crumble the saffron into a small bowl, add the milk, and leave to steep for 20 minutes. 7. Once cooked through and the sauce has thickened, pour in the saffron milk for added decadence, if using. Then add the garam masala. Garnish with the fresh coriander leaves and chopped almonds. You can also add a squeeze of lemon juice for added freshness, then serve.

Per Serving:
calories: 568 | fat: 23g | protein: 79g | carbs: 9g | fiber: 2g | sodium: 779mg

Hot Goan-Style Coconut Chicken

Prep time: 20 minutes | Cook time: 4 to 6 hours |
Serves 6

Spice Paste:	⅓ cup water
8 dried Kashmiri chiles, broken into pieces	Chicken:
2 tablespoons coriander seeds	12 chicken thigh and drumstick pieces, on the bone, skinless
2-inch piece cassia bark, broken into pieces	1 teaspoon salt (or to taste)
1 teaspoon black peppercorns	1 teaspoon turmeric
1 teaspoon cumin seeds	2 tablespoons coconut oil
1 teaspoon fennel seeds	2 medium onions, finely sliced
4 cloves	⅓ cup water
2 star anise	½ teaspoon ground nutmeg
1 tablespoon poppy seeds	2 teaspoons tamarind paste
1 cup freshly grated coconut, or desiccated coconut shreds	Handful fresh coriander leaves, chopped for garnish
6 garlic cloves	1 or 2 fresh red chiles, for garnish

Make the Spice Paste: 1. In a dry frying pan, roast the Kashmiri chiles, coriander seeds, cassia bark, peppercorns, cumin seeds, fennel seeds, cloves, and star anise until fragrant, about 1 minute. Add the poppy seeds and continue roasting for a few minutes. Then remove from the heat and leave to cool. 2. Once cooled, grind the toasted spices in your spice grinder and set aside. 3. In the same pan, add the dried coconut and toast it for 5 to 7 minutes, until it just starts to turn golden. 4. Transfer to a blender with the garlic, and add the water. Blend to make a thick, wet paste. 5. Add the ground spices and blend again to mix together. Make the Chicken: 6. In a large bowl, toss the chicken with the salt and turmeric. Marinate for 15 to 20 minutes. In the meantime, heat the slow cooker to high. 7. Heat the oil in a frying pan (or in the slow cooker if you have a sear setting). Cook the sliced onions for 10 minutes, and then add the spice and coconut paste. Cook until it becomes fragrant. 8. Transfer everything to the slow cooker. Add the chicken, then the water. Cover and cook on low for 6 hours, or on high for 4 hours. 9. Sprinkle in the nutmeg and stir in the tamarind paste. Cover and cook for another 5 minutes. 10. Garnish with fresh coriander leaves and whole red chiles to serve.

Per Serving:
calories: 583 | fat: 26g | protein: 77g | carbs: 7g | fiber: 3g | sodium: 762mg

Roasted Cornish Hen with Figs

Prep time: 10 minutes | Cook time: 45 minutes |
Serves 2

2 Cornish game hens
2 tablespoons olive oil
1 tablespoon Herbes de Provence

Sea salt and freshly ground pepper, to taste
1 pound (454 g) fresh figs
1 cup dry white wine

1. Preheat the oven to 350°F (180°C). 2. Place the Cornish hens in a shallow roasting pan and brush them with olive oil. 3. Season liberally with Herbes de Provence, sea salt, and freshly ground pepper. Roast the hens for 15 minutes, or until golden brown. 4. Add the figs and white wine, and cover the hens with aluminum foil. Cook an additional 20–30 minutes, or until the hens are cooked through. Allow to rest for 10 minutes before serving.

Per Serving:

calories: 660 | fat: 22g | protein: 50g | carbs: 48g | fiber: 7g | sodium: 166mg

Chicken with Lemon Asparagus

Prep time: 10 minutes | Cook time: 13 minutes |
Serves 4

2 tablespoons olive oil
4 (6-ounce / 170-g) boneless, skinless chicken breasts
½ teaspoon ground black pepper
¼ teaspoon salt
¼ teaspoon smoked paprika
2 cloves garlic, peeled and minced

2 sprigs thyme
2 sprigs oregano
1 tablespoon grated lemon zest
¼ cup lemon juice
¼ cup low-sodium chicken broth
1 bunch asparagus, trimmed
¼ cup chopped fresh parsley
4 lemon wedges

1. Press Sauté on the Instant Pot® and heat oil. Season chicken with pepper, salt, and smoked paprika. Brown chicken on both sides, about 4 minutes per side. Add garlic, thyme, oregano, lemon zest, lemon juice, and chicken broth. Press the Cancel button. 2. Close lid, set steam release to Sealing, press the Manual button, and set time to 5 minutes. 3. When the timer beeps, quick-release the pressure until the float valve drops. Press the Cancel button and open lid. Transfer chicken breasts to a serving platter. Tent with foil to keep warm. 4. Add asparagus to the Instant Pot®. Close lid, set steam release to Sealing, press the Manual button, and set time to 0. When the timer beeps, quick-release the pressure until the float valve drops. Open lid and remove asparagus. Arrange asparagus around chicken and garnish with parsley and lemon wedges. Serve immediately.

Per Serving:

calories: 227 | fat: 11g | protein: 35g | carbs: 0g | fiber: 0g | sodium: 426mg

Cajun-Breaded Chicken Bites

Prep time: 10 minutes | Cook time: 12 minutes |
Serves 4

1 pound (454 g) boneless, skinless chicken breasts, cut into 1-inch cubes
½ cup heavy whipping cream
½ teaspoon salt
¼ teaspoon ground black

pepper
1 ounce (28 g) plain pork rinds, finely crushed
¼ cup unflavored whey protein powder
½ teaspoon Cajun seasoning

1. Place chicken in a medium bowl and pour in cream. Stir to coat. Sprinkle with salt and pepper. 2. In a separate large bowl, combine pork rinds, protein powder, and Cajun seasoning. Remove chicken from cream, shaking off any excess, and toss in dry mix until fully coated. 3. Place bites into ungreased air fryer basket. Adjust the temperature to 400°F (204°C) and air fry for 12 minutes, shaking the basket twice during cooking. Bites will be done when golden brown and have an internal temperature of at least 165°F (74°C). Serve warm.

Per Serving:

calories: 272 | fat: 13g | protein: 35g | carbs: 2g | fiber: 1g | sodium: 513mg

Niçoise Chicken

Prep time: 20 minutes | Cook time: 50 minutes |
Serves 6

¼ cup olive oil
3 medium onions, coarsely chopped
3 cloves garlic, minced
4 pounds (1.8 kg) chicken breast from 1 cut-up chicken
5 Roma tomatoes, peeled and chopped
½ cup white wine
1 (14½-ounce / 411-g) can

chicken broth
½ cup black Niçoise olives, pitted
Juice of 1 lemon
¼ cup flat-leaf parsley, chopped
1 tablespoon fresh tarragon leaves, chopped
Sea salt and freshly ground pepper, to taste

1. Heat the olive oil in a deep saucepan or stew pot over medium heat. Cook the onions and garlic 5 minutes, or until tender and translucent. 2. Add the chicken and cook an additional 5 minutes to brown slightly. 3. Add the tomatoes, white wine, and chicken broth, cover, and simmer 30–45 minutes on medium-low heat, or until the chicken is tender and the sauce is thickened slightly. 4. Remove the lid and add the olives and lemon juice. 5. Cook an additional 10–15 minutes to thicken the sauce further. 6. Stir in the parsley and tarragon, and season to taste. Serve immediately with noodles or potatoes and a dark leafy salad.

Per Serving:

calories: 501 | fat: 15g | protein: 74g | carbs: 11g | fiber: 2g | sodium: 451mg

Chicken Cacciatore

Prep time: 20 minutes | Cook time: 1 hour 10 minutes | Serves 4 to6

2 tablespoons extra-virgin olive oil
½ cup diced carrots
2 garlic cloves, minced
½ cup chopped celery
2 onions, chopped
2 pounds (907 g) chicken

tenders
2 (14½-ounce / 411-g) cans Italian seasoned diced tomatoes, drained
2 cups cooked corkscrew pasta, such as whole-grain fusilli

1. In a large saucepan, heat the oil over medium-high heat and sauté the carrots, garlic, celery, and onions for about 5 minutes, until softened. Add the chicken and brown for 4 to 5 minutes on each side. 2. Add the diced tomatoes. Cover and reduce heat to simmer for an hour. Serve over pasta.

Per Serving:

calories: 416 | fat: 3g | protein: 58g | carbs: 38g | fiber: 7g | sodium: 159mg

Lemon Chicken with Artichokes and Crispy Kale

Prep time: 15 minutes | Cook time: 35 minutes | Serves 4

3 tablespoons extra-virgin olive oil, divided
2 tablespoons lemon juice
Zest of 1 lemon
2 garlic cloves, minced
2 teaspoons dried rosemary
½ teaspoon kosher salt
¼ teaspoon freshly ground

black pepper
1½ pounds (680 g) boneless, skinless chicken breast
2 (14-ounce / 397-g) cans artichoke hearts, drained
1 bunch (about 6 ounces / 170 g) lacinato kale, stemmed and torn or chopped into pieces

1. In a large bowl or zip-top bag, combine 2 tablespoons of the olive oil, the lemon juice, lemon zest, garlic, rosemary, salt, and black pepper. Mix well and then add the chicken and artichokes. Marinate for at least 30 minutes, and up to 4 hours in the refrigerator. 2. Preheat the oven to 350ºF (180ºC). Line a baking sheet with parchment paper or foil. Remove the chicken and artichokes from the marinade and spread them in a single layer on the baking sheet. Roast for 15 minutes, turn the chicken over, and roast another 15 minutes. Remove the baking sheet and put the chicken, artichokes, and juices on a platter or large plate. Tent with foil to keep warm. 3. Change the oven temperature to broil. In a large bowl, combine the kale with the remaining 1 tablespoon of the olive oil. Arrange the kale on the baking sheet and broil until golden brown in spots and as crispy as you like, about 3 to 5 minutes. Place the kale on top of the chicken and artichokes.

Per Serving:

calories: 430 | fat: 16g | protein: 46g | carbs: 29g | fiber: 19g | sodium: 350mg

Citrus and Spice Chicken

Prep time: 15 minutes | Cook time: 17 minutes | Serves 8

2 tablespoons olive oil
3 pounds (1.4 kg) boneless, skinless chicken thighs
1 teaspoon smoked paprika
½ teaspoon salt
⅛ teaspoon ground cinnamon
⅛ teaspoon ground ginger
⅛ teaspoon ground nutmeg
½ cup golden raisins

½ cup slivered almonds
1 cup orange juice
⅛ cup lemon juice
⅛ cup lime juice
1 pound (454 g) carrots, peeled and chopped
2 tablespoons water
1 tablespoon arrowroot powder

1. Press the Sauté button on the Instant Pot® and heat oil. Fry chicken thighs for 2 minutes on each side until browned. 2. Add paprika, salt, cinnamon, ginger, nutmeg, raisins, almonds, orange juice, lemon juice, lime juice, and carrots. Press the Cancel button. 3. Close lid, set steam release to Sealing, press the Manual button, and set time to 10 minutes. When the timer beeps, let pressure release naturally for 5 minutes. Quick-release any remaining pressure until the float valve drops and then open lid. Check chicken using a meat thermometer to make sure the internal temperature is at least 165ºF (74ºC). 4. Use a slotted spoon to remove chicken, carrots, and raisins, and transfer to a serving platter. Press the Cancel button. 5. In a small bowl, whisk together water and arrowroot to create a slurry. Add to liquid in the Instant Pot® and stir to combine. Press the Sauté button, press the Adjust button to change the temperature to Less, and simmer uncovered for 3 minutes until sauce is thickened. Pour sauce over chicken and serve.

Per Serving:

calories: 332 | fat: 14g | protein: 36g | carbs: 14g | fiber: 3g | sodium: 337mg

Harissa Yogurt Chicken Thighs

Prep time: 5 minutes | Cook time: 25 minutes | Serves 4

½ cup plain Greek yogurt
2 tablespoons harissa
1 tablespoon lemon juice
½ teaspoon kosher salt

¼ teaspoon freshly ground black pepper
1½ pounds (680 g) boneless, skinless chicken thighs

1. In a bowl, combine the yogurt, harissa, lemon juice, salt, and black pepper. Add the chicken and mix together. Marinate for at least 15 minutes, and up to 4 hours in the refrigerator. 2. Preheat the oven to 425ºF (220ºC). Line a baking sheet with parchment paper or foil. Remove the chicken thighs from the marinade and arrange in a single layer on the baking sheet. Roast for 20 minutes, turning the chicken over halfway. 3. Change the oven temperature to broil. Broil the chicken until golden brown in spots, 2 to 3 minutes.

Per Serving:

calories: 190 | fat: 10g | protein: 24g | carbs: 1g | fiber: 0g | sodium: 230mg

Bomba Chicken with Chickpeas

Prep time: 10 minutes | Cook time: 30 minutes |

Serves 4

2 pounds (907 g) boneless, skinless chicken thighs
Sea salt
Freshly ground black pepper
2 tablespoons olive oil, divided
1 onion, chopped
3 garlic cloves, minced

1 cup chicken broth
1 tablespoon bomba sauce or harissa
2 (15 ounces / 425 g) cans chickpeas, drained and rinsed
¼ cup chopped fresh Italian parsley

1. Season the chicken thighs generously with salt and pepper. 2. In a large skillet, heat 1 tablespoon of olive oil over medium-high heat. Add the chicken and cook until browned, 2 to 3 minutes per side. Transfer the chicken to a plate and set aside. 3. In the same skillet, heat the remaining 1 tablespoon of olive oil. Add the onion and garlic and sauté for 4 to 5 minutes, until softened. Return the chicken to the skillet, then add the broth and bomba sauce. Bring to a boil, reduce the heat to low, cover, and simmer for 15 minutes, or until the chicken is cooked through. 4. Add the chickpeas and simmer for 5 minutes more. 5. Garnish with the parsley and serve.

Per Serving:

calories: 552 | fat: 19g | protein: 56g | carbs: 37g | fiber: 10g | sodium: 267mg

Punjabi Chicken Curry

Prep time: 20 minutes | Cook time: 4 to 6 hours |

Serves 6

2 tablespoons vegetable oil
3 onions, finely diced
6 garlic cloves, finely chopped
1 heaped tablespoon freshly grated ginger
1 (14-ounce / 397-g) can plum tomatoes
1 teaspoon salt
1 teaspoon turmeric
1 teaspoon chili powder
Handful coriander stems, finely

chopped
3 fresh green chiles, finely chopped
12 pieces chicken, mixed thighs and drumsticks, or a whole chicken, skinned, trimmed, and chopped
2 teaspoons garam masala
Handful fresh coriander leaves, chopped

1. Heat the oil in a frying pan (or in the slow cooker if you have a sear setting). Add the diced onions and cook for 5 minutes. Add the garlic and continue to cook for 10 minutes until the onions are brown. 2. Heat the slow cooker to high and add the onion-and-garlic mixture. Stir in the ginger, tomatoes, salt, turmeric, chili powder, coriander stems, and chiles. 3. Add the chicken pieces. Cover and cook on low for 6 hours, or on high for 4 hours. 4. Once cooked, check the seasoning, and then stir in the garam masala and coriander leaves.

Per Serving:

calories: 298 | fat: 9g | protein: 35g | carbs: 19g | fiber: 3g | sodium: 539mg

Chicken Thighs with Cilantro

Prep time: 15 minutes | Cook time: 25 minutes |

Serves 4

1 tablespoon olive oil
Juice of ½ lime
1 tablespoon coconut aminos
1½ teaspoons Montreal chicken seasoning

8 bone-in chicken thighs, skin on
2 tablespoons chopped fresh cilantro

1. In a gallon-size resealable bag, combine the olive oil, lime juice, coconut aminos, and chicken seasoning. Add the chicken thighs, seal the bag, and massage the bag to ensure the chicken is thoroughly coated. Refrigerate for at least 2 hours, preferably overnight. 2. Preheat the air fryer to 400ºF (204ºC). 3. Remove the chicken from the marinade (discard the marinade) and arrange in a single layer in the air fryer basket. Pausing halfway through the cooking time to flip the chicken, air fry for 20 to 25 minutes, until a thermometer inserted into the thickest part registers 165ºF (74ºC). 4. Transfer the chicken to a serving platter and top with the cilantro before serving.

Per Serving:

calories: 692 | fat: 53g | protein: 49g | carbs: 2g | fiber: 0g | sodium: 242mg

Tuscan Turkey

Prep time: 15 minutes | Cook time: 6 to 8 hours |

Serves 4

1 pound (454 g) new potatoes, halved
1 red bell pepper, seeded and sliced
1 small onion, sliced
4 boneless, skinless turkey breast fillets (about 2 pounds / 907 g)
1 cup low-sodium chicken broth

½ cup grated Parmesan cheese
3 garlic cloves, minced
1 teaspoon dried oregano
1 teaspoon dried rosemary
½ teaspoon sea salt
½ teaspoon freshly ground black pepper
½ teaspoon dried thyme
¼ cup chopped fresh basil

1. In a slow cooker, combine the potatoes, bell pepper, and onion. Stir to mix well. 2. Place the turkey on top of the vegetables. 3. In a small bowl, whisk together the chicken broth, Parmesan cheese, garlic, oregano, rosemary, salt, black pepper, and thyme until blended. Pour the sauce over the turkey. 4. Cover the cooker and cook for 6 to 8 hours on Low heat. 5. Garnish with fresh basil for serving.

Per Serving:

calories: 402 | fat: 5g | protein: 65g | carbs: 24g | fiber: 3g | sodium: 673mg

Chicken Legs with Leeks

Prep time: 30 minutes | Cook time: 18 minutes | Serves 6

2 leeks, sliced

2 large-sized tomatoes, chopped

3 cloves garlic, minced

½ teaspoon dried oregano

6 chicken legs, boneless and skinless

½ teaspoon smoked cayenne pepper

2 tablespoons olive oil

A freshly ground nutmeg

1. In a mixing dish, thoroughly combine all ingredients, minus the leeks. Place in the refrigerator and let it marinate overnight. 2. Lay the leeks onto the bottom of the air fryer basket. Top with the chicken legs. 3. Roast chicken legs at 375ºF (191ºC) for 18 minutes, turning halfway through. Serve with hoisin sauce.

Per Serving:
calories: 390 | fat: 16g | protein: 52g | carbs: 7g | fiber: 1g | sodium: 264mg

Whole-Roasted Spanish Chicken

Prep time: 1 hour | Cook time: 55 minutes | Serves 4

4 tablespoons (½ stick) unsalted butter, softened

2 tablespoons lemon zest

2 tablespoons smoked paprika

2 tablespoons garlic, minced

1½ teaspoons salt

1 teaspoon freshly ground black pepper

1 (5-pound / 2.3-kg) whole chicken

1. In a small bowl, combine the butter with the lemon zest, paprika, garlic, salt, and pepper. 2. Pat the chicken dry using a paper towel. Using your hands, rub the seasoned butter all over the chicken. Refrigerate the chicken for 30 minutes. 3. Preheat the oven to 425°F(220ºC). Take the chicken out of the fridge and let it sit out for 20 minutes. 4. Put the chicken in a baking dish in the oven and let it cook for 20 minutes. Turn the temperature down to 350°F (180ºC) and let the chicken cook for another 35 minutes. 5. Take the chicken out of the oven and let it stand for 10 minutes before serving.

Per Serving:
calories: 705 | fat: 17g | protein: 126g | carbs: 4g | fiber: 1g | sodium: 880mg

Citrus Chicken with Pecan Wild Rice

Prep time: 15 minutes | Cook time: 10 minutes | Serves 4

4 boneless, skinless chicken breasts

Sea salt and freshly ground pepper, to taste

2 tablespoons olive oil

Juice and zest of 1 orange

2 cups wild rice, cooked

2 green onions, sliced

1 cup pecans, toasted and chopped

1. Season chicken breasts with sea salt and freshly ground pepper. 2. Heat a large skillet over medium heat. Add the oil and sear the chicken until browned on 1 side. 3. Flip the chicken and brown other side. 4. Add the orange juice to the skillet and let cook down. 5. In a large bowl, combine the rice, onions, pecans, and orange zest. Season with sea salt and freshly ground pepper to taste. 6. Serve the chicken alongside the rice and a green salad for a complete meal.

Per Serving:
calories: 870 | fat: 34g | protein: 76g | carbs: 66g | fiber: 8g | sodium: 128mg

Chapter 7 Beans and Grains

Domatorizo (Greek Tomato Rice)

Prep time: 10 minutes | Cook time: 12 minutes |

Serves 6

2 tablespoons extra-virgin olive oil
1 large onion, peeled and diced
1 cup Arborio rice
1 cup tomato juice
3 tablespoons dry white wine
2 cups water
1 tablespoon tomato paste

½ teaspoon salt
½ teaspoon ground black pepper
½ cup crumbled or cubed feta cheese
⅛ teaspoon dried Greek oregano
1 scallion, thinly sliced

1. Press the Sauté button on the Instant Pot® and heat oil. Add onion and cook until just tender, about 3 minutes. Stir in rice and cook for 2 minutes. 2. Add tomato juice and wine to rice. Cook, stirring often, until the liquid is absorbed, about 1 minute. 3. In a small bowl, whisk together water and tomato paste. Add to pot along with salt and pepper and stir well. Press the Cancel button. 4. Close lid, set steam release to Sealing, press the Manual button, and set time to 5 minutes. When the timer beeps, let pressure release naturally for 10 minutes, then quick-release any remaining pressure until the float valve drops. 5. Open lid and stir well. Spoon rice into bowls and top with feta, oregano, and scallion. Serve immediately.

Per Serving:

calories: 184 | fat: 9g | protein: 6g | carbs: 20g | fiber: 1g | sodium: 537mg

Two-Bean Bulgur Chili

Prep time: 10 minutes | Cook time: 30 minutes |

Serves 4 to 5

2 tablespoons olive oil
1 onion, diced
2 celery stalks, diced
1 carrot, diced
1 jalapeño pepper, seeded and chopped
3 garlic cloves, minced
1 (28-ounce/ 794-g) can diced tomatoes
1 tablespoon tomato paste
1½ teaspoons chili powder

2 teaspoons dried oregano
2 teaspoons ground cumin
1 (15-ounce/ 425-g) can black beans, drained and rinsed
1 (15-ounce/ 425-g) can cannellini beans, drained and rinsed
¾ cup dried bulgur
4 cups chicken broth
Sea salt
Freshly ground black pepper

1. In a Dutch oven, heat the olive oil over medium-high heat.

Add the onion, celery, carrot, jalapeño, and garlic and sauté until the vegetables are tender, about 4 minutes. 2. Reduce the heat to medium and add the diced tomatoes, tomato paste, chili powder, oregano, and cumin. Cook for 3 minutes, then add the black beans, cannellini beans, bulgur, and broth. 3. Increase the heat to high, cover, and bring to a boil. Reduce the heat to low and simmer until the chili is cooked to your desired thickness, about 30 minutes. Season with salt and black pepper and serve.

Per Serving:

calories: 385 | fat: 9g | protein: 16g | carbs: 64g | fiber: 20g | sodium: 325mg

Greek Chickpeas with Coriander and Sage

Prep time: 20 minutes | Cook time: 22 minutes |

Serves 6 to 8

1½ tablespoons table salt, for brining
1 pound (454 g) dried chickpeas, picked over and rinsed
2 tablespoons extra-virgin olive oil, plus extra for drizzling
2 onions, halved and sliced thin
¼ teaspoon table salt
1 tablespoon coriander seeds,

cracked
¼ to ½ teaspoon red pepper flakes
2½ cups chicken broth
¼ cup fresh sage leaves
2 bay leaves
1½ teaspoons grated lemon zest plus 2 teaspoons juice
2 tablespoons minced fresh parsley

1. Dissolve 1½ tablespoons salt in 2 quarts cold water in large container. Add chickpeas and soak at room temperature for at least 8 hours or up to 24 hours. Drain and rinse well. 2. Using highest sauté function, heat oil in Instant Pot until shimmering. Add onions and ¼ teaspoon salt and cook until onions are softened and well browned, 10 to 12 minutes. Stir in coriander and pepper flakes and cook until fragrant, about 30 seconds. Stir in broth, scraping up any browned bits, then stir in chickpeas, sage, and bay leaves. 3. Lock lid in place and close pressure release valve. Select low pressure cook function and cook for 10 minutes. Turn off Instant Pot and let pressure release naturally for 15 minutes. Quick-release any remaining pressure, then carefully remove lid, allowing steam to escape away from you. 4. Discard bay leaves. Stir lemon zest and juice into chickpeas and season with salt and pepper to taste. Sprinkle with parsley. Serve, drizzling individual portions with extra oil.

Per Serving:

calories: 190 | fat: 6g | protein: 11g | carbs: 40g | fiber: 1g | sodium: 360mg

Farro Salad with Tomatoes and Olives

Prep time: 10 minutes | Cook time: 20 minutes | Serves 6

10 ounces (283 g) farro, rinsed and drained
4 cups water
4 Roma tomatoes, seeded and chopped
4 scallions, green parts only, thinly sliced
½ cup sliced black olives
¼ cup minced fresh flat-leaf parsley
¼ cup extra-virgin olive oil
2 tablespoons balsamic vinegar
¼ teaspoon ground black pepper

1. Place farro and water in the Instant Pot®. Close lid and set steam release to Sealing. Press the Multigrain button and set time to 20 minutes. When the timer beeps, let pressure release naturally, about 30 minutes. 2. Open lid and fluff with a fork. Transfer to a bowl and cool 30 minutes. Add tomatoes, scallions, black olives, and parsley and mix well. 3. In a small bowl, whisk together oil, balsamic vinegar, and pepper. Pour over salad and toss to evenly coat. Refrigerate for at least 4 hours before serving. Serve chilled or at room temperature.

Per Serving:

calories: 288 | fat: 14g | protein: 7g | carbs: 31g | fiber: 3g | sodium: 159mg

Tomato Rice

Prep time: 10 minutes | Cook time: 25 minutes | Serves 3

2 tablespoons extra virgin olive oil
1 medium onion (any variety), chopped
1 garlic clove, finely chopped
1 cup uncooked medium-grain rice
1 tablespoon tomato paste
1 pound (454 g) canned crushed
tomatoes, or 1 pound (454 g) fresh tomatoes (puréed in a food processor)
¾ teaspoon fine sea salt
1 teaspoon granulated sugar
2 cups hot water
2 tablespoons chopped fresh mint or basil

1. Heat the olive oil in a wide, deep pan over medium heat. When the oil begins to shimmer, add the onion and sauté for 3–4 minutes or until soft, then add the garlic and sauté for an additional 30 seconds. 2. Add the rice and stir until the rice is coated with the oil, then add the tomato paste and stir rapidly. Add the tomatoes, sea salt, and sugar, and then stir again. 3. Add the hot water, stir, then reduce the heat to low and simmer, covered, for 20 minutes or until the rice is soft. (If the rice appears to need more cooking time, add a small amount of hot water to the pan and continue cooking.) Remove the pan from the heat. 4. Add the chopped mint or basil, and let the rice sit for 10 minutes before serving. Store covered in the refrigerator for up to 4 days.

Per Serving:

calories: 359 | fat: 11g | protein: 7g | carbs: 60g | fiber: 6g | sodium: 607mg

White Beans with Garlic and Tomatoes

Prep time: 10 minutes | Cook time: 40 minutes | Serves 6

1 cup dried cannellini beans, soaked overnight and drained
4 cups water
4 cups vegetable stock
1 tablespoon olive oil
1 teaspoon salt
2 cloves garlic, peeled and minced
½ cup diced tomato
½ teaspoon dried sage
½ teaspoon ground black pepper

1. Add beans and water to the Instant Pot®. Close lid, set steam release to Sealing, press the Bean button, and cook for default time of 30 minutes. When timer beeps, quick-release the pressure until the float valve drops. 2. Press the Cancel button, open lid, drain and rinse beans, and return to pot along with stock. Soak for 1 hour. 3. Add olive oil, salt, garlic, tomato, sage, and pepper to beans. Close lid, set steam release to Sealing, press the Manual button, and set time to 10 minutes. When the timer beeps, quick-release the pressure until the float valve drops and open lid. Serve hot.

Per Serving:

calories: 128 | fat: 2g | protein: 7g | carbs: 20g | fiber: 4g | sodium: 809mg

White Bean and Barley Soup

Prep time: 20 minutes | Cook time: 26 minutes | Serves 8

2 tablespoons light olive oil
½ medium onion, peeled and chopped
1 medium carrot, peeled and chopped
1 stalk celery, chopped
2 cloves garlic, peeled and minced
2 sprigs fresh thyme
1 bay leaf
½ teaspoon ground black pepper
1 (14-ounce / 397-g) can fire-roasted diced tomatoes, undrained
½ cup medium pearl barley, rinsed and drained
4 cups vegetable broth
2 cups water
2 (15-ounce / 425-g) cans Great Northern beans, drained and rinsed
½ teaspoon salt

1. Press the Sauté button on the Instant Pot® and heat oil. Add onion, carrot, and celery. Cook until just tender, about 5 minutes. Add garlic, thyme, bay leaf, and pepper, and cook until fragrant, about 30 seconds. Press the Cancel button. 2. Add the tomatoes, barley, broth, and water. Close lid, set steam release to Sealing, press the Soup button, and cook for default time of 20 minutes. 3. When the timer beeps, let pressure release naturally, about 20 minutes. Open lid, stir soup, then add beans and salt. Close lid and let stand on the Keep Warm setting for 10 minutes. Remove and discard bay leaf. Serve hot.

Per Serving:

calories: 129 | fat: 4g | protein: 5g | carbs: 20g | fiber: 5g | sodium: 636mg

White Bean Cassoulet

Prep time: 30 minutes | Cook time: 45 minutes |

Serves 8

1 tablespoon olive oil
1 medium onion, peeled and diced
2 cups dried cannellini beans, soaked overnight and drained
1 medium parsnip, peeled and diced
2 medium carrots, peeled and diced
2 stalks celery, diced
1 medium zucchini, trimmed
and chopped
½ teaspoon fennel seed
¼ teaspoon ground nutmeg
½ teaspoon garlic powder
1 teaspoon sea salt
½ teaspoon ground black pepper
2 cups vegetable broth
1 (14½-ounce / 411-g) can diced tomatoes, including juice
2 sprigs rosemary

1. Press the Sauté button on the Instant Pot® and heat oil. Add onion and cook until translucent, about 5 minutes. Add beans and toss. 2. Add a layer of parsnip, then a layer of carrots, and next a layer of celery. Finally, add a layer of zucchini. Sprinkle in fennel seed, nutmeg, garlic powder, salt, and pepper. Press the Cancel button. 3. Gently pour in broth and canned tomatoes. Top with rosemary. 4. Close lid, set steam release to Sealing, press the Bean button, and cook for the default time of 30 minutes. When the timer beeps, let pressure release naturally for 10 minutes. Quick-release any remaining pressure until the float valve drops and open lid. Press the Cancel button. 5. Press the Sauté button, then press the Adjust button to change the temperature to Less, and simmer bean mixture uncovered for 10 minutes to thicken. Transfer to a serving bowl and carefully toss. Remove and discard rosemary and serve.

Per Serving:

calories: 128 | fat: 2g | protein: 6g | carbs: 21g | fiber: 5g | sodium: 387mg

Herbed Polenta

Prep time: 10 minutes | Cook time: 3 to 5 hours |

Serves 4

1 cup stone-ground polenta
4 cups low-sodium vegetable stock or low-sodium chicken stock
1 tablespoon extra-virgin olive oil
1 small onion, minced
2 garlic cloves, minced
1 teaspoon sea salt
1 teaspoon dried parsley
1 teaspoon dried oregano
1 teaspoon dried thyme
½ teaspoon freshly ground black pepper
½ cup grated Parmesan cheese

1. In a slow cooker, combine the polenta, vegetable stock, olive oil, onion, garlic, salt, parsley, oregano, thyme, and pepper. Stir to mix well. 2. Cover the cooker and cook for 3 to 5 hours on Low heat. 3. Stir in the Parmesan cheese for serving.

Per Serving:

calories: 191 | fat: 9g | protein: 11g | carbs: 18g | fiber: 1g | sodium: 796mg

White Beans with Kale

Prep time: 15 minutes | Cook time: 7½ hours |

Serves 2

1 onion, chopped
1 leek, white part only, sliced
2 celery stalks, sliced
2 garlic cloves, minced
1 cup dried white lima beans or cannellini beans, sorted and rinsed
2 cups vegetable broth
½ teaspoon salt
½ teaspoon dried thyme leaves
⅛ teaspoon freshly ground black pepper
3 cups torn kale

1. In the slow cooker, combine all the ingredients except the kale. 2. Cover and cook on low for 7 hours, or until the beans are tender. 3. Add the kale and stir. 4. Cover and cook on high for 30 minutes, or until the kale is tender but still firm, and serve.

Per Serving:

calories: 176 | fat: 1g | protein: 9g | carbs: 36g | fiber: 9g | sodium: 616mg

Quinoa Salad with Chicken, Chickpeas, and Spinach

Prep time: 15 minutes | Cook time: 18 minutes |

Serves 6

4 tablespoons olive oil, divided
1 medium yellow onion, peeled and chopped
2 cloves garlic, peeled and minced
4 cups fresh baby spinach leaves
½ teaspoon salt
¼ teaspoon ground black pepper
1½ cups quinoa, rinsed and
drained
2 cups vegetable broth
1⅓ cups water
1 tablespoon apple cider vinegar
1 (15 ounces / 425 g) can chickpeas, drained and rinsed
1 (6-ounce / 170-g) boneless, skinless chicken breast, cooked and shredded

1. Press the Sauté button on the Instant Pot® and heat 2 tablespoons olive oil. Add onion and cook until tender, about 3 minutes. Add garlic, spinach, salt, and pepper and cook 3 minutes until spinach has wilted. Transfer spinach mixture to a large bowl. Press the Cancel button. 2. Add quinoa, broth, and water to the Instant Pot®. Close lid, set steam release to Sealing, press the Rice button, and set time to 12 minutes. 3. While quinoa cooks, add remaining 2 tablespoons olive oil, vinegar, chickpeas, and chicken to spinach mixture and toss to coat. Set aside. 4. When the timer beeps, let pressure release naturally, about 20 minutes. 5. Open lid and fluff quinoa with a fork. Press the Cancel button and let quinoa cool 10 minutes, then transfer to the bowl with chicken mixture. Mix well. Serve warm, at room temperature, or cold.

Per Serving:

calories: 232 | fat: 12g | protein: 14g | carbs: 20g | fiber: 6g | sodium: 463mg

Lebanese Rice and Broken Noodles with Cabbage

Prep time: 5 minutes |Cook time: 25 minutes|

Serves: 6

1 tablespoon extra-virgin olive oil
1 cup (about 3 ounces / 85 g) uncooked vermicelli or thin spaghetti, broken into 1- to 1½-inch pieces
3 cups shredded cabbage (about half a 14-ounce package of coleslaw mix or half a small head of cabbage)
3 cups low-sodium or no-salt-added vegetable broth
½ cup water
1 cup instant brown rice
2 garlic cloves
¼ teaspoon kosher or sea salt
⅛ to ¼ teaspoon crushed red pepper
½ cup loosely packed, coarsely chopped cilantro
Fresh lemon slices, for serving (optional)

1. In a large saucepan over medium-high heat, heat the oil. Add the pasta and cook for 3 minutes to toast, stirring often. Add the cabbage and cook for 4 minutes, stirring often. Add the broth, water, rice, garlic, salt, and crushed red pepper, and bring to a boil over high heat. Stir, cover, and reduce the heat to medium-low. Simmer for 10 minutes. 2. Remove the pan from the heat, but do not lift the lid. Let sit for 5 minutes. Fish out the garlic cloves, mash them with a fork, then stir the garlic back into the rice. Stir in the cilantro. Serve with the lemon slices (if using).

Per Serving:

calories: 150 | fat: 4g | protein: 3g | carbs: 27g | fiber: 3g | sodium: 664mg

Lentils with Cilantro and Lime

Prep time: 15 minutes | Cook time: 20 minutes |

Serves 6

2 tablespoons olive oil
1 medium yellow onion, peeled and chopped
1 medium carrot, peeled and chopped
¼ cup chopped fresh cilantro
½ teaspoon ground cumin
½ teaspoon salt
2 cups dried green lentils, rinsed and drained
4 cups low-sodium chicken broth
2 tablespoons lime juice

1. Press the Sauté button on the Instant Pot® and heat oil. Add onion and carrot, and cook until just tender, about 3 minutes. Add cilantro, cumin, and salt, and cook until fragrant, about 30 seconds. Press the Cancel button. 2. Add lentils and broth to pot. Close lid, set steam release to Sealing, press the Manual button, and set time to 15 minutes. 3. When the timer beeps, let pressure release naturally, about 25 minutes. Open lid and stir in lime juice. Serve warm.

Per Serving:

calories: 316 | fat: 5g | protein: 20g | carbs: 44g | fiber: 21g | sodium: 349mg

Rice and Lentils

Prep time: 10 minutes | Cook time: 55 minutes |

Serves 4

2 cups green or brown lentils
1 cup brown rice
5 cups water or chicken stock
½ teaspoon sea salt
½ teaspoon freshly ground
pepper
½ teaspoon dried thyme
¼ cup olive oil
3 onions, peeled and sliced

1. Place the lentils and rice in a large saucepan with water or chicken stock. Bring to a boil, cover, and simmer for 20 to 25 minutes, or until almost tender. 2. Add the seasonings and cook an additional 20 to 30 minutes, or until the rice is tender and the water is absorbed. 3. In another saucepan, heat the olive oil over medium heat. Add the onions and cook very slowly, stirring frequently, until the onions become browned and caramelized, about 20 minutes. 4. To serve, ladle the lentils and rice into bowls and top with the caramelized onions.

Per Serving:

calories: 661 | fat: 16g | protein: 28g | carbs: 104g | fiber: 13g | sodium: 303mg

Brown Rice Vegetable Bowl with Roasted Red Pepper Dressing

Prep time: 10 minutes | Cook time: 22 minutes |

Serves 2

¼ cup chopped roasted red bell pepper
2 tablespoons extra-virgin olive oil
1 tablespoon red wine vinegar
1 teaspoon honey
2 tablespoons light olive oil
2 cloves garlic, peeled and minced
½ teaspoon ground black pepper
¼ teaspoon salt
1 cup brown rice
1 cup vegetable broth
¼ cup chopped fresh flat-leaf parsley
2 tablespoons chopped fresh chives
2 tablespoons chopped fresh dill
½ cup diced tomato
½ cup chopped red onion
½ cup diced cucumber
½ cup chopped green bell pepper

1. Place roasted red pepper, extra-virgin olive oil, red wine vinegar, and honey in a blender. Purée until smooth, about 1 minute. Refrigerate until ready to serve. 2. Press the Sauté button on the Instant Pot® and heat light olive oil. Add garlic and cook until fragrant, about 30 seconds. Add black pepper, salt, and rice and stir well. Press the Cancel button. 3. Stir in broth. Close lid, set steam release to Sealing, press the Manual button, and set time to 22 minutes.

Per Serving:

calories: 561 | fat: 23g | protein: 10g | carbs: 86g | fiber: 5g | sodium: 505mg

Quinoa Salad in Endive Boats

Prep time: 10 minutes | Cook time: 3 minutes | Serves 4

1 tablespoon walnut oil
1 cup quinoa, rinsed and drained
2½ cups water
2 cups chopped jarred artichoke hearts
2 cups diced tomatoes

½ small red onion, peeled and thinly sliced
2 tablespoons olive oil
1 tablespoon balsamic vinegar
4 large Belgian endive leaves
1 cup toasted pecans

1. Press the Sauté button on the Instant Pot® and heat walnut oil. Add quinoa and toss for 1 minute until slightly browned. Add water and stir. Press the Cancel button. 2. Close lid, set steam release to Sealing, press the Manual button, and set time to 2 minutes. When the timer beeps, let pressure release naturally for 10 minutes. Quick-release any remaining pressure until the float valve drops and open lid. Drain liquid and transfer quinoa to a serving bowl. 3. Add artichoke hearts, tomatoes, onion, olive oil, and vinegar to quinoa and stir to combine. Cover and refrigerate mixture for 1 hour or up to overnight. 4. Place endive leaves on four plates. Top each with ¼ cup quinoa mixture. Sprinkle toasted pecans over the top of each endive boat and serve.

Per Serving:

calories: 536 | fat: 35g | protein: 13g | carbs: 46g | fiber: 13g | sodium: 657mg

Moroccan Date Pilaf

Prep time: 10 minutes | Cook time: 30 minutes | Serves 4

3 tablespoons olive oil
1 onion, chopped
3 garlic cloves, minced
1 cup uncooked long-grain rice
½ to 1 tablespoon harissa
5 or 6 Medjool dates (or another variety), pitted and chopped
¼ cup dried cranberries

¼ teaspoon ground cinnamon
½ teaspoon ground turmeric
¼ teaspoon sea salt
¼ teaspoon freshly ground black pepper
2 cups chicken broth
¼ cup shelled whole pistachios, for garnish

1. In a large stockpot, heat the olive oil over medium heat. Add the onion and garlic and sauté for 3 to 5 minutes, until the onion is soft. Add the rice and cook for 3 minutes, until the grains start to turn opaque. Add the harissa, dates, cranberries, cinnamon, turmeric, salt, and pepper and cook for 30 seconds. Add the broth and bring to a boil, then reduce the heat to low, cover, and simmer for 20 minutes, or until the liquid has been absorbed. 2. Remove the rice from the heat and stir in the nuts. Let stand for 10 minutes before serving.

Per Serving:

calories: 368 | fat: 15g | protein: 6g | carbs: 54g | fiber: 4g | sodium: 83mg

Garlic Shrimp with Quinoa

Prep time: 10 minutes | Cook time: 30 minutes | Serves 4

4 cups chicken broth
2 cups uncooked quinoa, rinsed
5 tablespoons olive oil
½ red onion, chopped
6 garlic cloves, minced
1 tablespoon tomato paste
1 teaspoon chili powder

Sea salt
Freshly ground black pepper
1½ pounds (680 g) medium shrimp (36/40 count), peeled and deveined
½ cup crumbled feta cheese, for garnish

1. In a large stockpot, combine the broth and quinoa and bring to a boil over high heat. Reduce the heat to low, cover, and simmer for 20 to 25 minutes, until the quinoa is cooked. Drain the quinoa and set aside in a medium bowl. 2. Rinse and dry the pot. Pour in the olive oil and heat over medium heat. Add the onion, garlic, tomato paste, and chili powder and cook for 1 minute. Season with salt and pepper and stir to combine. Add the shrimp and cook until the shrimp are pink and just cooked through, 5 to 7 minutes. 3. Return the quinoa to the pot and stir everything together. Remove from the heat. 4. Serve topped with the feta.

Per Serving:

calories: 712 | fat: 28g | protein: 54g | carbs: 62g | fiber: 7g | sodium: 474mg

Fava Beans with Ground Meat

Prep time: 15 minutes | Cook time: 6 to 8 hours | Serves 6

8 ounces (227 g) raw ground meat
1 pound (454 g) dried fava beans, rinsed well under cold water and picked over to remove debris, or 1 (15-ounce/425-g) can fava beans, drained and rinsed
10 cups water or 5 cups water and 5 cups low-sodium vegetable broth
1 small onion, diced

1 bell pepper, any color, seeded and diced
1 teaspoon sea salt
1 teaspoon garlic powder
1 teaspoon dried parsley
1 teaspoon dried oregano
1 teaspoon paprika
1 teaspoon cayenne pepper
½ teaspoon freshly ground black pepper
½ teaspoon dried thyme

1. In a large skillet over medium-high heat, cook the ground meat for 3 to 5 minutes, stirring and breaking it up with a spoon, until it has browned and is no longer pink. Drain any grease and put the meat in a slow cooker. 2. Add the fava beans, water, onion, bell pepper, salt, garlic powder, parsley, oregano, paprika, cayenne pepper, black pepper, and thyme to the meat. Stir to mix well. 3. Cover the cooker and cook for 6 to 8 hours on Low heat, or until the beans are tender.

Per Serving:

calories: 308 | fat: 4g | protein: 26g | carbs: 43g | fiber: 19g | sodium: 417mg

Cilantro Lime Rice

Prep time: 10 minutes | Cook time: 32 minutes |

Serves 8

2 tablespoons extra-virgin olive oil

½ medium yellow onion, peeled and chopped

2 cloves garlic, peeled and minced

½ cup chopped fresh cilantro, divided

2 cups brown rice

2¼ cups water

2 tablespoons lime juice

1 tablespoon grated lime zest

¼ teaspoon salt

½ teaspoon ground black pepper

1. Press the Sauté button on the Instant Pot® and heat oil. Add onion and cook until soft, about 6 minutes. Add garlic and ¼ cup cilantro and cook until fragrant, about 30 seconds. Add rice and cook, stirring constantly, until well coated and starting to toast, about 3 minutes. Press the Cancel button. 2. Stir in water. Close lid, set steam release to Sealing, press the Manual button, and set time to 22 minutes. When the timer beeps, let pressure release naturally for 10 minutes, then quick-release the remaining pressure. Open lid and fluff rice with a fork. Fold in remaining ¼ cup cilantro, lime juice, lime zest, salt, and pepper. Serve warm.

Per Serving:

calories: 95 | fat: 4g | protein: 1g | carbs: 14g | fiber: 1g | sodium: 94mg

No-Stir Polenta with Arugula, Figs, and Blue Cheese

Prep time: 15 minutes | Cook time: 40 minutes |

Serves 4

1 cup coarse-ground cornmeal

½ cup oil-packed sun-dried tomatoes, chopped

1 teaspoon minced fresh thyme or ¼ teaspoon dried

½ teaspoon table salt

¼ teaspoon pepper

3 tablespoons extra-virgin olive

oil, divided

2 ounces (57 g) baby arugula

4 figs, cut into ½-inch-thick wedges

1 tablespoon balsamic vinegar

2 ounces (57 g) blue cheese, crumbled (½ cup)

2 tablespoons pine nuts, toasted

1. Arrange trivet included with Instant Pot in base of insert and add 1 cup water. Fold sheet of aluminum foil into 16 by 6-inch sling, then rest 1½-quart round soufflé dish in center of sling. Whisk 4 cups water, cornmeal, tomatoes, thyme, salt, and pepper together in bowl, then transfer mixture to soufflé dish. Using sling, lower soufflé dish into pot and onto trivet; allow narrow edges of sling to rest along sides of insert. 2. Lock lid in place and close pressure release valve. Select high pressure cook function and cook for 40 minutes. Turn off Instant Pot and quick-release pressure. Carefully remove lid, allowing steam to escape away from you. 3. Using sling, transfer soufflé dish to wire rack. Whisk 1 tablespoon oil into polenta, smoothing out any lumps. Let sit until thickened slightly, about 10 minutes. Season with salt and pepper to taste. 4. Toss arugula and figs with vinegar and remaining 2 tablespoons oil in bowl, and season with salt and pepper to taste. Divide polenta among individual serving plates and top with arugula mixture, blue cheese, and pine nuts. Serve.

Per Serving:

calories: 360 | fat: 21g | protein: 7g | carbs: 38g | fiber: 8g | sodium: 510mg

Pilaf with Eggplant and Raisins

Prep time: 10 minutes | Cook time: 30 minutes |

Serves 4

4 eggplant (preferably thinner, about 6 ounces/170g each) cut into ¼-inch (.5cm) thick slices (if the slices are too large, cut them in half)

1½ teaspoons fine sea salt, divided

½ cup extra virgin olive oil

1 medium onion (any variety), diced

4 garlic cloves, thinly sliced

¼ cup white wine

1 cup uncooked medium-grain rice

1 (15 ounces / 425 g) can crushed tomatoes

3 cups hot water

4 tablespoons black raisins

4 teaspoons finely chopped fresh parsley

4 teaspoons finely chopped fresh mint

¼ teaspoon freshly ground black pepper to serve

1. Place the eggplant in a colander and sprinkle with ½ teaspoon of the sea salt. Set aside to rest for 10 minutes, then rinse well and squeeze to remove any remaining water. 2. Add the olive oil to a medium pot placed over medium heat. When the oil begins to shimmer, add the eggplant and sauté for 7 minutes or until soft, moving the eggplant continuously, then add the onions and continue sautéing and stirring for 2 more minutes. 3. Add the garlic and sauté for 1 additional minute, then add the white wine and deglaze the pan. After about 1 minute, add the rice and stir until the rice is coated with the oil. 4. Add the crushed tomatoes, hot water, and remaining sea salt. Stir and bring to a boil, then reduce the heat to low and simmer for 20 minutes. Add more hot water, ¼ cup at a time, if the water level gets too low. 5. Add the raisins, stir, then cover the pot and remove from the heat. Set aside to cool for 15 minutes. 6. To serve, sprinkle 1 teaspoon of the mint and 1 teaspoon of the parsley over each serving, then season each serving with black pepper. Store covered in the refrigerator for up to 3 days.

Per Serving:

calories: 612 | fat: 29g | protein: 11g | carbs: 84g | fiber: 21g | sodium: 859mg

Garbanzo and Pita No-Bake Casserole

Prep time: 10 minutes | Cook time: 10 minutes | Serves 4

4 cups Greek yogurt

3 cloves garlic, minced

1 teaspoon salt

2 (16-ounce/ 454-g) cans garbanzo beans, rinsed and drained

2 cups water

4 cups pita chips

5 tablespoons unsalted butter

1. In a large bowl, whisk together the yogurt, garlic, and salt. Set aside. 2. Put the garbanzo beans and water in a medium pot. Bring to a boil; let beans boil for about 5 minutes. 3. Pour the garbanzo beans and the liquid into a large casserole dish. 4. Top the beans with pita chips. Pour the yogurt sauce over the pita chip layer. 5. In a small saucepan, melt and brown the butter, about 3 minutes. Pour the brown butter over the yogurt sauce.

Per Serving:

calories: 772 | fat: 36g | protein: 39g | carbs: 73g | fiber: 13g | sodium: 1,003mg

Barley Salad with Lemon-Tahini Dressing

Prep time: 15 minutes | Cook time: 10 minutes | Serves 4 to 6

1½ cups pearl barley

5 tablespoons extra-virgin olive oil, divided

1½ teaspoons table salt, for cooking barley

¼ cup tahini

1 teaspoon grated lemon zest plus ¼ cup juice (2 lemons)

1 tablespoon sumac, divided

1 garlic clove, minced

¾ teaspoon table salt

1 English cucumber, cut into ½-inch pieces

1 carrot, peeled and shredded

1 red bell pepper, stemmed, seeded, and chopped

4 scallions, sliced thin

2 tablespoons finely chopped jarred hot cherry peppers

¼ cup coarsely chopped fresh mint

1. Combine 6 cups water, barley, 1 tablespoon oil, and 1½ teaspoons salt in Instant Pot. Lock lid in place and close pressure release valve. Select high pressure cook function and cook for 8 minutes. Turn off Instant Pot and let pressure release naturally for 15 minutes. Quick-release any remaining pressure, then carefully remove lid, allowing steam to escape away from you. Drain barley, spread onto rimmed baking sheet, and let cool completely, about 15 minutes. 2. Meanwhile, whisk remaining ¼ cup oil, tahini, 2 tablespoons water, lemon zest and juice, 1 teaspoon sumac, garlic, and ¾ teaspoon salt in large bowl until combined; let sit for 15 minutes. 3. Measure out and reserve ½ cup dressing for serving. Add barley, cucumber, carrot, bell pepper, scallions, and cherry peppers to bowl with dressing and gently toss to combine. Season with salt and pepper to taste. Transfer salad to serving dish and sprinkle with mint and remaining 2 teaspoons sumac. Serve, passing reserved dressing separately.

Per Serving:

calories: 370 | fat: 18g | protein: 8g | carbs: 47g | fiber: 10g | sodium: 510mg

Chapter 8 Vegetables and Sides

Sautéed Kale with Tomato and Garlic

Prep time: 5 minutes | Cook time: 10 minutes |
Serves 4

1 tablespoon extra-virgin olive oil
4 garlic cloves, sliced
¼ teaspoon red pepper flakes
2 bunches kale, stemmed and

chopped or torn into pieces
1 (14½-ounce / 411-g) can no-salt-added diced tomatoes
½ teaspoon kosher salt

1. Heat the olive oil in a wok or large skillet over medium-high heat. Add the garlic and red pepper flakes, and sauté until fragrant, about 30 seconds. Add the kale and sauté, about 3 to 5 minutes, until the kale shrinks down a bit. 2. Add the tomatoes and the salt, stir together, and cook for 3 to 5 minutes, or until the liquid reduces and the kale cooks down further and becomes tender.

Per Serving:
calories: 110 | fat: 5g | protein: 6g | carbs: 15g | fiber: 6g | sodium: 222mg

Braised Cauliflower

Prep time: 10 minutes | Cook time: 35 minutes |
Serves 3

½ cup extra virgin olive oil
1 medium head cauliflower (about 2 pounds / 907 g), washed and cut into medium-sized florets
1 medium russet or white potato, cut into 1-inch pieces
¼ teaspoon freshly ground

black pepper
3 allspice berries
1 cinnamon stick
3 cloves
2 tablespoons tomato paste
1 teaspoon fine sea salt
¾ cup hot water

1. Add the olive oil to a large pot over medium heat. When the oil begins to shimmer, add the cauliflower, potatoes, black pepper, allspice berries, cinnamon stick, and cloves. Sauté for 4 minutes or until the cauliflower begins to brown. 2. Add the tomato paste and sea salt. Continue heating, using a wooden spoon to swirl the tomato paste around the pan until the color changes to a brick red. 3. Add the hot water and stir gently. Reduce the heat to low, cover, and simmer for about 30 minutes or until the cauliflower is tender and the sauce has thickened. (If the sauce is still watery, remove the lid and simmer until the sauce has thickened.) Remove the allspice berries, cinnamon stick, and cloves. 4. Remove the cauliflower from the heat and set it aside to cool for at least 10 minutes before serving. When ready to serve, transfer the cauliflower to a large

serving bowl and spoon the sauce over the top. Store covered in the refrigerator for up to 3 days.

Per Serving:
calories: 406 | fat: 36g | protein: 4g | carbs: 19g | fiber: 3g | sodium: 813mg

Sesame-Ginger Broccoli

Prep time: 10 minutes | Cook time: 15 minutes |
Serves 4

3 tablespoons toasted sesame oil
2 teaspoons sesame seeds
1 tablespoon chili-garlic sauce
2 teaspoons minced fresh ginger

½ teaspoon kosher salt
½ teaspoon black pepper
1 (16-ounce / 454-g) package frozen broccoli florets (do not thaw)

1. In a large bowl, combine the sesame oil, sesame seeds, chili-garlic sauce, ginger, salt, and pepper. Stir until well combined. Add the broccoli and toss until well coated. 2. Arrange the broccoli in the air fryer basket. Set the air fryer to 325ºF (163ºC) for 15 minutes, or until the broccoli is crisp, tender, and the edges are lightly browned, gently tossing halfway through the cooking time.

Per Serving:
calories: 143 | fat: 11g | protein: 4g | carbs: 9g | fiber: 4g | sodium: 385mg

Coriander-Cumin Roasted Carrots

Prep time: 10 minutes | Cook time: 20 minutes |
Serves 2

½ pound (227 g) rainbow carrots (about 4)
2 tablespoons fresh orange juice

1 tablespoon honey
½ teaspoon coriander
Pinch salt

1. Preheat oven to 400°F(205ºC) and set the oven rack to the middle position. 2. Peel the carrots and cut them lengthwise into slices of even thickness. Place them in a large bowl. 3. In a small bowl, mix together the orange juice, honey, coriander, and salt. 4. Pour the orange juice mixture over the carrots and toss well to coat. 5. Spread carrots onto a baking dish in a single layer. 6. Roast for 15 to 20 minutes, or until fork-tender.

Per Serving:
calories: 85 | fat: 0g | protein: 1g | carbs: 21g | fiber: 3g | sodium: 156mg

Vegetable Vindaloo

Prep time: 15 minutes | Cook time: 2 to 4 hours |

Serves 6

Spice Paste:
1 teaspoon mustard seeds
1 teaspoon cumin seeds
2 teaspoons coriander seeds
4 cloves
4 dried Kashmiri chiles
1 teaspoon black peppercorns
2 onions, roughly chopped
6 garlic cloves
1-inch piece fresh ginger
4 tablespoons malt vinegar
Vindaloo:
1 tablespoon vegetable oil
1 teaspoon mustard seeds
4 medium potatoes, peeled and cut into 1-inch cubes
4 ounces (113 g) cauliflower florets
1 zucchini, diced
4 ounces (113 g) mushrooms, sliced
1 carrot, peeled and sliced
1 (14-ounce / 397-g) can kidney beans, drained and rinsed
1 teaspoon salt
1 teaspoon turmeric
½ teaspoon sugar

Make the Spice Paste: 1. Preheat the slow cooker on high for 15 minutes. 2. In a blender, make the spice paste by grinding the mustard seeds, cumin seeds, coriander seeds, cloves, chiles, and peppercorns to a fine powder. 3. Then add the onions, garlic, ginger, vinegar, and a splash of water to the powder. Blend to make a paste. Make the Vindaloo: 4. Heat the oil in a frying pan (or in the slow cooker if you have a sear setting). Add the mustard seeds and cook until they pop. Add all of the spice paste and cook until the paste is fragrant. 5. Put everything in the slow cooker. Add the potatoes, cauliflower florets, zucchini, mushrooms, carrot, and beans. Then stir in the salt, turmeric, and sugar, plus a splash of water if needed. 6. Cover and cook on low for 3 to 4 hours, or on high for 2 hours. 7. Check the seasoning and adjust if required. Serve hot.

Per Serving:

calories: 279 | fat: 4g | protein: 11g | carbs: 53g | fiber: 10g | sodium: 570mg

Walnut and Freekeh Pilaf

Prep time: 15 minutes | Cook time: 15 minutes |

Serves 4

2½ cups freekeh
3 tablespoons extra-virgin olive oil, divided
2 medium onions, diced
¼ teaspoon ground cinnamon
¼ teaspoon ground allspice
5 cups chicken stock
½ cup chopped walnuts
Salt
Freshly ground black pepper
½ cup plain, unsweetened, full-fat Greek yogurt
1½ teaspoons freshly squeezed lemon juice
½ teaspoon garlic powder

1. In a small bowl, soak the freekeh covered in cold water for 5 minutes. Drain and rinse the freekeh, then rinse one more time. 2. In a large sauté pan or skillet, heat 2 tablespoons oil, then add the onions and cook until fragrant. Add the freekeh, cinnamon, and allspice. Stir periodically for 1 minute. 3. Add the stock and walnuts

and season with salt and pepper. Bring to a simmer. 4. Cover and reduce the heat to low. Cook for 15 minutes. Once freekeh is tender, remove from the heat and allow to rest for 5 minutes. 5. In a small bowl, combine the yogurt, lemon juice, and garlic powder. You may need to add salt to bring out the flavors. Add the yogurt mixture to the freekeh and serve immediately.

Per Serving:

calories: 653 | fat: 25g | protein: 23g | carbs: 91g | fiber: 12g | sodium: 575mg

Parmesan-Rosemary Radishes

Prep time: 5 minutes | Cook time: 15 to 20 minutes |

Serves 4

1 bunch radishes, stemmed, trimmed, and quartered
1 tablespoon avocado oil
2 tablespoons finely grated fresh Parmesan cheese
1 tablespoon chopped fresh rosemary
Sea salt and freshly ground black pepper, to taste

1. Place the radishes in a medium bowl and toss them with the avocado oil, Parmesan cheese, rosemary, salt, and pepper. 2. Set the air fryer to 375°F (191°C). Arrange the radishes in a single layer in the air fryer basket. Roast for 15 to 20 minutes, until golden brown and tender. Let cool for 5 minutes before serving.

Per Serving:

calories: 58 | fat: 4g | protein: 1g | carbs: 4g | fiber: 2g | sodium: 63mg

Grits Casserole

Prep time: 5 minutes | Cook time: 28 to 30 minutes |

Serves 4

10 fresh asparagus spears, cut into 1-inch pieces
2 cups cooked grits, cooled to room temperature
1 egg, beaten
2 teaspoons Worcestershire sauce
½ teaspoon garlic powder
¼ teaspoon salt
2 slices provolone cheese (about 1½ ounces / 43 g)
Oil for misting or cooking spray

1. Mist asparagus spears with oil and air fry at 390°F (199°C) for 5 minutes, until crisp-tender. 2. In a medium bowl, mix together the grits, egg, Worcestershire, garlic powder, and salt. 3. Spoon half of grits mixture into a baking pan and top with asparagus. 4. Tear cheese slices into pieces and layer evenly on top of asparagus. 5. Top with remaining grits. 6. Bake at 360°F (182°C) for 23 to 25 minutes. The casserole will rise a little as it cooks. When done, the top will have browned lightly with just a hint of crispiness.

Per Serving:

calories: 161 | fat: 6g | protein: 8g | carbs: 20g | fiber: 2g | sodium: 704mg

Roasted Asparagus and Fingerling Potatoes with Thyme

Prep time: 5 minutes | Cook time: 20 minutes |

Serves 4

1 pound (454 g) asparagus, trimmed	3 tablespoons olive oil
1 pound (454 g) fingerling potatoes, cut into thin rounds	¾ teaspoon salt
2 scallions, thinly sliced	¼ teaspoon freshly ground black pepper
	1 tablespoon fresh thyme leaves

1. Preheat the oven to 450°F (235°C). 2. In a large baking dish, combine the asparagus, potatoes, and scallions and toss to mix. Add the olive oil, salt, and pepper and toss again to coat all of the vegetables in the oil. Spread the vegetables out in as thin a layer as possible and roast in the preheated oven, stirring once, until the vegetables are tender and nicely browned, about 20 minutes. Just before serving, sprinkle with the thyme leaves. Serve hot.

Per Serving:

calories: 197 | fat: 11g | protein: 5g | carbs: 24g | fiber: 5g | sodium: 449mg

Braised Whole Cauliflower with North African Spices

Prep time: 15 minutes | Cook time: 10 minutes |

Serves 4

2 tablespoons extra-virgin olive oil	juice reserved, chopped coarse
6 garlic cloves, minced	1 large head cauliflower (3 pounds / 1.4 kg)
3 anchovy fillets, rinsed and minced (optional)	½ cup pitted brine-cured green olives, chopped coarse
2 teaspoons ras el hanout	¼ cup golden raisins
⅛ teaspoon red pepper flakes	¼ cup fresh cilantro leaves
1 (28-ounce / 794-g) can whole peeled tomatoes, drained with	¼ cup pine nuts, toasted

1. Using highest sauté function, cook oil, garlic, anchovies (if using), ras el hanout, and pepper flakes in Instant Pot until fragrant, about 3 minutes. Turn off Instant Pot, then stir in tomatoes and reserved juice. 2. Trim outer leaves of cauliflower and cut stem flush with bottom florets. Using paring knife, cut 4-inch-deep cross in stem. Nestle cauliflower stem side down into pot and spoon some of sauce over top. Lock lid in place and close pressure release valve. Select high pressure cook function and cook for 3 minutes. 3. Turn off Instant Pot and quick-release pressure. Carefully remove lid, allowing steam to escape away from you. Using tongs and slotted spoon, transfer cauliflower to serving dish and tent with aluminum foil. Stir olives and raisins into sauce and cook, using highest sauté function, until sauce has thickened slightly, about 5 minutes. Season with salt and pepper to taste. Cut cauliflower into wedges and spoon some of sauce over top. Sprinkle with cilantro

and pine nuts. Serve, passing remaining sauce separately.

Per Serving:

calories: 265 | fat: 16g | protein: 8g | carbs: 29g | fiber: 9g | sodium: 319mg

Root Vegetable Hash

Prep time: 20 minutes | Cook time: 8 hours | Makes

9 (¾-cup) servings

4 carrots, peeled and cut into 1-inch cubes	⅛ teaspoon freshly ground black pepper
3 large russet potatoes, peeled and cut into 1-inch cubes	½ teaspoon dried thyme leaves
1 onion, diced	1 sprig rosemary
3 garlic cloves, minced	½ cup vegetable broth
½ teaspoon salt	3 plums, cut into 1-inch pieces

1. In the slow cooker, combine the carrots, potatoes, onion, and garlic. Sprinkle with the salt, pepper, and thyme, and stir. 2. Imbed the rosemary sprig in the vegetables. 3. Pour the broth over everything. 4. Cover and cook on low for 7½ hours, or until the vegetables are tender. 5. Stir in the plums, cover, and cook on low for 30 minutes, until tender. 6. Remove and discard the rosemary sprig, and serve.

Per Serving:

calories: 137 | fat: 0g | protein: 3g | carbs: 32g | fiber: 4g | sodium: 204mg

White Beans with Rosemary, Sage, and Garlic

Prep time: 10 minutes | Cook time: 10 minutes |

Serves 2

1 tablespoon olive oil	1 teaspoon minced fresh rosemary (from 1 sprig) plus 1 whole fresh rosemary sprig
2 garlic cloves, minced	
1 (15 ounces / 425 g) can white cannellini beans, drained and rinsed	½ cup low-sodium chicken stock
¼ teaspoon dried sage	Salt

1. Heat the olive oil in a sauté pan over medium-high heat. Add the garlic and sauté for 30 seconds. 2. Add the beans, sage, minced and whole rosemary, and chicken stock and bring the mixture to a boil. 3. Reduce the heat to medium and simmer the beans for 10 minutes, or until most of the liquid is evaporated. If desired, mash some of the beans with a fork to thicken them. 4. Season with salt. Remove the rosemary sprig before serving

Per Serving:

calories: 155 | fat: 7g | protein: 6g | carbs: 17g | fiber: 8g | sodium: 153mg

Chermoula-Roasted Beets

Prep time: 15 minutes | Cook time: 25 minutes | Serves 4

Chermoula:
1 cup packed fresh cilantro leaves
½ cup packed fresh parsley leaves
6 cloves garlic, peeled
2 teaspoons smoked paprika
2 teaspoons ground cumin
1 teaspoon ground coriander
½ to 1 teaspoon cayenne pepper
Pinch crushed saffron (optional)
½ cup extra-virgin olive oil
Kosher salt, to taste
Beets:
3 medium beets, trimmed, peeled, and cut into 1-inch chunks
2 tablespoons chopped fresh cilantro
2 tablespoons chopped fresh parsley

1. For the chermoula: In a food processor, combine the cilantro, parsley, garlic, paprika, cumin, coriander, and cayenne. Pulse until coarsely chopped. Add the saffron, if using, and process until combined. With the food processor running, slowly add the olive oil in a steady stream; process until the sauce is uniform. Season to taste with salt. 2. For the beets: In a large bowl, drizzle the beets with ½ cup of the chermoula, or enough to coat. Arrange the beets in the air fryer basket. Set the air fryer to 375ºF (191ºC) for 25 to minutes, or until the beets are tender. 3. Transfer the beets to a serving platter. Sprinkle with chopped cilantro and parsley and serve.

Per Serving:

calories: 61 | fat: 2g | protein: 2g | carbs: 9g | fiber: 3g | sodium: 59mg

Green Veg & Macadamia Smash

Prep time: 25 minutes | Cook time: 15 minutes | Serves 6

⅔ cup macadamia nuts
Enough water to cover and soak the macadamias
7 ounces (198 g) cavolo nero or kale, stalks removed and chopped
1 medium head broccoli, cut into florets, or broccolini
2 cloves garlic, crushed
¼ cup extra-virgin olive oil
2 tablespoons fresh lemon juice
4 medium spring onions, sliced
¼ cup chopped fresh herbs, such as parsley, dill, basil, or mint
Salt and black pepper, to taste

1. Place the macadamias in a small bowl and add enough water to cover them. Soak for about 2 hours, then drain. Discard the water. 2. Fill a large pot with about 1½ cups (360 ml) of water, then insert a steamer colander. Bring to a boil over high heat, then reduce to medium-high. Add the cavolo nero and cook for 6 minutes. Add the broccoli and cook for 8 minutes or until fork-tender. Remove the lid, let the steam escape, and let cool slightly. 3. Place the cooked vegetables in a blender or a food processor. Add the soaked macadamias, garlic, olive oil, lemon juice, spring onions, and fresh

herbs (you can reserve some for topping). 4. Process to the desired consistency (smooth or chunky). Season with salt and pepper to taste and serve. To store, let cool completely and store in a sealed container in the fridge for up to 5 days.

Per Serving:

calories: 250 | fat: 22g | protein: 5g | carbs: 12g | fiber: 5g | sodium: 44mg

Stuffed Cucumbers

Prep time: 10 minutes | Cook time: 0 minutes | Serves 2

1 English cucumber
1 tomato, diced
1 avocado, diced
Dash of lime juice
Sea salt and freshly ground pepper, to taste
Small bunch cilantro, chopped

1. Cut the cucumber in half lengthwise and scoop out the flesh and seeds into a small bowl. 2. Without mashing too much, gently combine the cucumber flesh and seeds with the tomato, avocado, and lime juice. 3. Season with sea salt and freshly ground pepper to taste. 4. Put mixture back into cucumber halves and cut each piece in half. Garnish with the cilantro and serve.

Per Serving:

calories: 189 | fat: 15g | protein: 3g | carbs: 15g | fiber: 8g | sodium: 13mg

Nordic Stone Age Bread

Prep time: 10 minutes | Cook time: 1 hour | Serves 14

½ cup flaxseeds
½ cup chia seeds
½ cup sesame seeds
¼ cup pumpkin seeds
¼ cup sunflower seeds
½ cup whole almonds, chopped
½ cup blanched hazelnuts,
chopped
½ cup pecans or walnuts
1 teaspoon salt, or to taste
1 teaspoon coarse black pepper
4 large eggs
½ cup extra-virgin olive oil or melted ghee

1. Preheat the oven to 285ºF (140ºC) fan assisted or 320ºF (160ºC) conventional. Line a loaf pan with parchment paper. 2. In a mixing bowl, combine all of the dry ingredients. Add the eggs and olive oil and stir through until well combined. Pour the dough into the loaf pan. Transfer to the oven and bake for about 1 hour or until the top is crisp. 3. Remove from the oven and let cool slightly in the pan before transferring to a wire rack to cool completely before slicing. Store at room temperature for up to 3 days loosely covered with a kitchen towel, refrigerate for up to 10 days, or freeze for up to 3 months.

Per Serving:

calories: 251 | fat: 23g | protein: 7g | carbs: 7g | fiber: 5g | sodium: 192mg

Corn Croquettes

Prep time: 10 minutes | Cook time: 12 to 14 minutes | Serves 4

½ cup leftover mashed potatoes
2 cups corn kernels (if frozen, thawed, and well drained)
¼ teaspoon onion powder
⅛ teaspoon ground black

pepper
¼ teaspoon salt
½ cup panko bread crumbs
Oil for misting or cooking spray

1. Place the potatoes and half the corn in food processor and pulse until corn is well chopped. 2. Transfer mixture to large bowl and stir in remaining corn, onion powder, pepper and salt. 3. Shape mixture into 16 balls. 4. Roll balls in panko crumbs, mist with oil or cooking spray, and place in air fryer basket. 5. Air fry at 360°F (182°C) for 12 to 14 minutes, until golden brown and crispy.

Per Serving:
calories: 149 | fat: 1g | protein: 5g | carbs: 33g | fiber: 3g | sodium: 250mg

Rustic Cauliflower and Carrot Hash

Prep time: 10 minutes | Cook time: 10 minutes | Serves 4

3 tablespoons extra-virgin olive oil
1 large onion, chopped
1 tablespoon garlic, minced
2 cups carrots, diced

4 cups cauliflower pieces, washed
1 teaspoon salt
½ teaspoon ground cumin

1. In a large skillet over medium heat, cook the olive oil, onion, garlic, and carrots for 3 minutes. 2. Cut the cauliflower into 1-inch or bite-size pieces. Add the cauliflower, salt, and cumin to the skillet and toss to combine with the carrots and onions. 3. Cover and cook for 3 minutes. 4. Toss the vegetables and continue to cook uncovered for an additional 3 to 4 minutes. 5. Serve warm.

Per Serving:
calories: 159 | fat: 11g | protein: 3g | carbs: 15g | fiber: 5g | sodium: 657mg

Tingly Chili-Roasted Broccoli

Prep time: 5 minutes | Cook time: 10 minutes | Serves 2

12 ounces (340 g) broccoli florets
2 tablespoons Asian hot chili oil
1 teaspoon ground Sichuan peppercorns (or black pepper)

2 garlic cloves, finely chopped
1 (2-inch) piece fresh ginger, peeled and finely chopped
Kosher salt and freshly ground black pepper, to taste

1. In a bowl, toss together the broccoli, chili oil, Sichuan peppercorns, garlic, ginger, and salt and black pepper to taste. 2. Transfer to the air fryer and roast at 375°F (191°C), shaking the basket halfway through, until lightly charred and tender, about 10 minutes. Remove from the air fryer and serve warm.

Per Serving:
calories: 141 | fat: 9g | protein: 5g | carbs: 13g | fiber: 5g | sodium: 57mg

Hearty Minestrone Soup

Prep time: 20 minutes | Cook time: 20 minutes | Serves 8

2 cups dried Great Northern beans, soaked overnight and drained
1 cup orzo
2 large carrots, peeled and diced
1 bunch Swiss chard, ribs removed and roughly chopped
1 medium zucchini, trimmed and diced
2 stalks celery, diced
1 medium onion, peeled and

diced
1 teaspoon minced garlic
1 tablespoon Italian seasoning
1 teaspoon salt
½ teaspoon ground black pepper
2 bay leaves
1 (14½-ounce / 411-g) can diced tomatoes, including juice
4 cups vegetable broth
1 cup tomato juice

1. Place all ingredients in the Instant Pot® and stir to combine. Close lid, set steam release to Sealing, press the Soup button, and cook for the default time of 20 minutes. 2. When the timer beeps, let pressure release naturally for 10 minutes. Quick-release any remaining pressure until the float valve drops and open lid. Remove and discard bay leaves. 3. Ladle into bowls and serve warm.

Per Serving:
calories: 207 | fat: 1g | protein: 12g | carbs: 47g | fiber: 10g | sodium: 814mg

Zucchini Casserole

Prep time: 20 minutes | Cook time: 3 hours | Serves 4

1 medium red onion, sliced
1 green bell pepper, cut into thin strips
4 medium zucchini, sliced
1 (15 ounces / 425 g) can diced tomatoes, with the juice

1 teaspoon sea salt
½ teaspoon black pepper
½ teaspoon basil
1 tablespoon extra-virgin olive oil
¼ cup grated Parmesan cheese

1. Combine the onion slices, bell pepper strips, zucchini slices, and tomatoes in the slow cooker. Sprinkle with the salt, pepper, and basil. 2. Cover and cook on low for 3 hours. 3. Drizzle the olive oil over the casserole and sprinkle with the Parmesan. Cover and cook on low for 1½ hours more. Serve hot.

Per Serving:
calories: 124 | fat: 6g | protein: 6g | carbs: 15g | fiber: 5g | sodium: 723mg

Roasted Broccolini with Garlic and Romano

Prep time: 5 minutes | Cook time: 10 minutes |

Serves 2

1 bunch broccolini (about 5 ounces / 142 g)
1 tablespoon olive oil
½ teaspoon garlic powder

¼ teaspoon salt
2 tablespoons grated Romano cheese

1. Preheat the oven to 400°F(205ºC) and set the oven rack to the middle position. Line a sheet pan with parchment paper or foil. 2. Slice the tough ends off the broccolini and place in a medium bowl. Add the olive oil, garlic powder, and salt and toss to combine. Arrange broccolini on the lined sheet pan. 3. Roast for 7 minutes, flipping pieces over halfway through the roasting time. 4. Remove the pan from the oven and sprinkle the cheese over the broccolini. With a pair of tongs, carefully flip the pieces over to coat all sides. Return to the oven for another 2 to 3 minutes, or until the cheese melts and starts to turn golden.

Per Serving:

calories: 114 | fat: 9g | protein: 4g | carbs: 5g | fiber: 2g | sodium: 400mg

Parsnip Fries with Romesco Sauce

Prep time: 20 minutes | Cook time: 24 minutes |

Serves 4

Romesco Sauce:
1 red bell pepper, halved and seeded
1 (1-inch) thick slice of Italian bread, torn into pieces (about 1 to 1½ cups)
1 cup almonds, toasted
Olive oil
½ Jalapeño pepper, seeded
1 tablespoon fresh parsley leaves
1 clove garlic

2 Roma tomatoes, peeled and seeded (or ⅓ cup canned crushed tomatoes)
1 tablespoon red wine vinegar
¼ teaspoon smoked paprika
½ teaspoon salt
¾ cup olive oil
3 parsnips, peeled and cut into long strips
2 teaspoons olive oil
Salt and freshly ground black pepper, to taste

1. Preheat the air fryer to 400ºF (204ºC). 2. Place the red pepper halves, cut side down, in the air fryer basket and air fry for 8 to 10 minutes, or until the skin turns black all over. Remove the pepper from the air fryer and let it cool. When it is cool enough to handle, peel the pepper. 3. Toss the torn bread and almonds with a little olive oil and air fry for 4 minutes, shaking the basket a couple times throughout the cooking time. When the bread and almonds are nicely toasted, remove them from the air fryer and let them cool for just a minute or two. 4. Combine the toasted bread, almonds, roasted red pepper, Jalapeño pepper, parsley, garlic, tomatoes, vinegar, smoked paprika and salt in a food processor or blender. Process until smooth. With the processor running, add the olive oil through the feed tube until the sauce comes together in a smooth paste that is barely pourable. 5. Toss the parsnip strips with the olive oil, salt and freshly ground black pepper and air fry at 400ºF (204ºC) for 10 minutes, shaking the basket a couple times during the cooking process so they brown and cook evenly. Serve the parsnip fries warm with the Romesco sauce to dip into.

Per Serving:

calories: 604 | fat: 55g | protein: 7g | carbs: 55g | fiber: 8g | sodium: 319mg

Herb Vinaigrette Potato Salad

Prep time: 10 minutes | Cook time: 4 minutes |

Serves 10

¼ cup olive oil
3 tablespoons red wine vinegar
¼ cup chopped fresh flat-leaf parsley
2 tablespoons chopped fresh dill
2 tablespoons chopped fresh chives
1 clove garlic, peeled and

minced
½ teaspoon dry mustard powder
¼ teaspoon ground black pepper
2 pounds (907 g) baby Yukon Gold potatoes
1 cup water
1 teaspoon salt

1. Whisk together oil, vinegar, parsley, dill, chives, garlic, mustard, and pepper in a small bowl. Set aside. 2. Place potatoes in a steamer basket. Place the rack in the Instant Pot®, add water and salt, then top with the steamer basket. Close lid, set steam release to Sealing, press the Manual button, and set time to 4 minutes. When the timer beeps, quick-release the pressure until the float valve drops. Press the Cancel button and open lid. 3. Transfer hot potatoes to a serving bowl. Pour dressing over potatoes and gently toss to coat. Serve warm or at room temperature.

Per Serving:

calories: 116 | fat: 6g | protein: 2g | carbs: 16g | fiber: 1g | sodium: 239mg

Crispy Green Beans

Prep time: 5 minutes | Cook time: 8 minutes | Serves 4

2 teaspoons olive oil
½ pound (227 g) fresh green beans, ends trimmed

¼ teaspoon salt
¼ teaspoon ground black pepper

1. In a large bowl, drizzle olive oil over green beans and sprinkle with salt and pepper. 2. Place green beans into ungreased air fryer basket. Adjust the temperature to 350ºF (177ºC) and set the timer for 8 minutes, shaking the basket two times during cooking. Green beans will be dark golden and crispy at the edges when done. Serve warm.

Per Serving:

calories: 33 | fat: 3g | protein: 1g | carbs: 3g | fiber: 1g | sodium: 147mg

Individual Asparagus and Goat Cheese Frittatas

Prep time: 15 minutes | Cook time: 15 minutes | Serves 4

1 tablespoon extra-virgin olive oil
8 ounces (227 g) asparagus, trimmed and sliced ¼ inch thick
1 red bell pepper, stemmed, seeded, and chopped
2 shallots, minced
2 ounces (57 g) goat cheese, crumbled (½ cup)
1 tablespoon minced fresh tarragon
1 teaspoon grated lemon zest
8 large eggs
½ teaspoon table salt

1. Using highest sauté function, heat oil in Instant Pot until shimmering. Add asparagus, bell pepper, and shallots; cook until softened, about 5 minutes. Turn off Instant Pot and transfer vegetables to bowl. Stir in goat cheese, tarragon, and lemon zest. 2. Arrange trivet included with Instant Pot in base of now-empty insert and add 1 cup water. Spray four 6-ounce ramekins with vegetable oil spray. Beat eggs, ¼ cup water, and salt in large bowl until thoroughly combined. Divide vegetable mixture between prepared ramekins, then pour egg mixture over top (you may have some left over). Set ramekins on trivet. Lock lid in place and close pressure release valve. Select high pressure cook function and cook for 10 minutes. 3. Turn off Instant Pot and quick-release pressure. Carefully remove lid, allowing steam to escape away from you. Using tongs, transfer ramekins to wire rack and let cool slightly. Run paring knife around inside edge of ramekins to loosen frittatas, then invert onto individual serving plates. Serve.

Per Serving:

calories: 240 | fat: 16g | protein: 17g | carbs: 6g | fiber: 2g | sodium: 500mg

Roasted Fennel with Parmesan

Prep time: 5 minutes | Cook time: 30 minutes | Serves 4

2 fennel bulbs (about 2 pounds / 907 g), cored and cut into 8 wedges each (reserve fronds for garnish)
¼ cup olive oil
Salt
Freshly ground black pepper
1¼ teaspoons red pepper flakes
½ cup freshly grated Parmesan cheese

1. Preheat the oven to 350ºF (180ºC). 2. Arrange the fennel wedges on a large, rimmed baking sheet and drizzle the oil over the top. 3. Sprinkle each wedge with a pinch each of salt, black pepper, and red pepper flakes. Sprinkle the cheese over the top. 4. Bake in the preheated oven for about 30 minutes, until the fennel is tender and the cheese is golden brown. Remove from the oven and let cool in the oil until just warm. Using a slotted metal spatula, transfer the fennel to plates and garnish with the reserved fennel fronds.

Per Serving:

calories: 237 | fat: 19g | protein: 11g | carbs: 10g | fiber: 4g | sodium: 363mg

Dandelion Greens

Prep time: 10 minutes | Cook time: 1 minute | Serves 6

4 pounds (1.8 kg) dandelion greens, stalks cut and discarded, and greens washed
½ cup water
¼ cup extra-virgin olive oil
¼ cup lemon juice
½ teaspoon salt
½ teaspoon ground black pepper

1. Add dandelion greens and water to the Instant Pot®. Close lid, set steam release to Sealing, press the Manual button, and set time to 1 minute. When the timer beeps, quick-release the pressure until the float valve drops. Open lid and drain well. 2. Combine olive oil, lemon juice, salt, and pepper in a small bowl. Pour over greens and toss to coat.

Per Serving:

calories: 39 | fat: 12g | protein: 1g | carbs: 7g | fiber: 3g | sodium: 253mg

Braised Fennel

Prep time: 10 minutes | Cook time: 50 minutes | Serves 4

2 large fennel bulbs
¼ cup extra-virgin avocado oil or ghee, divided
1 small shallot or red onion
1 clove garlic, sliced
4 to 6 thyme sprigs
1 small bunch fresh parsley,
leaves and stalks separated
1 cup water
3 tablespoons fresh lemon juice
Salt and black pepper, to taste
¼ cup extra-virgin olive oil, to drizzle

1. Cut off the fennel stalks where they attach to the bulb. Reserve the stalks. Cut the fennel bulb in half, trim the hard bottom part, and cut into wedges. 2. Heat a saucepan greased with 2 tablespoons of the avocado oil over medium-high heat. Sauté the shallot, garlic, thyme sprigs, parsley stalks, and hard fennel stalks for about 5 minutes. Add the water, bring to a boil, and simmer over medium heat for 10 minutes. Remove from the heat, set aside for 10 minutes, and then strain the stock, discarding the aromatics. 3. Preheat the oven to 350ºF (180ºC) fan assisted or 400ºF (205ºC) conventional. 4. Heat an ovenproof skillet greased with the remaining 2 tablespoons of avocado oil over medium-high heat and add the fennel wedges. Sear until caramelized, about 5 minutes, turning once. Pour the stock and the lemon juice over the fennel wedges, and season with salt and pepper. Loosely cover with a piece of aluminum foil. Bake for about 30 minutes. When done, the fennel should be easy to pierce with the tip of a knife. 5. Remove from the oven and scatter with the chopped parsley leaves and drizzle with the olive oil. To store, let cool and refrigerate for up to 5 days.

Per Serving:

calories: 225 | fat: 20g | protein: 2g | carbs: 12g | fiber: 5g | sodium: 187mg

Summer Squash Ribbons with Lemon and Ricotta

Prep time: 20 minutes | Cook time: 0 minutes |

Serves 4

2 medium zucchini or yellow squash
½ cup ricotta cheese
2 tablespoons fresh mint, chopped, plus additional mint leaves for garnish
2 tablespoons fresh parsley, chopped

Zest of ½ lemon
2 teaspoons lemon juice
½ teaspoon kosher salt
¼ teaspoon freshly ground black pepper
1 tablespoon extra-virgin olive oil

1. Using a vegetable peeler, make ribbons by peeling the summer squash lengthwise. The squash ribbons will resemble the wide pasta, pappardelle. 2. In a medium bowl, combine the ricotta cheese, mint, parsley, lemon zest, lemon juice, salt, and black pepper. 3. Place mounds of the squash ribbons evenly on 4 plates then dollop the ricotta mixture on top. Drizzle with the olive oil and garnish with the mint leaves.

Per Serving:

calories: 90 | fat: 6g | protein: 5g | carbs: 5g | fiber: 1g | sodium: 180mg

Roasted Brussels Sprouts with Tahini-Yogurt Sauce

Prep time: 10 minutes | Cook time: 35 minutes |

Serves 4

1 pound (454 g) Brussels sprouts, trimmed and halved lengthwise
6 tablespoons extra-virgin olive oil, divided
1 teaspoon salt, divided
½ teaspoon garlic powder

¼ teaspoon freshly ground black pepper
¼ cup plain whole-milk Greek yogurt
¼ cup tahini
Zest and juice of 1 lemon

1. Preheat the oven to 425ºF (220ºC). Line a baking sheet with aluminum foil or parchment paper and set aside. 2. Place the Brussels sprouts in a large bowl. Drizzle with 4 tablespoons olive oil, ½ teaspoon salt, the garlic powder, and pepper and toss well to coat. 3. Place the Brussels sprouts in a single layer on the baking sheet, reserving the bowl, and roast for 20 minutes. Remove from the oven and give the sprouts a toss to flip. Return to the oven and continue to roast until browned and crispy, another 10 to 15 minutes. Remove from the oven and return to the reserved bowl. 4. In a small bowl, whisk together the yogurt, tahini, lemon zest and juice, remaining 2 tablespoons olive oil, and remaining ½ teaspoon salt. Drizzle over the roasted sprouts and toss to coat. Serve warm.

Per Serving:

calories: 330 | fat: 29g | protein: 7g | carbs: 15g | fiber: 6g | sodium: 635mg

Eggplant Caponata

Prep time: 20 minutes | Cook time: 5 minutes |

Serves 8

¼ cup extra-virgin olive oil
¼ cup white wine
2 tablespoons red wine vinegar
1 teaspoon ground cinnamon
1 large eggplant, peeled and diced
1 medium onion, peeled and diced
1 medium green bell pepper, seeded and diced
1 medium red bell pepper, seeded and diced

2 cloves garlic, peeled and minced
1 (14½-ounce / 411-g) can diced tomatoes
3 stalks celery, diced
½ cup chopped oil-cured olives
½ cup golden raisins
2 tablespoons capers, rinsed and drained
½ teaspoon salt
½ teaspoon ground black pepper

1. Place all ingredients in the Instant Pot®. Stir well to mix. Close lid, set steam release to Sealing, press the Manual button, and set time to 5 minutes. 2. When the timer beeps, quick-release the pressure until the float valve drops. Open the lid and stir well. Serve warm or at room temperature.

Per Serving:

calories: 90 | fat: 1g | protein: 2g | carbs: 17g | fiber: 4g | sodium: 295mg

Sautéed Fava Beans with Olive Oil, Garlic, and Chiles

Prep time: 10 minutes | Cook time: 7 minutes |

Serves 4

3½ pounds (1.6 kg) fresh fava beans, shelled (4 cups)
2 tablespoons olive oil
2 cloves garlic, minced
2 teaspoons fresh lemon juice
1 teaspoon finely grated lemon

zest
½ teaspoon crushed red pepper flakes
½ teaspoon salt
¼ teaspoon freshly ground black pepper

1. Bring a medium saucepan of lightly salted water to a boil. Add the shelled favas and cook for 3 to 4 minutes, until tender. Drain the favas and immediately place them in an ice water bath to stop their cooking. When cool, peel the tough outer skin off the beans. 2. Heat the olive oil in a large skillet over medium-high heat. Add the garlic and cook, stirring, until it is aromatic but not browned, about 30 seconds. Add the beans and cook, stirring, until heated through, about 2 minutes. Stir in the lemon juice, lemon zest, red pepper flakes, salt, and pepper and remove from the heat. Serve immediately.

Per Serving:

calories: 576 | fat: 9g | protein: 39g | carbs: 88g | fiber: 38g | sodium: 311mg

Turkish Stuffed Eggplant

Prep time: 10 minutes | Cook time: 2 hours 10 minutes | Serves 6

½ cup extra-virgin olive oil
3 small eggplants
1 teaspoon sea salt
½ teaspoon black pepper
1 large yellow onion, finely chopped
4 garlic cloves, minced

1 (15 ounces / 425 g) can diced tomatoes, with the juice
¼ cup finely chopped fresh flat-leaf parsley
6 (8-inch) round pita breads, quartered and toasted
1 cup plain Greek yogurt

1. Pour ¼ cup of the olive oil into the slow cooker, and generously coat the interior of the crock. 2. Cut each eggplant in half lengthwise. You can leave the stem on. Score the cut side of each half every ¼ inch, being careful not to cut through the skin. 3. Arrange the eggplant halves, skin-side down, in the slow cooker. Sprinkle with 1 teaspoon salt and ½ teaspoon pepper. 4. In a large skillet, heat the remaining ¼ cup olive oil over medium-high heat. Sauté the onion and garlic for 3 minutes, or until the onion begins to soften. 5. Add the tomatoes and parsley to the skillet. Season with salt and pepper. Sauté for another 5 minutes, until the liquid has almost evaporated. 6. Using a large spoon, spoon the tomato mixture over the eggplants, covering each half with some of the mixture. 7. Cover and cook on high for 2 hours or on low for 4 hours. When the dish is finished, the eggplant should feel very tender when you insert the tip of a sharp knife into the thickest part. 8. Uncover the slow cooker, and let the eggplant rest for 10 minutes. Then transfer the eggplant to a serving dish. If there is any juice in the bottom of the cooker, spoon it over the eggplant. Serve hot with toasted pita wedges and yogurt on the side.

Per Serving:
calories: 449 | fat: 22g | protein: 11g | carbs: 59g | fiber: 15g | sodium: 706mg

Baked Turkey Kibbeh

Prep time: 15 minutes | Cook time: 45 minutes | Serves 8

Outer Layer:
1½ cups bulgur wheat
1¼ pounds (567 g) ground turkey
1 yellow onion, grated on a box grater
½ cup finely chopped fresh mint
1 teaspoon ground allspice
½ teaspoon ground cinnamon
1 teaspoon kosher salt
¼ teaspoon ground black

pepper
Filling:
4 tablespoons olive oil, divided
1 yellow onion, finely chopped
3 cloves garlic, minced
1 pound (454 g) ground turkey
¼ cup finely chopped fresh flat-leaf parsley
½ cup pine nuts, toasted
½ teaspoon ground allspice
½ teaspoon kosher salt
¼ teaspoon ground black

pepper
Assembly and Serving:
1 tablespoon olive oil

8 tablespoons low-fat Greek yogurt or labneh
¼ cup thinly sliced fresh mint

1. To make the outer layer: Soak the bulgur overnight in a bowl with enough water to cover by 2'. 2. Drain, squeezing the bulgur until there is no excess moisture. Transfer to a large bowl. 3. With your hands, mix in the turkey, onion, mint, allspice, cinnamon, salt, and pepper until thoroughly combined. 4. To make the filling: In a medium cast-iron skillet over medium heat, warm 2 tablespoons of the oil. Cook the onion and garlic until translucent, about 8 minutes. Add the turkey and cook until no longer pink, about 5 minutes. 5. Stir in the parsley, pine nuts, allspice, salt, and pepper. Drizzle in the remaining 2 tablespoons oil. Transfer to a bowl and wipe out the skillet. 6. To assemble the kibbeh: Preheat an oven to 350°F(180ºC). Lightly coat the cast-iron skillet with olive oil. 7. Press half of the outer layer into the bottom of the skillet in an even layer about ¾' thick. Spread the filling evenly over the top. Using wet fingers, use the remaining half of the outer layer to cover the filling. Once the filling is completely covered, smooth with wet hands. 8. Score the surface of the kibbeh into 8 wedges to make it easier to cut and portion after baking. Drizzle the oil over the top and bake until deep brown, about 30 minutes. 9. Serve hot with the yogurt or labneh and a sprinkle of the mint.

Per Serving:
calories: 395 | fat: 21g | protein: 31g | carbs: 24g | fiber: 6g | sodium: 462mg

Puff Pastry Turnover with Roasted Vegetables

Prep time: 10 minutes | Cook time: 35 minutes | Serves 4 to 6

Nonstick cooking spray
1 zucchini, cut in ¼-inch-thick slices
½ bunch asparagus, cut into quarters

1 package (6-inch) whole-grain pastry discs, in the freezer section (Goya brand preferred), at room temperature
1 large egg, beaten

1. Preheat the oven to 350°F(180ºC). 2. Spray a baking sheet with cooking spray and arrange the zucchini and asparagus on it in a single layer. Roast for 15 to 20 minutes, until tender. Set aside to cool. 3. Allow the pastry dough to warm to room temperature. Place the discs on a floured surface. 4. Place a roasted zucchini slice on one half of each disc, then top with asparagus. Fold the empty side over the full side and pinch the turnover closed with a fork. 5. Once all discs are full and closed, brush the turnovers with the beaten egg and put them onto a baking sheet. Bake for 10 to 15 minutes, until golden brown. Let cool completely before eating.

Per Serving:
calories: 334 | fat: 15g | protein: 9g | carbs: 42g | fiber: 4g | sodium: 741mg

Crispy Garlic Oven Potatoes

Prep time: 30 minutes | Cook time: 30 minutes |

Serves 2

10 ounces (283 g) golden mini potatoes, halved
4 tablespoons extra-virgin olive oil
2 teaspoons dried, minced garlic

1 teaspoon onion salt
½ teaspoon paprika
¼ teaspoon freshly ground black pepper
¼ teaspoon red pepper flakes
¼ teaspoon dried dill

1. Preheat the oven to 400°F(205°C). 2. Soak the potatoes and put in a bowl of ice water for 30 minutes. Change the water if you return and the water is milky. 3. Rinse and dry the potatoes, then put them on a baking sheet. 4. Drizzle the potatoes with oil and sprinkle with the garlic, onion salt, paprika, pepper, red pepper flakes, and dill. Using tongs or your hands, toss well to coat. 5. Lower the heat to 375°F(190°C), add potatoes to the oven, and bake for 20 minutes. 6. At 20 minutes, check and flip potatoes. Bake for another 10 minutes, or until the potatoes are fork-tender.

Per Serving:

½ cup: calories: 344 | fat: 28g | protein: 3g | carbs: 24g | fiber: 4g | sodium: 723mg

Asparagus Fries

Prep time: 15 minutes | Cook time: 5 to 7 minutes

per batch | Serves 4

12 ounces (340 g) fresh asparagus spears with tough ends trimmed off
2 egg whites
¼ cup water

¾ cup panko bread crumbs
¼ cup grated Parmesan cheese, plus 2 tablespoons
¼ teaspoon salt
Oil for misting or cooking spray

1. Preheat the air fryer to 390ºF (199ºC). 2. In a shallow dish, beat egg whites and water until slightly foamy. 3. In another shallow dish, combine panko, Parmesan, and salt. 4. Dip asparagus spears in egg, then roll in crumbs. Spray with oil or cooking spray. 5. Place a layer of asparagus in air fryer basket, leaving just a little space in between each spear. Stack another layer on top, crosswise. Air fry at 390ºF (199ºC) for 5 to 7 minutes, until crispy and golden brown. 6. Repeat to cook remaining asparagus.

Per Serving:

calories: 132 | fat: 3g | protein: 8g | carbs: 19g | fiber: 3g | sodium: 436mg

Roasted Salsa

Prep time: 15 minutes | Cook time: 30 minutes |

Makes 2 cups

2 large San Marzano tomatoes, cored and cut into large chunks
½ medium white onion, peeled and large-diced
½ medium jalapeño, seeded and large-diced

2 cloves garlic, peeled and diced
½ teaspoon salt
1 tablespoon coconut oil
¼ cup fresh lime juice

1. Place tomatoes, onion, and jalapeño into an ungreased round nonstick baking dish. Add garlic, then sprinkle with salt and drizzle with coconut oil. 2. Place dish into air fryer basket. Adjust the temperature to 300ºF (149ºC) and bake for 30 minutes. Vegetables will be dark brown around the edges and tender when done. 3. Pour mixture into a food processor or blender. Add lime juice. Process on low speed 30 seconds until only a few chunks remain. 4. Transfer salsa to a sealable container and refrigerate at least 1 hour. Serve chilled.

Per Serving:

calories: 115 | fat: 7g | protein: 2g | carbs: 13g | fiber: 3g | sodium: 593mg

Cucumbers with Feta, Mint, and Sumac

Prep time: 15 minutes | Cook time: 0 minutes |

Serves 4

1 tablespoon extra-virgin olive oil
1 tablespoon lemon juice
2 teaspoons ground sumac
½ teaspoon kosher salt
2 hothouse or English cucumbers, diced

¼ cup crumbled feta cheese
1 tablespoon fresh mint, chopped
1 tablespoon fresh parsley, chopped
⅛ teaspoon red pepper flakes

1. In a large bowl, whisk together the olive oil, lemon juice, sumac, and salt. Add the cucumber and feta cheese and toss well. 2. Transfer to a serving dish and sprinkle with the mint, parsley, and red pepper flakes.

Per Serving:

calories: 85 | fat: 6g | protein: 3g | carbs: 8g | fiber: 1g | sodium: 230mg

Chapter 9 Vegetarian Mains

Broccoli Crust Pizza

Prep time: 15 minutes | Cook time: 12 minutes |
Serves 4

3 cups riced broccoli, steamed and drained well
1 large egg
½ cup grated vegetarian Parmesan cheese

3 tablespoons low-carb Alfredo sauce
½ cup shredded Mozzarella cheese

1. In a large bowl, mix broccoli, egg, and Parmesan. 2. Cut a piece of parchment to fit your air fryer basket. Press out the pizza mixture to fit on the parchment, working in two batches if necessary. Place into the air fryer basket. 3. Adjust the temperature to 370°F (188°C) and air fry for 5 minutes. 4. The crust should be firm enough to flip. If not, add 2 additional minutes. Flip crust. 5. Top with Alfredo sauce and Mozzarella. Return to the air fryer basket and cook an additional 7 minutes or until cheese is golden and bubbling. Serve warm.

Per Serving:
calories: 87 | fat: 2g | protein: 11g | carbs: 5g | fiber: 1g | sodium: 253mg

Sheet Pan Roasted Chickpeas and Vegetables with Harissa Yogurt

Prep time: 10 minutes | Cook time: 30 minutes |
Serves 2

4 cups cauliflower florets (about ½ small head)
2 medium carrots, peeled, halved, and then sliced into quarters lengthwise
2 tablespoons olive oil, divided
½ teaspoon garlic powder, divided

½ teaspoon salt, divided
2 teaspoons za'atar spice mix, divided
1 (15 ounces / 425 g) can chickpeas, drained, rinsed, and patted dry
¾ cup plain Greek yogurt
1 teaspoon harissa spice paste

1. Preheat the oven to 400°F (205°C) and set the rack to the middle position. Line a sheet pan with foil or parchment paper. 2. Place the cauliflower and carrots in a large bowl. Drizzle with 1 tablespoon olive oil and sprinkle with ¼ teaspoon of garlic powder, ¼ teaspoon of salt, and 1 teaspoon of za'atar. Toss well to combine. 3. Spread the vegetables onto one half of the sheet pan in a single layer. 4. Place the chickpeas in the same bowl and season with the remaining 1 tablespoon of oil, ¼ teaspoon of garlic powder, and ¼ teaspoon of salt, and the remaining za'atar. Toss well to combine. 5. Spread the chickpeas onto the other half of the sheet pan. 6. Roast for 30 minutes, or until the vegetables are tender and the chickpeas start to turn golden. Flip the vegetables halfway through the cooking time, and give the chickpeas a stir so they cook evenly. 7. The chickpeas may need an extra few minutes if you like them crispy. If so, remove the vegetables and leave the chickpeas in until they're cooked to desired crispiness. 8. While the vegetables are roasting, combine the yogurt and harissa in a small bowl. Taste, and add additional harissa as desired.

Per Serving:
calories: 467 | fat: 23g | protein: 18g | carbs: 54g | fiber: 15g | sodium: 632mg

Crustless Spanakopita

Prep time: 15 minutes | Cook time: 45 minutes |
Serves 6

12 tablespoons extra-virgin olive oil, divided
1 small yellow onion, diced
1 (32-ounce / 907-g) bag frozen chopped spinach, thawed, fully drained, and patted dry (about 4 cups)
4 garlic cloves, minced

½ teaspoon salt
½ teaspoon freshly ground black pepper
1 cup whole-milk ricotta cheese
4 large eggs
¾ cup crumbled traditional feta cheese
¼ cup pine nuts

1. Preheat the oven to 375°F (190°C). 2. In a large skillet, heat 4 tablespoons olive oil over medium-high heat. Add the onion and sauté until softened, 6 to 8 minutes. 3. Add the spinach, garlic, salt, and pepper and sauté another 5 minutes. Remove from the heat and allow to cool slightly. 4. In a medium bowl, whisk together the ricotta and eggs. Add to the cooled spinach and stir to combine. 5. Pour 4 tablespoons olive oil in the bottom of a 9-by-13-inch glass baking dish and swirl to coat the bottom and sides. Add the spinach-ricotta mixture and spread into an even layer. 6. Bake for 20 minutes or until the mixture begins to set. Remove from the oven and crumble the feta evenly across the top of the spinach. Add the pine nuts and drizzle with the remaining 4 tablespoons olive oil. Return to the oven and bake for an additional 15 to 20 minutes, or until the spinach is fully set and the top is starting to turn golden brown. Allow to cool slightly before cutting to serve.

Per Serving:
calories: 497 | fat: 44g | protein: 18g | carbs: 11g | fiber: 5g | sodium: 561mg

Spinach-Artichoke Stuffed Mushrooms

Prep time: 10 minutes | Cook time: 10 to 14 minutes | Serves 4

2 tablespoons olive oil
4 large portobello mushrooms, stems removed and gills scraped out
½ teaspoon salt
¼ teaspoon freshly ground pepper
4 ounces (113 g) goat cheese, crumbled
½ cup chopped marinated artichoke hearts
1 cup frozen spinach, thawed and squeezed dry
½ cup grated Parmesan cheese
2 tablespoons chopped fresh parsley

1. Preheat the air fryer to 400ºF (204ºC). 2. Rub the olive oil over the portobello mushrooms until thoroughly coated. Sprinkle both sides with the salt and black pepper. Place top-side down on a clean work surface. 3. In a small bowl, combine the goat cheese, artichoke hearts, and spinach. Mash with the back of a fork until thoroughly combined. Divide the cheese mixture among the mushrooms and sprinkle with the Parmesan cheese. 4. Air fry for 10 to 14 minutes until the mushrooms are tender and the cheese has begun to brown. Top with the fresh parsley just before serving.

Per Serving:
calories: 284 | fat: 21g | protein: 16g | carbs: 10g | fiber: 4g | sodium: 686mg

Fava Bean Purée with Chicory

Prep time: 5 minutes | Cook time: 2 hours 10 minutes | Serves 4

½ pound (227 g) dried fava beans, soaked in water overnight and drained
1 pound (454 g) chicory leaves
¼ cup olive oil
1 small onion, chopped
1 clove garlic, minced
Salt

1. In a saucepan, cover the fava beans by at least an inch of water and bring to a boil over medium-high heat. Reduce the heat to low, cover, and simmer until very tender, about 2 hours. Check the pot from time to time to make sure there is enough water and add more as needed. 2. Drain off any excess water and then mash the beans with a potato masher. 3. While the beans are cooking, bring a large pot of salted water to a boil. Add the chicory and cook for about 3 minutes, until tender. Drain. 4. In a medium skillet, heat the olive oil over medium-high heat. Add the onion and a pinch of salt and cook, stirring frequently, until softened and beginning to brown, about 5 minutes. Add the garlic and cook, stirring, for another minute. Transfer half of the onion mixture, along with the oil, to the bowl with the mashed beans and stir to mix. Taste and add salt as needed. 5. Serve the purée topped with some of the remaining onions and oil, with the chicory leaves on the side.

Per Serving:
calories: 336 | fat: 14g | protein: 17g | carbs: 40g | fiber: 19g | sodium: 59mg

Grilled Eggplant Stacks

Prep time: 20 minutes | Cook time: 10 minutes | Serves 2

1 medium eggplant, cut crosswise into 8 slices
¼ teaspoon salt
1 teaspoon Italian herb seasoning mix
2 tablespoons olive oil
1 large tomato, cut into 4 slices
4 (1-ounce / 28-g) slices of buffalo mozzarella
Fresh basil, for garnish

1. Place the eggplant slices in a colander set in the sink or over a bowl. Sprinkle both sides with the salt. Let the eggplant sit for 15 minutes. 2. While the eggplant is resting, heat the grill to medium-high heat (about 350ºF / 180ºC). 3. Pat the eggplant dry with paper towels and place it in a mixing bowl. Sprinkle it with the Italian herb seasoning mix and olive oil. Toss well to coat. 4. Grill the eggplant for 5 minutes, or until it has grill marks and is lightly charred. Flip each eggplant slice over, and grill on the second side for another 5 minutes. 5. Flip the eggplant slices back over and top four of the slices with a slice of tomato and a slice of mozzarella. Top each stack with one of the remaining four slices of eggplant. 6. Turn the grill down to low and cover it to let the cheese melt. Check after 30 seconds and remove when the cheese is soft and mostly melted. 7. Sprinkle with fresh basil slices.

Per Serving:
calories: 354 | fat: 29g | protein: 13g | carbs: 19g | fiber: 9g | sodium: 340mg

Moroccan Red Lentil and Pumpkin Stew

Prep time: 10 minutes | Cook time: 30 minutes | Serves 4

2 tablespoons olive oil
1 teaspoon ground cumin
1 teaspoon ground turmeric
1 tablespoon curry powder
1 large onion, diced
1 teaspoon salt
2 tablespoons minced fresh ginger
4 cloves garlic, minced
1 pound (454 g) pumpkin, peeled, seeded, and cut into 1-inch dice
1 red bell pepper, seeded and diced
1½ cups red lentils, rinsed
6 cups vegetable broth
¼ cup chopped cilantro, for garnish

1. Heat the olive oil in a stockpot over medium heat. Add the cumin, turmeric, and curry powder and cook, stirring, for 1 minute, until fragrant. Add the onion and salt and cook, stirring frequently, until softened, about 5 minutes. Add the ginger and garlic and cook, stirring frequently, for 2 more minutes. Stir in the pumpkin and bell pepper, and then the lentils and broth and bring to a boil. 2. Reduce the heat to low and simmer, uncovered, for about 20 minutes, until the lentils are very tender. Serve hot, garnished with cilantro.

Per Serving:
calories: 405 | fat: 9g | protein: 20g | carbs: 66g | fiber: 11g | sodium: 594mg

Tangy Asparagus and Broccoli

Prep time: 25 minutes | Cook time: 22 minutes |
Serves 4

½ pound (227 g) asparagus, cut into 1½-inch pieces
½ pound (227 g) broccoli, cut into 1½-inch pieces
2 tablespoons olive oil

Salt and white pepper, to taste
½ cup vegetable broth
2 tablespoons apple cider vinegar

1. Place the vegetables in a single layer in the lightly greased air fryer basket. Drizzle the olive oil over the vegetables. 2. Sprinkle with salt and white pepper. 3. Cook at 380°F (193°C) for 15 minutes, shaking the basket halfway through the cooking time. 4. Add ½ cup of vegetable broth to a saucepan; bring to a rapid boil and add the vinegar. Cook for 5 to 7 minutes or until the sauce has reduced by half. 5. Spoon the sauce over the warm vegetables and serve immediately. Bon appétit!

Per Serving:

calories: 93 | fat: 7g | protein: 3g | carbs: 6g | fiber: 3g | sodium: 89mg

Broccoli-Cheese Fritters

Prep time: 5 minutes | Cook time: 20 to 25 minutes |
Serves 4

1 cup broccoli florets
1 cup shredded Mozzarella cheese
¾ cup almond flour
½ cup flaxseed meal, divided
2 teaspoons baking powder

1 teaspoon garlic powder
Salt and freshly ground black pepper, to taste
2 eggs, lightly beaten
½ cup ranch dressing

1. Preheat the air fryer to 400°F (204°C). 2. In a food processor fitted with a metal blade, pulse the broccoli until very finely chopped. 3. Transfer the broccoli to a large bowl and add the Mozzarella, almond flour, ¼ cup of the flaxseed meal, baking powder, and garlic powder. Stir until thoroughly combined. Season to taste with salt and black pepper. Add the eggs and stir again to form a sticky dough. Shape the dough into 1¼-inch fritters. 4. Place the remaining ¼ cup flaxseed meal in a shallow bowl and roll the fritters in the meal to form an even coating. 5. Working in batches if necessary, arrange the fritters in a single layer in the basket of the air fryer and spray generously with olive oil. Pausing halfway through the cooking time to shake the basket, air fry for 20 to 25 minutes until the fritters are golden brown and crispy. Serve with the ranch dressing for dipping.

Per Serving:

calories: 388 | fat: 30g | protein: 19g | carbs: 14g | fiber: 7g | sodium: 526mg

Crispy Tofu

Prep time: 30 minutes | Cook time: 15 to 20 minutes
| Serves 4

1 (16-ounce / 454-g) block extra-firm tofu
2 tablespoons coconut aminos
1 tablespoon toasted sesame oil
1 tablespoon olive oil

1 tablespoon chili-garlic sauce
1½ teaspoons black sesame seeds
1 scallion, thinly sliced

1. Press the tofu for at least 15 minutes by wrapping it in paper towels and setting a heavy pan on top so that the moisture drains. 2. Slice the tofu into bite-size cubes and transfer to a bowl. Drizzle with the coconut aminos, sesame oil, olive oil, and chili-garlic sauce. Cover and refrigerate for 1 hour or up to overnight. 3. Preheat the air fryer to 400°F (204°C). 4. Arrange the tofu in a single layer in the air fryer basket. Pausing to shake the pan halfway through the cooking time, air fry for 15 to 20 minutes until crisp. Serve with any juices that accumulate in the bottom of the air fryer, sprinkled with the sesame seeds and sliced scallion.

Per Serving:

calories: 173 | fat: 14g | protein: 12g | carbs: 3g | fiber: 1g | sodium: 49mg

One-Pan Mushroom Pasta with Mascarpone

Prep time: 10 minutes | Cook time: 20 minutes |
Serves 2

2 tablespoons olive oil
1 large shallot, minced
8 ounces (227 g) baby bella (cremini) mushrooms, sliced
¼ cup dry sherry
1 teaspoon dried thyme
2 cups low-sodium vegetable

stock
6 ounces (170 g) dry pappardelle pasta
2 tablespoons mascarpone cheese
Salt
Freshly ground black pepper

1. Heat olive oil in a large sauté pan over medium-high heat. Add the shallot and mushrooms and sauté for 10 minutes, or until the mushrooms have given up much of their liquid. 2. Add the sherry, thyme, and vegetable stock. Bring the mixture to a boil. 3. Add the pasta, breaking it up as needed so it fits into the pan and is covered by the liquid. Return the mixture to a boil. Cover, and reduce the heat to medium-low. Let the pasta cook for 10 minutes, or until al dente. Stir it occasionally so it doesn't stick. If the sauce gets too dry, add some water or additional chicken stock. 4. When the pasta is tender, stir in the mascarpone cheese and season with salt and pepper. 5. The sauce will thicken up a bit when it's off the heat.

Per Serving:

calories: 517 | fat: 18g | protein: 16g | carbs: 69g | fiber: 3g | sodium: 141mg

Tortellini in Red Pepper Sauce

Prep time: 15 minutes | Cook time: 10 minutes |

Serves 4

1 (16-ounce / 454-g) container fresh cheese tortellini (usually green and white pasta)
1 (16-ounce / 454-g) jar roasted red peppers, drained
1 teaspoon garlic powder
¼ cup tahini
1 tablespoon red pepper oil (optional)

1. Bring a large pot of water to a boil and cook the tortellini according to package directions. 2. In a blender, combine the red peppers with the garlic powder and process until smooth. Once blended, add the tahini until the sauce is thickened. If the sauce gets too thick, add up to 1 tablespoon red pepper oil (if using). 3. Once tortellini are cooked, drain and leave pasta in colander. Add the sauce to the bottom of the empty pot and heat for 2 minutes. Then, add the tortellini back into the pot and cook for 2 more minutes. Serve and enjoy!

Per Serving:

calories: 350 | fat: 11g | protein: 12g | carbs: 46g | fiber: 4g | sodium: 192mg

Baked Tofu with Sun-Dried Tomatoes and Artichokes

Prep time: 15 minutes | Cook time: 30 minutes |

Serves 4

1 (16-ounce / 454-g) package extra-firm tofu, drained and patted dry, cut into 1-inch cubes
2 tablespoons extra-virgin olive oil, divided
2 tablespoons lemon juice, divided
1 tablespoon low-sodium soy sauce or gluten-free tamari
1 onion, diced
½ teaspoon kosher salt
2 garlic cloves, minced
1 (14-ounce / 397-g) can artichoke hearts, drained
8 sun-dried tomato halves packed in oil, drained and chopped
¼ teaspoon freshly ground black pepper
1 tablespoon white wine vinegar
Zest of 1 lemon
¼ cup fresh parsley, chopped

1. Preheat the oven to 400ºF (205ºC). Line a baking sheet with foil or parchment paper. 2. In a bowl, combine the tofu, 1 tablespoon of the olive oil, 1 tablespoon of the lemon juice, and the soy sauce. Allow to sit and marinate for 15 to 30 minutes. Arrange the tofu in a single layer on the prepared baking sheet and bake for 20 minutes, turning once, until light golden brown. 3. Heat the remaining 1 tablespoon olive oil in a large skillet or sauté pan over medium heat. Add the onion and salt; sauté until translucent, 5 to 6 minutes. Add the garlic and sauté for 30 seconds. Add the artichoke hearts, sun-dried tomatoes, and black pepper and sauté for 5 minutes. Add the white wine vinegar and the remaining 1 tablespoon lemon juice and deglaze the pan, scraping up any brown bits. Remove the pan

from the heat and stir in the lemon zest and parsley. Gently mix in the baked tofu.

Per Serving:

calories: 230 | fat: 14g | protein: 14g | carbs: 13g | fiber: 5g | sodium: 500mg

Mozzarella and Sun-Dried Portobello Mushroom Pizza

Prep time: 10 minutes | Cook time: 10 minutes |

Serves 4

4 large portobello mushroom caps
3 tablespoons extra-virgin olive oil
Salt
Freshly ground black pepper
4 sun-dried tomatoes
1 cup mozzarella cheese, divided
½ to ¾ cup low-sodium tomato sauce

1. Preheat the broiler on high. 2. On a baking sheet, drizzle the mushroom caps with the olive oil and season with salt and pepper. Broil the portobello mushrooms for 5 minutes on each side, flipping once, until tender. 3. Fill each mushroom cap with 1 sun-dried tomato, 2 tablespoons of cheese, and 2 to 3 tablespoons of sauce. Top each with 2 tablespoons of cheese. Place the caps back under the broiler for a final 2 to 3 minutes, then quarter the mushrooms and serve.

Per Serving:

calories: 218| fat: 16g | protein: 11g | carbs: 12g | fiber: 2g | sodium: 244mg

Pistachio Mint Pesto Pasta

Prep time: 10 minutes | Cook time: 10 minutes |

Serves 4

8 ounces (227 g) whole-wheat pasta
1 cup fresh mint
½ cup fresh basil
⅓ cup unsalted pistachios,
shelled
1 garlic clove, peeled
½ teaspoon kosher salt
Juice of ½ lime
⅓ cup extra-virgin olive oil

1. Cook the pasta according to the package directions. Drain, reserving ½ cup of the pasta water, and set aside. 2. In a food processor, add the mint, basil, pistachios, garlic, salt, and lime juice. Process until the pistachios are coarsely ground. Add the olive oil in a slow, steady stream and process until incorporated. 3. In a large bowl, mix the pasta with the pistachio pesto; toss well to incorporate. If a thinner, more saucy consistency is desired, add some of the reserved pasta water and toss well.

Per Serving:

calories: 420 | fat: 3g | protein: 11g | carbs: 48g | fiber: 2g | sodium: 150mg

Cheese Stuffed Zucchini

Prep time: 20 minutes | Cook time: 8 minutes |
Serves 4

1 large zucchini, cut into four pieces
2 tablespoons olive oil
1 cup Ricotta cheese, room temperature
2 tablespoons scallions, chopped
1 heaping tablespoon fresh

parsley, roughly chopped
1 heaping tablespoon coriander, minced
2 ounces (57 g) Cheddar cheese, preferably freshly grated
1 teaspoon celery seeds
½ teaspoon salt
½ teaspoon garlic pepper

1. Cook your zucchini in the air fryer basket for approximately 10 minutes at 350°F (177°C). Check for doneness and cook for 2-3 minutes longer if needed. 2. Meanwhile, make the stuffing by mixing the other items. 3. When your zucchini is thoroughly cooked, open them up. Divide the stuffing among all zucchini pieces and bake an additional 5 minutes.

Per Serving:
calories: 242 | fat: 20g | protein: 12g | carbs: 5g | fiber: 1g | sodium: 443mg

Zucchini Lasagna

Prep time: 15 minutes | Cook time: 1 hour | Serves 8

½ cup extra-virgin olive oil, divided
4 to 5 medium zucchini squash
1 teaspoon salt
8 ounces (227 g) frozen spinach, thawed and well drained (about 1 cup)
2 cups whole-milk ricotta cheese
¼ cup chopped fresh basil or 2 teaspoons dried basil

1 teaspoon garlic powder
½ teaspoon freshly ground black pepper
2 cups shredded fresh whole-milk mozzarella cheese
1¾ cups shredded Parmesan cheese
½ (24 ounces / 680 g) jar low-sugar marinara sauce (less than 5 grams sugar)

1. Preheat the oven to 425°F (220°C). 2. Line two baking sheets with parchment paper or aluminum foil and drizzle each with 2 tablespoons olive oil, spreading evenly. 3. Slice the zucchini lengthwise into ¼-inch-thick long slices and place on the prepared baking sheet in a single layer. Sprinkle with ½ teaspoon salt per sheet. Bake until softened, but not mushy, 15 to 18 minutes. Remove from the oven and allow to cool slightly before assembling the lasagna. 4. Reduce the oven temperature to 375°F (190°C). 5. While the zucchini cooks, prep the filling. In a large bowl, combine the spinach, ricotta, basil, garlic powder, and pepper. In a small bowl, mix together the mozzarella and Parmesan cheeses. In a medium bowl, combine the marinara sauce and remaining ¼ cup olive oil and stir to fully incorporate the oil into sauce. 6. To assemble the lasagna, spoon a third of the marinara sauce mixture into the bottom of a 9-by-13-inch glass baking dish and spread evenly. Place 1 layer of softened zucchini slices to fully cover the sauce, then add a third of the ricotta-spinach mixture and spread evenly on top of the zucchini. Sprinkle a third of the mozzarella-Parmesan mixture on top of the ricotta. Repeat with 2 more cycles of these layers: marinara, zucchini, ricotta-spinach, then cheese blend. 7. Bake until the cheese is bubbly and melted, 30 to 35 minutes. Turn the broiler to low and broil until the top is golden brown, about 5 minutes. Remove from the oven and allow to cool slightly before slicing.

Per Serving:
calories: 473 | fat: 36g | protein: 23g | carbs: 17g | fiber: 3g | sodium: 868mg

Stuffed Portobellos

Prep time: 10 minutes | Cook time: 8 minutes |
Serves 4

3 ounces (85 g) cream cheese, softened
½ medium zucchini, trimmed and chopped
¼ cup seeded and chopped red bell pepper
1½ cups chopped fresh spinach

leaves
4 large portobello mushrooms, stems removed
2 tablespoons coconut oil, melted
½ teaspoon salt

1. In a medium bowl, mix cream cheese, zucchini, pepper, and spinach. 2. Drizzle mushrooms with coconut oil and sprinkle with salt. Scoop ¼ zucchini mixture into each mushroom. 3. Place mushrooms into ungreased air fryer basket. Adjust the temperature to 400°F (204°C) and air fry for 8 minutes. Portobellos will be tender and tops will be browned when done. Serve warm.

Per Serving:
calories: 151 | fat: 13g | protein: 4g | carbs: 6g | fiber: 2g | sodium: 427mg

Cauliflower Rice-Stuffed Peppers

Prep time: 10 minutes | Cook time: 15 minutes |
Serves 4

2 cups uncooked cauliflower rice
¾ cup drained canned petite diced tomatoes
2 tablespoons olive oil
1 cup shredded Mozzarella

cheese
¼ teaspoon salt
¼ teaspoon ground black pepper
4 medium green bell peppers, tops removed, seeded

1. In a large bowl, mix all ingredients except bell peppers. Scoop mixture evenly into peppers. 2. Place peppers into ungreased air fryer basket. Adjust the temperature to 350°F (177°C) and air fry for 15 minutes. Peppers will be tender and cheese will be melted when done. Serve warm.

Per Serving:
calories: 144 | fat: 7g | protein: 11g | carbs: 11g | fiber: 5g | sodium: 380mg

Root Vegetable Soup with Garlic Aioli

Prep time: 10 minutes | Cook time 25 minutes |

Serves 4

For the Soup:
8 cups vegetable broth
½ teaspoon salt
1 medium leek, cut into thick rounds
1 pound (454 g) carrots, peeled and diced
1 pound (454 g) potatoes, peeled and diced

1 pound (454 g) turnips, peeled and cut into 1-inch cubes
1 red bell pepper, cut into strips
2 tablespoons fresh oregano
For the Aioli:
5 garlic cloves, minced
¼ teaspoon salt
⅔ cup olive oil
1 drop lemon juice

1. Bring the broth and salt to a boil and add the vegetables one at a time, letting the water return to a boil after each addition. Add the carrots first, then the leeks, potatoes, turnips, and finally the red bell peppers. Let the vegetables cook for about 3 minutes after adding the green beans and bringing to a boil. The process will take about 20 minutes in total. 2. Meanwhile, make the aioli. In a mortar and pestle, grind the garlic to a paste with the salt. Using a whisk and whisking constantly, add the olive oil in a thin stream. Continue whisking until the mixture thickens to the consistency of mayonnaise. Add the lemon juice. 3. Serve the vegetables in the broth, dolloped with the aioli and garnished with the fresh oregano.

Per Serving:

calories: 538 | fat: 37g | protein: 5g | carbs: 50g | fiber: 9g | sodium: 773mg

Pesto Spinach Flatbread

Prep time: 10 minutes | Cook time: 8 minutes |

Serves 4

1 cup blanched finely ground almond flour
2 ounces (57 g) cream cheese
2 cups shredded Mozzarella

cheese
1 cup chopped fresh spinach leaves
2 tablespoons basil pesto

1. Place flour, cream cheese, and Mozzarella in a large microwave-safe bowl and microwave on high 45 seconds, then stir. 2. Fold in spinach and microwave an additional 15 seconds. Stir until a soft dough ball forms. 3. Cut two pieces of parchment paper to fit air fryer basket. Separate dough into two sections and press each out on ungreased parchment to create 6-inch rounds. 4. Spread 1 tablespoon pesto over each flatbread and place rounds on parchment into ungreased air fryer basket. Adjust the temperature to 350°F (177°C) and air fry for 8 minutes, turning crusts halfway through cooking. Flatbread will be golden when done. 5. Let cool 5 minutes before slicing and serving.

Per Serving:

calories: 387 | fat: 28g | protein: 28g | carbs: 10g | fiber: 5g | sodium: 556mg

Kate's Warm Mediterranean Farro Bowl

Prep time: 15 minutes | Cook time: 10 minutes |

Serves 4 to 6

⅓ cup extra-virgin olive oil
½ cup chopped red bell pepper
⅓ cup chopped red onions
2 garlic cloves, minced
1 cup zucchini, cut in ½-inch slices
½ cup canned chickpeas, drained and rinsed
½ cup coarsely chopped artichokes
3 cups cooked farro

Salt
Freshly ground black pepper
¼ cup sliced olives, for serving (optional)
½ cup crumbled feta cheese, for serving (optional)
2 tablespoons fresh basil, chiffonade, for serving (optional)
3 tablespoons balsamic reduction, for serving (optional)

1. In a large sauté pan or skillet, heat the oil over medium heat and sauté the pepper, onions, and garlic for about 5 minutes, until tender. 2. Add the zucchini, chickpeas, and artichokes, then stir and continue to sauté vegetables, approximately 5 more minutes, until just soft. 3. Stir in the cooked farro, tossing to combine and cooking enough to heat through. Season with salt and pepper and remove from the heat. 4. Transfer the contents of the pan into the serving vessels or bowls. 5. Top with olives, feta, and basil (if using). Drizzle with balsamic reduction (if using) to finish.

Per Serving:

calories: 367 | fat: 20g | protein: 9g | carbs: 51g | fiber: 9g | sodium: 87mg

Freekeh, Chickpea, and Herb Salad

Prep time: 15 minutes | Cook time: 10 minutes |

Serves 4 to 6

1 (15 ounces / 425 g) can chickpeas, rinsed and drained
1 cup cooked freekeh
1 cup thinly sliced celery
1 bunch scallions, both white and green parts, finely chopped
½ cup chopped fresh flat-leaf parsley
¼ cup chopped fresh mint

3 tablespoons chopped celery leaves
½ teaspoon kosher salt
⅓ cup extra-virgin olive oil
¼ cup freshly squeezed lemon juice
¼ teaspoon cumin seeds
1 teaspoon garlic powder

1. In a large bowl, combine the chickpeas, freekeh, celery, scallions, parsley, mint, celery leaves, and salt and toss lightly. 2. In a small bowl, whisk together the olive oil, lemon juice, cumin seeds, and garlic powder. Once combined, add to freekeh salad.

Per Serving:

calories: 350 | fat: 19g | protein: 9g | carbs: 38g | fiber: 9g | sodium: 329mg

Three-Cheese Zucchini Boats

Prep time: 15 minutes | Cook time: 20 minutes |
Serves 2

2 medium zucchini
1 tablespoon avocado oil
¼ cup low-carb, no-sugar-added pasta sauce
¼ cup full-fat ricotta cheese
¼ cup shredded Mozzarella

cheese
¼ teaspoon dried oregano
¼ teaspoon garlic powder
½ teaspoon dried parsley
2 tablespoons grated vegetarian Parmesan cheese

1. Cut off 1 inch from the top and bottom of each zucchini. Slice zucchini in half lengthwise and use a spoon to scoop out a bit of the inside, making room for filling. Brush with oil and spoon 2 tablespoons pasta sauce into each shell. 2. In a medium bowl, mix ricotta, Mozzarella, oregano, garlic powder, and parsley. Spoon the mixture into each zucchini shell. Place stuffed zucchini shells into the air fryer basket. 3. Adjust the temperature to 350ºF (177ºC) and air fry for 20 minutes. 4. To remove from the basket, use tongs or a spatula and carefully lift out. Top with Parmesan. Serve immediately.

Per Serving:

calories: 208 | fat: 14g | protein: 12g | carbs: 11g | fiber: 3g | sodium: 247mg

Cheesy Cauliflower Pizza Crust

Prep time: 15 minutes | Cook time: 11 minutes |
Serves 2

1 (12 ounces / 340 g) steamer bag cauliflower
½ cup shredded sharp Cheddar cheese
1 large egg

2 tablespoons blanched finely ground almond flour
1 teaspoon Italian blend seasoning

1. Cook cauliflower according to package instructions. Remove from bag and place into cheesecloth or paper towel to remove excess water. Place cauliflower into a large bowl. 2. Add cheese, egg, almond flour, and Italian seasoning to the bowl and mix well. 3. Cut a piece of parchment to fit your air fryer basket. Press cauliflower into 6-inch round circle. Place into the air fryer basket. 4. Adjust the temperature to 360ºF (182ºC) and air fry for 11 minutes. 5. After 7 minutes, flip the pizza crust. 6. Add preferred toppings to pizza. Place back into air fryer basket and cook an additional 4 minutes or until fully cooked and golden. Serve immediately.

Per Serving:

calories: 251 | fat: 17g | protein: 15g | carbs: 12g | fiber: 5g | sodium: 375mg

Cauliflower Steaks with Olive Citrus Sauce

Prep time: 15 minutes | Cook time: 30 minutes |
Serves 4

1 or 2 large heads cauliflower (at least 2 pounds / 907 g, enough for 4 portions)
⅓ cup extra-virgin olive oil
¼ teaspoon kosher salt
⅛ teaspoon ground black pepper
Juice of 1 orange

Zest of 1 orange
¼ cup black olives, pitted and chopped
1 tablespoon Dijon or grainy mustard
1 tablespoon red wine vinegar
½ teaspoon ground coriander

1. Preheat the oven to 400ºF (205ºC). Line a baking sheet with parchment paper or foil. 2. Cut off the stem of the cauliflower so it will sit upright. Slice it vertically into four thick slabs. Place the cauliflower on the prepared baking sheet. Drizzle with the olive oil, salt, and black pepper. Bake for about 30 minutes, turning over once, until tender and golden brown. 3. In a medium bowl, combine the orange juice, orange zest, olives, mustard, vinegar, and coriander; mix well. 4. Serve the cauliflower warm or at room temperature with the sauce.

Per Serving:

calories: 265 | fat: 21g | protein: 5g | carbs: 19g | fiber: 4g | sodium: 310mg

Vegetable Burgers

Prep time: 10 minutes | Cook time: 12 minutes |
Serves 4

8 ounces (227 g) cremini mushrooms
2 large egg yolks
½ medium zucchini, trimmed and chopped
¼ cup peeled and chopped

yellow onion
1 clove garlic, peeled and finely minced
½ teaspoon salt
¼ teaspoon ground black pepper

1. Place all ingredients into a food processor and pulse twenty times until finely chopped and combined. 2. Separate mixture into four equal sections and press each into a burger shape. Place burgers into ungreased air fryer basket. Adjust the temperature to 375ºF (191ºC) and air fry for 12 minutes, turning burgers halfway through cooking. Burgers will be browned and firm when done. 3. Place burgers on a large plate and let cool 5 minutes before serving.

Per Serving:

calories: 50 | fat: 3g | protein: 3g | carbs: 4g | fiber: 1g | sodium: 299mg

Stuffed Pepper Stew

Prep time: 20 minutes | Cook time: 50 minutes | Serves 2

2 tablespoons olive oil	vegetarian Worcestershire sauce
2 sweet peppers, diced (about 2 cups)	1 cup low-sodium vegetable stock
½ large onion, minced	1 cup low-sodium tomato juice
1 garlic clove, minced	¼ cup brown lentils
1 teaspoon oregano	¼ cup brown rice
1 tablespoon gluten-free	Salt

1. Heat olive oil in a Dutch oven over medium-high heat. Add the sweet peppers and onion and sauté for 10 minutes, or until the peppers are wilted and the onion starts to turn golden. 2. Add the garlic, oregano, and Worcestershire sauce, and cook for another 30 seconds. Add the vegetable stock, tomato juice, lentils, and rice. 3. Bring the mixture to a boil. Cover, and reduce the heat to medium-low. Simmer for 45 minutes, or until the rice is cooked and the lentils are softened. Season with salt.

Per Serving:

calories: 379 | fat: 16g | protein: 11g | carbs: 53g | fiber: 7g | sodium: 392mg

Eggplants Stuffed with Walnuts and Feta

Prep time: 10 minutes | Cook time: 55 minutes | Serves 6

3 medium eggplants, halved lengthwise	pieces
2 teaspoons salt, divided	2¼ teaspoons ground cinnamon
¼ cup olive oil, plus 2 tablespoons, divided	1½ teaspoons dried oregano
2 medium onions, diced	½ teaspoon freshly ground black pepper
1½ pints cherry or grape tomatoes, halved	¼ cup whole-wheat breadcrumbs
¾ cup roughly chopped walnut	⅔ cup (about 3 ounces / 85 g) crumbled feta cheese

1. Scoop out the flesh of the eggplants, leaving a ½-inch thick border of flesh in the skins. Dice the flesh that you removed and place it in a colander set over the sink. Sprinkle 1½ teaspoons of salt over the diced eggplant and inside the eggplant shells and let stand for 30 minutes. Rinse the shells and the pieces and pat dry with paper towels. 2. Heat ¼ cup of olive oil in a large skillet over medium heat. Add the eggplant shells, skin-side down, and cook for about 4 minutes, until browned and softened. Turn over and cook on the cut side until golden brown and soft, about 4 minutes more. Transfer to a plate lined with paper towel to drain. 3. Drain off all but about 1 to 2 tablespoons of the oil in the skillet and heat over medium-high heat. Add the onions and cook, stirring, until beginning to soften, about 3 minutes. Add the diced eggplant, tomatoes, walnuts, cinnamon, oregano, ¼ cup water, the remaining ½ teaspoon of salt, and the pepper. Cook, stirring occasionally, until the vegetables are golden brown and softened, about 8 minutes. 4. Preheat the broiler to high. 5. In a small bowl, toss together the breadcrumbs and 1 tablespoon olive oil. 6. Arrange the eggplant shells cut-side up on a large, rimmed baking sheet. Brush each shell with about ½ teaspoon of olive oil. Cook under the broiler until tender and just starting to turn golden brown, about 5 minutes. Remove the eggplants from the broiler and reduce the heat of the oven to 375ºF (190ºC). 7. Spoon the sautéed vegetable mixture into the eggplant shells, dividing equally. Sprinkle the breadcrumbs over the tops of the filled eggplants, dividing equally. Sprinkle the cheese on top, again dividing equally. Bake in the oven until the filling and shells are heated through and the topping is nicely browned and crisp, about 35 minutes.

Per Serving:

calories: 274 | fat: 15g | protein: 7g | carbs: 34g | fiber: 13g | sodium: 973mg

Crustless Spinach Cheese Pie

Prep time: 10 minutes | Cook time: 20 minutes | Serves 4

6 large eggs	1 cup shredded sharp Cheddar cheese
¼ cup heavy whipping cream	
1 cup frozen chopped spinach, drained	¼ cup diced yellow onion

1. In a medium bowl, whisk eggs and add cream. Add remaining ingredients to bowl. 2. Pour into a round baking dish. Place into the air fryer basket. 3. Adjust the temperature to 320ºF (160ºC) and bake for 20 minutes. 4. Eggs will be firm and slightly browned when cooked. Serve immediately.

Per Serving:

calories: 263 | fat: 20g | protein: 18g | carbs: 4g | fiber: 1g | sodium: 321mg

Chapter 10 Pizzas, Wraps, and Sandwiches

Sautéed Mushroom, Onion, and Pecorino Romano Panini

Prep time: 10 minutes | Cook time: 20 minutes | Serves 4

3 tablespoons olive oil, divided
1 small onion, diced
10 ounces (283 g) button or cremini mushrooms, sliced
½ teaspoon salt
¼ teaspoon freshly ground black pepper
4 crusty Italian sandwich rolls
4 ounces (113 g) freshly grated Pecorino Romano

1. Heat 1 tablespoon of the olive oil in a skillet over medium-high heat. Add the onion and cook, stirring, until it begins to soften, about 3 minutes. Add the mushrooms, season with salt and pepper, and cook, stirring, until they soften and the liquid they release evaporates, about 7 minutes. 2. To make the panini, heat a skillet or grill pan over high heat and brush with 1 tablespoon olive oil. Brush the inside of the rolls with the remaining 1 tablespoon olive oil. Divide the mushroom mixture evenly among the rolls and top each with ¼ of the grated cheese. 3. Place the sandwiches in the hot pan and place another heavy pan, such as a cast-iron skillet, on top to weigh them down. Cook for about 3 to 4 minutes, until crisp and golden on the bottom, and then flip over and repeat on the second side, cooking for an additional 3 to 4 minutes until golden and crisp. Slice each sandwich in half and serve hot.

Per Serving:
calories: 348 | fat: 20g | protein: 14g | carbs: 30g | fiber: 2g | sodium: 506mg

Grilled Eggplant and Chopped Greek Salad Wraps

Prep time: 10 minutes | Cook time: 20 minutes | Serves 4

15 small tomatoes, such as cherry or grape tomatoes, halved
10 pitted Kalamata olives, chopped
1 medium red onion, halved and thinly sliced
¾ cup crumbled feta cheese (about 4 ounces / 113 g)
2 tablespoons balsamic vinegar
1 tablespoon chopped fresh parsley
1 clove garlic, minced
2 tablespoons olive oil, plus 2 teaspoons, divided
¾ teaspoon salt, divided
1 medium cucumber, peeled, halved lengthwise, seeded, and diced
1 large eggplant, sliced ½-inch thick
½ teaspoon freshly ground black pepper
4 whole-wheat sandwich wraps or whole-wheat flour tortillas

1. In a medium bowl, toss together the tomatoes, olives, onion, cheese, vinegar, parsley, garlic, 2 teaspoons olive oil, and ¼ teaspoon of salt. Let sit at room temperature for 20 minutes. Add the cucumber, toss to combine, and let sit another 10 minutes. 2. While the salad is resting, grill the eggplant. Heat a grill or grill pan to high heat. Brush the remaining 2 tablespoons olive oil onto both sides of the eggplant slices. Grill for about 8 to 10 minutes per side, until grill marks appear and the eggplant is tender and cooked through. Transfer to a plate and season with the remaining ½ teaspoon of salt and the pepper. 3. Heat the wraps in a large, dry skillet over medium heat just until warm and soft, about 1 minute on each side. Place 2 or 3 eggplant slices down the center of each wrap. Spoon some of the salad mixture on top of the eggplant, using a slotted spoon so that any excess liquid is drained off. Fold in the sides of the wrap and roll up like a burrito. Serve immediately.

Per Serving:
calories: 233 | fat: 10g | protein: 8g | carbs: 29g | fiber: 7g | sodium: 707mg

Beans and Greens Pizza

Prep time: 11 minutes | Cook time: 14 to 19 minutes | Serves 4

¾ cup whole-wheat pastry flour
½ teaspoon low-sodium baking powder
1 tablespoon olive oil, divided
1 cup chopped kale
2 cups chopped fresh baby spinach
1 cup canned no-salt-added cannellini beans, rinsed and drained
½ teaspoon dried thyme
1 piece low-sodium string cheese, torn into pieces

1. In a small bowl, mix the pastry flour and baking powder until well combined. 2. Add ¼ cup of water and 2 teaspoons of olive oil. Mix until a dough forms. 3. On a floured surface, press or roll the dough into a 7-inch round. Set aside while you cook the greens. 4. In a baking pan, mix the kale, spinach, and remaining teaspoon of the olive oil. Air fry at 350ºF (177ºC) for 3 to 5 minutes, until the greens are wilted. Drain well. 5. Put the pizza dough into the air fryer basket. Top with the greens, cannellini beans, thyme, and string cheese. Air fry for 11 to 14 minutes, or until the crust is golden brown and the cheese is melted. Cut into quarters to serve.

Per Serving:
calories: 181 | fat: 6g | protein: 8g | carbs: 27g | fiber: 6g | sodium: 103mg

Dill Salmon Salad Wraps

Prep time: 10 minutes |Cook time: 10 minutes|

Serves:6

1 pound (454 g) salmon filet, cooked and flaked, or 3 (5-ounce / 142-g) cans salmon
½ cup diced carrots (about 1 carrot)
½ cup diced celery (about 1 celery stalk)
3 tablespoons chopped fresh dill
3 tablespoons diced red onion (a little less than ⅛ onion)

2 tablespoons capers
1½ tablespoons extra-virgin olive oil
1 tablespoon aged balsamic vinegar
½ teaspoon freshly ground black pepper
¼ teaspoon kosher or sea salt
4 whole-wheat flatbread wraps or soft whole-wheat tortillas

1. In a large bowl, mix together the salmon, carrots, celery, dill, red onion, capers, oil, vinegar, pepper, and salt. 2. Divide the salmon salad among the flatbreads. Fold up the bottom of the flatbread, then roll up the wrap and serve.

Per Serving:

calories: 185 | fat: 8g | protein: 17g | carbs: 12g | fiber: 2g | sodium: 237mg

Margherita Open-Face Sandwiches

Prep time: 10 minutes |Cook time: 5 minutes|

Serves: 4

2 (6- to 7-inch) whole-wheat submarine or hoagie rolls, sliced open horizontally
1 tablespoon extra-virgin olive oil
1 garlic clove, halved
1 large ripe tomato, cut into 8 slices

¼ teaspoon dried oregano
1 cup fresh mozzarella (about 4 ounces / 113 g), patted dry and sliced
¼ cup lightly packed fresh basil leaves, torn into small pieces
¼ teaspoon freshly ground black pepper

1. Preheat the broiler to high with the rack 4 inches under the heating element. 2. Place the sliced bread on a large, rimmed baking sheet. Place under the broiler for 1 minute, until the bread is just lightly toasted. Remove from the oven. 3. Brush each piece of the toasted bread with the oil, and rub a garlic half over each piece. 4. Place the toasted bread back on the baking sheet. Evenly distribute the tomato slices on each piece, sprinkle with the oregano, and layer the cheese on top. 5. Place the baking sheet under the broiler. Set the timer for 1½ minutes, but check after 1 minute. When the cheese is melted and the edges are just starting to get dark brown, remove the sandwiches from the oven (this can take anywhere from 1½ to 2 minutes). 6. Top each sandwich with the fresh basil and pepper.

Per Serving:

calories: 176 | fat: 9g | protein: 10g | carbs: 14g | fiber: 2g | sodium: 119mg

Grilled Eggplant and Feta Sandwiches

Prep time: 10 minutes | Cook time: 8 minutes |

Serves 2

1 medium eggplant, sliced into ½-inch-thick slices
2 tablespoons olive oil
Sea salt and freshly ground pepper, to taste
5 to 6 tablespoons hummus

4 slices whole-wheat bread, toasted
1 cup baby spinach leaves
2 ounces (57 g) feta cheese, softened

1. Preheat a gas or charcoal grill to medium-high heat. 2. Salt both sides of the sliced eggplant, and let sit for 20 minutes to draw out the bitter juices. 3. Rinse the eggplant and pat dry with a paper towel. 4. Brush the eggplant slices with olive oil and season with sea salt and freshly ground pepper. 5. Grill the eggplant until lightly charred on both sides but still slightly firm in the middle, about 3–4 minutes a side. 6. Spread the hummus on the bread and top with the spinach leaves, feta, and eggplant. Top with the other slice of bread and serve warm.

Per Serving:

calories: 516 | fat: 27g | protein: 14g | carbs: 59g | fiber: 14g | sodium: 597mg

Open-Faced Eggplant Parmesan Sandwich

Prep time: 10 minutes | Cook time: 10 minutes |

Serves 2

1 small eggplant, sliced into ¼-inch rounds
Pinch sea salt
2 tablespoons olive oil
Sea salt and freshly ground pepper, to taste

2 slices whole-grain bread, thickly cut and toasted
1 cup marinara sauce (no added sugar)
¼ cup freshly grated, low-fat Parmesan cheese

1. Preheat broiler to high heat. 2. Salt both sides of the sliced eggplant, and let sit for 20 minutes to draw out the bitter juices. 3. Rinse the eggplant and pat dry with a paper towel. 4. Brush the eggplant with the olive oil, and season with sea salt and freshly ground pepper. 5. Lay the eggplant on a sheet pan, and broil until crisp, about 4 minutes. Flip over and crisp the other side. 6. Lay the toasted bread on a sheet pan. Spoon some marinara sauce on each slice of bread, and layer the eggplant on top. 7. Sprinkle half of the cheese on top of the eggplant and top with more marinara sauce. 8. Sprinkle with remaining cheese. 9. Put the sandwiches under the broiler until the cheese has melted, about 2 minutes. 10. Using a spatula, transfer the sandwiches to plates and serve.

Per Serving:

calories: 355 | fat: 19g | protein: 10g | carbs: 38g | fiber: 13g | sodium: 334mg

Roasted Vegetable Bocadillo with Romesco Sauce

Prep time: 10 minutes | Cook time: 20 minutes |

Serves 4

2 small yellow squash, sliced lengthwise
2 small zucchini, sliced lengthwise
1 medium red onion, thinly sliced
4 large button mushrooms, sliced
2 tablespoons olive oil
1 teaspoon salt, divided
½ teaspoon freshly ground

black pepper, divided
2 roasted red peppers from a jar, drained
2 tablespoons blanched almonds
1 tablespoon sherry vinegar
1 small clove garlic
4 crusty multigrain rolls
4 ounces (113 g) goat cheese, at room temperature
1 tablespoon chopped fresh basil

1. Preheat the oven to 400°F(205°C). 2. In a medium bowl, toss the yellow squash, zucchini, onion, and mushrooms with the olive oil, ½ teaspoon salt, and ¼ teaspoon pepper. Spread on a large baking sheet. Roast the vegetables in the oven for about 20 minutes, until softened. 3. Meanwhile, in a food processor, combine the roasted peppers, almonds, vinegar, garlic, the remaining ½ teaspoon salt, and the remaining ¼ teaspoon pepper and process until smooth. 4. Split the rolls and spread ¼ of the goat cheese on the bottom of each. Place the roasted vegetables on top of the cheese, dividing equally. Top with chopped basil. Spread the top halves of the rolls with the roasted red pepper sauce and serve immediately.

Per Serving:
calories: 379 | fat: 21g | protein: 17g | carbs: 32g | fiber: 4g | sodium: 592mg

Greek Salad Wraps

Prep time: 15 minutes |Cook time: 0 minutes|

Serves: 4

1½ cups seedless cucumber, peeled and chopped (about 1 large cucumber)
1 cup chopped tomato (about 1 large tomato)
½ cup finely chopped fresh mint
1 (2¼ ounces / 64 g) can sliced black olives (about ½ cup), drained
¼ cup diced red onion (about ¼

onion)
2 tablespoons extra-virgin olive oil
1 tablespoon red wine vinegar
¼ teaspoon freshly ground black pepper
¼ teaspoon kosher or sea salt
½ cup crumbled goat cheese (about 2 ounces / 57 g)
4 whole-wheat flatbread wraps or soft whole-wheat tortillas

1. In a large bowl, mix together the cucumber, tomato, mint, olives, and onion until well combined. 2. In a small bowl, whisk together the oil, vinegar, pepper, and salt. Drizzle the dressing over the salad, and mix gently. 3. With a knife, spread the goat cheese evenly over the four wraps. Spoon a quarter of the salad filling down the middle

of each wrap. 4. Fold up each wrap: Start by folding up the bottom, then fold one side over and fold the other side over the top. Repeat with the remaining wraps and serve.

Per Serving:
calories: 217 | fat: 14g | protein: 7g | carbs: 17g | fiber: 3g | sodium: 329mg

Mediterranean Tuna Salad Sandwiches

Prep time: 10 minutes | Cook time: 5 minutes |

Serves 2

1 can white tuna, packed in water or olive oil, drained
1 roasted red pepper, diced
½ small red onion, diced
10 low-salt olives, pitted and finely chopped
¼ cup plain Greek yogurt

1 tablespoon flat-leaf parsley, chopped
Juice of 1 lemon
Sea salt and freshly ground pepper, to taste
4 whole-grain pieces of bread

1. In a small bowl, combine all of the ingredients except the bread, and mix well. 2. Season with sea salt and freshly ground pepper to taste. Toast the bread or warm in a pan. 3. Make the sandwich and serve immediately.

Per Serving:
calories: 307 | fat: 7g | protein: 30g | carbs: 31g | fiber: 5g | sodium: 564mg

Herbed Focaccia Panini with Anchovies and Burrata

Prep time: 5 minutes | Cook time: 8 minutes | Serves 4

8 ounces (227 g) burrata cheese, chilled and sliced
1 pound (454 g) whole-wheat herbed focaccia, cut crosswise into 4 rectangles and split horizontally

1 can anchovy fillets packed in oil, drained
8 slices tomato, sliced
2 cups arugula
1 tablespoon olive oil

1. Divide the cheese evenly among the bottom halves of the focaccia rectangles. Top each with 3 or 4 anchovy fillets, 2 slices of tomato, and ½ cup arugula. Place the top halves of the focaccia on top of the sandwiches. 2. To make the panini, heat a skillet or grill pan over high heat and brush with the olive oil. 3. Place the sandwiches in the hot pan and place another heavy pan, such as a cast-iron skillet, on top to weigh them down. Cook for about 3 to 4 minutes, until crisp and golden on the bottom, and then flip over and repeat on the second side, cooking for an additional 3 to 4 minutes until golden and crisp. Slice each sandwich in half and serve hot.

Per Serving:
calories: 596 | fat: 30g | protein: 27g | carbs: 58g | fiber: 5g | sodium: 626mg

Chicken and Goat Cheese Pizza

Prep time: 10 minutes | Cook time: 10 minutes |
Serves 4

All-purpose flour, for dusting
1 pound (454 g) premade pizza dough
2 tablespoons olive oil
1 cup shredded cooked chicken

3 ounces (85 g) goat cheese, crumbled
Sea salt
Freshly ground black pepper

1. Preheat the oven to 475°F (245°C) . 2. On a floured surface, roll out the dough to a 12-inch round and place it on a lightly floured pizza pan or baking sheet. Drizzle the dough with the olive oil and spread it out evenly. Top the dough with the chicken and goat cheese. 3. Bake the pizza for 8 to 10 minutes, until the crust is cooked through and golden. 4. Season with salt and pepper and serve.

Per Serving:
calories: 555 | fat: 23g | protein: 24g | carbs: 60g | fiber: 2g | sodium: 660mg

Za'atar Pizza

Prep time: 10 minutes | Cook time: 15 minutes |
Serves 4 to 6

1 sheet puff pastry
¼ cup extra-virgin olive oil

⅓ cup za'atar seasoning

1. Preheat the oven to 350°F(180°C). 2. Put the puff pastry on a parchment-lined baking sheet. Cut the pastry into desired slices. 3. Brush the pastry with olive oil. Sprinkle with the za'atar. 4. Put the pastry in the oven and bake for 10 to 12 minutes or until edges are lightly browned and puffed up. Serve warm or at room temperature.

Per Serving:
calories: 374 | fat: 30g | protein: 3g | carbs: 20g | fiber: 1g | sodium: 166mg

Vegetable Pita Sandwiches

Prep time: 15 minutes | Cook time: 9 to 12 minutes |
Serves 4

1 baby eggplant, peeled and chopped
1 red bell pepper, sliced
½ cup diced red onion
½ cup shredded carrot

1 teaspoon olive oil
⅓ cup low-fat Greek yogurt
½ teaspoon dried tarragon
2 low-sodium whole-wheat pita breads, halved crosswise

1. In a baking pan, stir together the eggplant, red bell pepper, red onion, carrot, and olive oil. Put the vegetable mixture into the air fryer basket and roast at 390°F (199°C) for 7 to 9 minutes, stirring once, until the vegetables are tender. Drain if necessary. 2. In a small bowl, thoroughly mix the yogurt and tarragon until well combined. 3. Stir the yogurt mixture into the vegetables. Stuff one-fourth of this mixture into each pita pocket. 4. Place the sandwiches in the air fryer and cook for 2 to 3 minutes, or until the bread is toasted. Serve immediately.

Per Serving:
calories: 115 | fat: 2g | protein: 4g | carbs: 22g | fiber: 6g | sodium: 90mg

Pesto Chicken Mini Pizzas

Prep time: 5 minutes | Cook time: 10 minutes |
Serves 4

2 cups shredded cooked chicken
¾ cup pesto
4 English muffins, split

2 cups shredded Mozzarella cheese

1. In a medium bowl, toss the chicken with the pesto. Place one-eighth of the chicken on each English muffin half. Top each English muffin with ¼ cup of the Mozzarella cheese. 2. Put four pizzas at a time in the air fryer and air fry at 350°F (177°C) for 5 minutes. Repeat this process with the other four pizzas.

Per Serving:
calories: 617 | fat: 36g | protein: 45g | carbs: 29g | fiber: 3g | sodium: 544mg

Grilled Chicken Salad Pita

Prep time: 15 minutes | Cook time: 16 minutes |
Serves 1

1 boneless, skinless chicken breast
Sea salt and freshly ground pepper, to taste
1 cup baby spinach
1 roasted red pepper, sliced
1 tomato, chopped

½ small red onion, thinly sliced
½ small cucumber, chopped
1 tablespoon olive oil
Juice of 1 lemon
1 whole-wheat pita pocket
2 tablespoons crumbled feta cheese

1. Preheat a gas or charcoal grill to medium-high heat. 2. Season the chicken breast with sea salt and freshly ground pepper, and grill until cooked through, about 7–8 minutes per side. 3. Allow chicken to rest for 5 minutes before slicing into strips. 4. While the chicken is cooking, put all the chopped vegetables into a medium-mixing bowl and season with sea salt and freshly ground pepper. 5. Chop the chicken into cubes and add to salad. Add the olive oil and lemon juice and toss well. 6. Stuff the mixture onto a pita pocket and top with the feta cheese. Serve immediately.

Per Serving:
calories: 653 | fat: 26g | protein: 71g | carbs: 34g | fiber: 6g | sodium: 464mg

Flatbread Pizza with Roasted Cherry Tomatoes, Artichokes, and Feta

Prep time: 5 minutes | Cook time: 20 minutes | Serves 4

1½ pounds (680 g) cherry or grape tomatoes, halved
3 tablespoons olive oil, divided
½ teaspoon salt
½ teaspoon freshly ground black pepper
4 Middle Eastern–style flatbread rounds

1 can artichoke hearts, rinsed, well drained, and cut into thin wedges
8 ounces (227 g) crumbled feta cheese
¼ cup chopped fresh Greek oregano

1. Preheat the oven to 500°F(260°C). 2. In a medium bowl, toss the tomatoes with 1 tablespoon olive oil, the salt, and the pepper. Spread out on a large baking sheet. Roast in the preheated oven until the tomato skins begin to blister and crack, about 10 to 12 minutes. Remove the tomatoes from the oven and reduce the heat to 450°F(235°C). 3. Place the flatbreads on a large baking sheet (or two baking sheets if necessary) and brush the tops with the remaining 2 tablespoons of olive oil. Top with the artichoke hearts, roasted tomatoes, and cheese, dividing equally. 4. Bake the flatbreads in the oven for about 8 to 10 minutes, until the edges are lightly browned and the cheese is melted. Sprinkle the oregano over the top and serve immediately.

Per Serving:
calories: 436 | fat: 27g | protein: 16g | carbs: 34g | fiber: 6g | sodium: 649mg

Moroccan Lamb Wrap with Harissa

Prep time: 10 minutes | Cook time: 10 minutes | Serves 4

1 clove garlic, minced
2 teaspoons ground cumin
2 teaspoons chopped fresh thyme
¼ cup olive oil, divided
1 lamb leg steak, about 12 ounces (340 g)
4 (8-inch) pocketless pita rounds or naan, preferably whole-wheat

1 medium eggplant, sliced ½-inch thick
1 medium zucchini, sliced lengthwise into 4 slices
1 bell pepper (any color), roasted and skinned
6 to 8 Kalamata olives, sliced
Juice of 1 lemon
2 to 4 tablespoons harissa
2 cups arugula

1. In a large bowl, combine the garlic, cumin, thyme, and 1 tablespoon of the olive oil. Add the lamb, turn to coat, cover, refrigerate, and marinate for at least an hour. 2. Preheat the oven to 400°F(205°C). 3. Heat a grill or grill pan to high heat. Remove the lamb from the marinade and grill for about 4 minutes per side, until medium-rare. Transfer to a plate and let rest for about 10 minutes before slicing thinly across the grain. 4. While the meat is resting, wrap the bread rounds in aluminum foil and heat in the oven for about 10 minutes. 5. Meanwhile, brush the eggplant and zucchini slices with the remaining olive oil and grill until tender, about 3 minutes. Dice them and the bell pepper. Toss in a large bowl with the olives and lemon juice. 6. Spread some of the harissa onto each warm flatbread round and top each evenly with roasted vegetables, a few slices of lamb, and a handful of the arugula. 7. Roll up the wraps, cut each in half crosswise, and serve immediately.

Per Serving:
calories: 553 | fat: 24g | protein: 33g | carbs: 53g | fiber: 11g | sodium: 531mg

Barbecue Chicken Pita Pizza

Prep time: 5 minutes | Cook time: 5 to 7 minutes per batch | Makes 4 pizzas

1 cup barbecue sauce, divided
4 pita breads
2 cups shredded cooked chicken
2 cups shredded Mozzarella

cheese
½ small red onion, thinly sliced
2 tablespoons finely chopped fresh cilantro

1. Measure ½ cup of the barbecue sauce in a small measuring cup. Spread 2 tablespoons of the barbecue sauce on each pita. 2. In a medium bowl, mix together the remaining ½ cup of barbecue sauce and chicken. Place ½ cup of the chicken on each pita. Top each pizza with ½ cup of the Mozzarella cheese. Sprinkle the tops of the pizzas with the red onion. 3. Place one pizza in the air fryer. Air fry at 400°F (204°C) for 5 to 7 minutes. Repeat this process with the remaining pizzas. 4. Top the pizzas with the cilantro.

Per Serving:
calories: 530 | fat: 19g | protein: 40g | carbs: 47g | fiber: 2g | sodium: 672mg

Cucumber Basil Sandwiches

Prep time: 10 minutes | Cook time: 0 minutes | Serves 2

Cucumber Basil Sandwiches
4 slices whole-grain bread
¼ cup hummus

1 large cucumber, thinly sliced
4 whole basil leaves

1. Spread the hummus on 2 slices of bread, and layer the cucumbers onto it. Top with the basil leaves and close the sandwiches. 2. Press down lightly and serve immediately.

Per Serving:
calories: 209 | fat: 5g | protein: 9g | carbs: 32g | fiber: 6g | sodium: 275mg

Chapter 11 Salads

Beets with Goat Cheese and Chermoula

Prep time: 10 minutes | Cook time: 40 minutes | Serves 4

6 beets, trimmed	1 teaspoon smoked paprika
Chermoula:	½ teaspoon kosher salt
1 cup fresh cilantro leaves	¼ teaspoon chili powder
1 cup fresh flat-leaf parsley	(optional)
leaves	¼ cup extra-virgin olive oil
¼ cup fresh lemon juice	2 ounces (57 g) goat cheese,
3 cloves garlic, minced	crumbled
2 teaspoons ground cumin	

1. Preheat the oven to 400°F(205°C). 2. Wrap the beets in a piece of foil and place on a baking sheet. Roast until the beets are tender enough to be pierced with a fork, 30 to 40 minutes. When cool enough to handle, remove the skins and slice the beets into ¼' rounds. Arrange the beet slices on a large serving platter. 3. To make the chermoula: In a food processor, pulse the cilantro, parsley, lemon juice, garlic, cumin, paprika, salt, and chili powder (if using) until the herbs are just coarsely chopped and the ingredients are combined. Stir in the oil. 4. To serve, dollop the chermoula over the beets and scatter the cheese on top.

Per Serving:

calories: 249 | fat: 19g | protein: 6g | carbs: 15g | fiber: 5g | sodium: 472mg

Roasted Cauliflower Salad with Tahini-Yogurt Dressing

Prep time: 10 minutes | Cook time: 35 minutes | Serves 8 to 10

10 cups cauliflower florets (1-	temperature
to 2-inch florets, from 1 to 2	¼ cup lemon juice, plus more
heads)	to taste
1½ tablespoons olive oil	¼ cup water
¾ teaspoon kosher salt, divided	1 tablespoon honey
½ cup walnuts	¼ cup chopped fresh dill
½ cup yogurt	1 tablespoon minced shallot
¼ cup tahini, at room	

1. Preheat the oven to 450°F(235°C). 2. On a large baking sheet, toss the cauliflower with the olive oil and ¼ teaspoon of the salt. Spread the cauliflower out in a single layer and roast in the preheated oven for about 30 minutes, until it is tender and browned on the bottom. Place the cooked cauliflower in a large bowl and set aside to cool while you prepare the rest of the salad. 3. Toast the walnuts in a skillet over medium heat until fragrant and golden, about 5 minutes. Chop and set aside. 4. In a blender or food processor, combine the yogurt, tahini, lemon juice, water, and honey and process until smooth. If the mixture is too thick, add a tablespoon or two of additional water. 5. Add the dill, shallot, and the remaining ½ teaspoon of salt to the cauliflower and toss to combine. Add the dressing and toss again to coat well. 6. Serve the salad at room temperature, garnished with the toasted walnuts.

Per Serving:

calories: 153 | fat: 10g | protein: 6g | carbs: 12g | fiber: 4g | sodium: 249mg

Spinach Salad with Pomegranate, Lentils, and Pistachios

Prep time: 10 minutes | Cook time: 30 minutes | Serves 4

1 tablespoon extra-virgin olive	rinsed
oil	3 cups water
1 shallot, finely chopped	6 cups baby spinach
1 small red chile pepper, such as	½ cup pomegranate seeds
a Fresno, finely chopped (wear	¼ cup chopped fresh cilantro
plastic gloves when handling)	¼ cup chopped fresh flat-leaf
½ teaspoon ground cumin	parsley
¼ teaspoon ground coriander	¼ cup chopped pistachi os
seeds	2 tablespoons fresh lemon juice
¼ teaspoon ground cinnamon	1 teaspoon finely grated lemon
Pinch of kosher salt	peel
1 cup French green lentils,	Ground black pepper, to taste

1. In a medium saucepan over medium heat, warm the oil until shimmering. Cook the shallot and chile pepper, stirring, until the shallot is translucent, about 8 minutes. Stir in the cumin, coriander, cinnamon, and salt until fragrant, about 1 minute. Add the lentils and water and bring to a boil. Cover and reduce the heat to a simmer. Cook, stirring occasionally, until the lentils are completely tender and the liquid has been absorbed, about 30 minutes. 2. In a large bowl, toss the lentils with the spinach, pomegranate seeds, cilantro, parsley, pistachios, lemon juice, lemon peel, and pepper to taste.

Per Serving:

calories: 279 | fat: 7g | protein: 15g | carbs: 39g | fiber: 10g | sodium: 198mg

Tricolor Tomato Summer Salad

Prep time: 10 minutes | Cook time: 0 minutes |
Serves 3 to 4

¼ cup while balsamic vinegar
2 tablespoons Dijon mustard
1 tablespoon sugar
½ teaspoon freshly ground black pepper
½ teaspoon garlic salt

¼ cup extra-virgin olive oil
1½ cups chopped orange, yellow, and red tomatoes
½ cucumber, peeled and diced
1 small red onion, thinly sliced
¼ cup crumbled feta (optional)

1. In a small bowl, whisk the vinegar, mustard, sugar, pepper, and garlic salt. Next, slowly whisk in the olive oil. 2. In a large bowl, add the tomatoes, cucumber, and red onion. Add the dressing. Toss once or twice, and serve with feta crumbles (if using) on top.

Per Serving:

calories: 246 | fat: 18g | protein: 1g | carbs: 19g | fiber: 2g | sodium: 483mg

Wild Rice Salad with Chickpeas and Pickled Radish

Prep time: 20 minutes | Cook time: 45 minutes |
Serves 6

For the Rice:
1 cup water
4 ounces (113 g) wild rice
¼ teaspoon kosher salt
For the Pickled Radish:
1 bunch radishes (6 to 8 small), thinly sliced
½ cup white wine vinegar
½ teaspoon kosher salt
For the Dressing:
2 tablespoons extra-virgin olive oil
2 tablespoons white wine vinegar
½ teaspoon pure maple syrup

½ teaspoon kosher salt
¼ teaspoon freshly ground black pepper
For the Salad:
1 (15 ounces / 425 g) can no-salt-added or low-sodium chickpeas, rinsed and drained
1 bulb fennel, diced
¼ cup walnuts, chopped and toasted
¼ cup crumbled feta cheese
¼ cup currants
2 tablespoons fresh dill, chopped

Make the Rice: Bring the water, rice, and salt to a boil in a medium saucepan. Cover, reduce the heat, and simmer for 45 minutes. Make the Pickled Radish: In a medium bowl, combine the radishes, vinegar, and salt. Let sit for 15 to 30 minutes. Make the Dressing: In a large bowl, whisk together the olive oil, vinegar, maple syrup, salt, and black pepper. Make the Salad: 1. While still warm, add the rice to the bowl with the dressing and mix well. 2. Add the chickpeas, fennel, walnuts, feta, currants, and dill. Mix well. 3. Garnish with the pickled radishes before serving.

Per Serving:

calories: 310 | fat: 16g | protein: 10g | carbs: 36g | fiber: 7g | sodium: 400mg

Italian Tuna and Olive Salad

Prep time : 5 minutes | Cook time: 0 minutes |
Serves 4

¼ cup olive oil
3 tablespoons white wine vinegar
1 teaspoon salt
1 cup pitted green olives
1 medium red bell pepper,

seeded and diced
1 small clove garlic, minced
2 (6-ounce / 170-g) cans or jars tuna in olive oil, well drained
Several leaves curly green or red lettuce

1. In a large bowl, whisk together the olive oil, vinegar, and salt. 2. Add the olives, bell pepper, and garlic to the dressing and toss to coat. Stir in the tuna, cover, and chill in the refrigerator for at least 1 hour to let the flavors meld. 3. To serve, line a serving bowl with the lettuce leaves and spoon the salad on top. Serve chilled.

Per Serving:

calories: 339 | fat: 24g | protein: 25g | carbs: 4g | fiber: 2g | sodium: 626mg

Panzanella (Tuscan Bread and Tomatoes Salad)

Prep time: 10 minutes | Cook time: 20 minutes |
Serves 6

4 ounces (113 g) sourdough bread, cut into 1' slices
3 tablespoons extra-virgin olive oil, divided
2 tablespoons red wine vinegar
2 cloves garlic, mashed to a paste
1 teaspoon finely chopped fresh oregano or ½ teaspoon dried
1 teaspoon fresh thyme leaves
½ teaspoon Dijon mustard
Pinch of kosher salt

Few grinds of ground black pepper
2 pounds (907 g) ripe tomatoes (mixed colors)
6 ounces (170 g) fresh mozzarella pearls
1 cucumber, cut into ½'-thick half-moons
1 small red onion, thinly sliced
1 cup baby arugula
½ cup torn fresh basil

1. Coat a grill rack or grill pan with olive oil and prepare to medium-high heat. 2. Brush 1 tablespoon of the oil all over the bread slices. Grill the bread on both sides until grill marks appear, about 2 minutes per side. Cut the bread into 1' cubes. 3. In a large bowl, whisk together the vinegar, garlic, oregano, thyme, mustard, salt, pepper, and the remaining 2 tablespoons oil until emulsified. 4. Add the bread, tomatoes, mozzarella, cucumber, onion, arugula, and basil. Toss to combine and let sit for 10 minutes to soak up the flavors.

Per Serving:

calories: 219 | fat: 12g | protein: 10g | carbs: 19g | fiber: 3g | sodium: 222mg

Easy Greek Salad

Prep time: 10 minutes | Cook time: 0 minutes |
Serves 4 to 6

1 head iceberg lettuce	1 teaspoon salt
1 pint (2 cups) cherry tomatoes	1 clove garlic, minced
1 large cucumber	1 cup Kalamata olives, pitted
1 medium onion	1 (6-ounce / 170-g) package
½ cup extra-virgin olive oil	feta cheese, crumbled
¼ cup lemon juice	

1. Cut the lettuce into 1-inch pieces and put them in a large salad bowl. 2. Cut the tomatoes in half and add them to the salad bowl. 3. Slice the cucumber into bite-size pieces and add them to the salad bowl. 4. Thinly slice the onion and add it to the salad bowl. 5. In another small bowl, whisk together the olive oil, lemon juice, salt, and garlic. Pour the dressing over the salad and gently toss to evenly coat. 6. Top the salad with the Kalamata olives and feta cheese and serve.

Per Serving:

calories: 297 | fat: 27g | protein: 6g | carbs: 11g | fiber: 3g | sodium: 661mg

Quinoa with Zucchini, Mint, and Pistachios

Prep time: 20 to 30 minutes | Cook time: 20 minutes | Serves 4

For the Quinoa:	¾ teaspoon kosher salt
1½ cups water	¼ teaspoon freshly ground
1 cup quinoa	black pepper
¼ teaspoon kosher salt	2 garlic cloves, sliced
For the Salad:	Zest of 1 lemon
2 tablespoons extra-virgin olive	2 tablespoons lemon juice
oil	¼ cup fresh mint, chopped
1 zucchini, thinly sliced into	¼ cup fresh basil, chopped
rounds	¼ cup pistachios, shelled and
6 small radishes, sliced	toasted
1 shallot, julienned	

Make the Quinoa: Bring the water, quinoa, and salt to a boil in a medium saucepan. Reduce to a simmer, cover, and cook for 10 to 12 minutes. Fluff with a fork. Make the Salad: 1. Heat the olive oil in a large skillet or sauté pan over medium-high heat. Add the zucchini, radishes, shallot, salt, and black pepper, and sauté for 7 to 8 minutes. Add the garlic and cook 30 seconds to 1 minute more. 2. In a large bowl, combine the lemon zest and lemon juice. Add the quinoa and mix well. Add the cooked zucchini mixture and mix well. Add the mint, basil, and pistachios and gently mix.

Per Serving:

calories: 220 | fat: 12g | protein: 6g | carbs: 25g | fiber: 5g | sodium: 295mg

Israeli Salad with Nuts and Seeds

Prep time: 15 minutes | Cook time: 0 minutes |
Serves 4

¼ cup pine nuts	chopped
¼ cup shelled pistachios	½ cup finely chopped fresh flat-
¼ cup coarsely chopped	leaf Italian parsley
walnuts	¼ cup extra-virgin olive oil
¼ cup shelled pumpkin seeds	2 to 3 tablespoons freshly
¼ cup shelled sunflower seeds	squeezed lemon juice (from 1
2 large English cucumbers,	lemon)
unpeeled and finely chopped	1 teaspoon salt
1 pint cherry tomatoes, finely	¼ teaspoon freshly ground
chopped	black pepper
½ small red onion, finely	4 cups baby arugula

1. In a large dry skillet, toast the pine nuts, pistachios, walnuts, pumpkin seeds, and sunflower seeds over medium-low heat until golden and fragrant, 5 to 6 minutes, being careful not to burn them. Remove from the heat and set aside. 2. In a large bowl, combine the cucumber, tomatoes, red onion, and parsley. 3. In a small bowl, whisk together olive oil, lemon juice, salt, and pepper. Pour over the chopped vegetables and toss to coat. 4. Add the toasted nuts and seeds and arugula and toss with the salad to blend well. Serve at room temperature or chilled.

Per Serving:

calories: 404 | fat: 36g | protein: 10g | carbs: 16g | fiber: 5g | sodium: 601mg

Riviera Tuna Salad

Prep time: 15 minutes | Cook time: 0 minutes |
Serves 4

¼ cup olive oil	1 (6-ounce / 170-g) can solid
¼ cup balsamic vinegar	white albacore tuna, drained
½ teaspoon minced garlic	1 cup canned garbanzo beans,
¼ teaspoon dried oregano	rinsed and drained
Sea salt and freshly ground	¼ cup low-salt olives, pitted
pepper, to taste	and quartered
2 tablespoons capers, drained	2 Roma tomatoes, chopped
4 to 6 cups baby greens	

1. To make the vinaigrette, whisk together the olive oil, balsamic vinegar, garlic, oregano, sea salt, and pepper until emulsified. 2. Stir in the capers. Refrigerate for up to 6 hours before serving. 3. Place the baby greens in a salad bowl or on individual plates, and top with the tuna, beans, olives, and tomatoes. 4. Drizzle the vinaigrette over all, and serve immediately.

Per Serving:

calories: 300 | fat: 19g | protein: 16g | carbs: 17g | fiber: 5g | sodium: 438mg

Traditional Greek Salad

Prep time: 10 minutes | Cook time: 0 minutes |

Serves 4

2 large English cucumbers	lemon juice
4 Roma tomatoes, quartered	1 tablespoon red wine vinegar
1 green bell pepper, cut into 1- to 1½-inch chunks	1 tablespoon chopped fresh oregano or 1 teaspoon dried oregano
¼ small red onion, thinly sliced	
4 ounces (113 g) pitted Kalamata olives	¼ teaspoon freshly ground black pepper
¼ cup extra-virgin olive oil	4 ounces (113 g) crumbled traditional feta cheese
2 tablespoons freshly squeezed	

1. Cut the cucumbers in half lengthwise and then into ½-inch-thick half-moons. Place in a large bowl. 2. Add the quartered tomatoes, bell pepper, red onion, and olives. 3. In a small bowl, whisk together the olive oil, lemon juice, vinegar, oregano, and pepper. Drizzle over the vegetables and toss to coat. 4. Divide between salad plates and top each with 1 ounce (28 g) of feta.

Per Serving:
calories: 256 | fat: 22g | protein: 6g | carbs: 11g | fiber: 3g | sodium: 476mg

Pistachio Quinoa Salad with Pomegranate Citrus Vinaigrette

Prep time: 15 minutes | Cook time: 15 minutes |

Serves 6

For the Quinoa:	¼ teaspoon freshly ground black pepper
1½ cups water	
1 cup quinoa	For the Salad:
¼ teaspoon kosher salt	3 cups baby spinach
For the Dressing:	½ cup fresh parsley, coarsely chopped
1 cup extra-virgin olive oil	
½ cup pomegranate juice	½ cup fresh mint, coarsely chopped
½ cup freshly squeezed orange juice	Approximately ¾ cup pomegranate seeds, or 2 pomegranates
1 small shallot, minced	
1 teaspoon pure maple syrup	
1 teaspoon za'atar	¼ cup pistachios, shelled and toasted
½ teaspoon ground sumac	
½ teaspoon kosher salt	¼ cup crumbled blue cheese

Make the Quinoa: Bring the water, quinoa, and salt to a boil in a small saucepan. Reduce the heat and cover; simmer for 10 to 12 minutes. Fluff with a fork. Make the Dressing: 1. In a medium bowl, whisk together the olive oil, pomegranate juice, orange juice, shallot, maple syrup, za'atar, sumac, salt, and black pepper. 2. In a large bowl, add about ½ cup of dressing. 3. Store the remaining dressing in a glass jar or airtight container and refrigerate. The dressing can be kept up to 2 weeks. Let the chilled dressing reach room temperature before using. Make the Salad: 4. Combine the spinach, parsley, and mint in the bowl with the dressing and toss gently together. 5. Add the quinoa. Toss gently. 6. Add the pomegranate seeds. 7. Or, if using whole pomegranates: Cut the pomegranates in half. Fill a large bowl with water and hold the pomegranate half, cut side-down. Using a wooden spoon, hit the back of the pomegranate so the seeds fall into the water. Immerse the pomegranate in the water and gently pull out any remaining seeds. Repeat with the remaining pomegranate. Skim the white pith off the top of the water. Drain the seeds and add them to the greens. 8. Add the pistachios and cheese and toss gently.

Per Serving:
calories: 300 | fat: 19g | protein: 8g | carbs: 28g | fiber: 5g | sodium: 225mg

Double-Apple Spinach Salad

Prep time: 15 minutes | Cook time: 0 minutes |

Serves 4

8 cups baby spinach	2 ounces (57 g) low-fat, sharp white cheddar cheese, cubed
1 medium Granny Smith apple, diced	
	3 tablespoons olive oil
1 medium red apple, diced	1 tablespoon red wine vinegar or apple cider vinegar
½ cup toasted walnuts	

1. Toss the spinach, apples, walnuts, and cubed cheese together. Lightly drizzle olive oil and vinegar over top and serve.

Per Serving:
calories: 275 | fat: 22g | protein: 7g | carbs: 16g | fiber: 4g | sodium: 140mg

No-Mayo Florence Tuna Salad

Prep time: 10 minutes | Cook time: 0 minutes |

Serves 4

4 cups spring mix greens	olives
1 (15 ounces / 425 g) can cannellini beans, drained	¼ cup thinly sliced scallions, both green and white parts
2 (5-ounce / 142-g) cans water-packed, white albacore tuna, drained (I prefer Wild Planet brand)	3 tablespoons extra-virgin olive oil
	½ teaspoon dried cilantro
⅔ cup crumbled feta cheese	2 or 3 leaves thinly chopped fresh sweet basil
½ cup thinly sliced sun-dried tomatoes	1 lime, zested and juiced
	Kosher salt
¼ cup sliced pitted kalamata	Freshly ground black pepper

1. In a large bowl, combine greens, beans, tuna, feta, tomatoes, olives, scallions, olive oil, cilantro, basil, and lime juice and zest. Season with salt and pepper, mix, and enjoy!

Per Serving:
1 cup: calories: 355 | fat: 19g | protein: 22g | carbs: 25g | fiber: 8g | sodium: 744mg

Roasted Broccoli Panzanella Salad

Prep time: 10 minutes |Cook time: 20 minutes|

Serves: 4

1 pound (454 g) broccoli (about 3 medium stalks), trimmed, cut into 1-inch florets and ½-inch stem slices	crusty bread
	1 tablespoon balsamic vinegar
	½ teaspoon freshly ground black pepper
3 tablespoons extra-virgin olive oil, divided	¼ teaspoon kosher or sea salt
1 pint cherry or grape tomatoes (about 1½ cups)	Grated Parmesan cheese (or other hard cheese) and chopped fresh oregano leaves, for serving (optional)
1½ teaspoons honey, divided	
3 cups cubed whole-grain	

1. Place a large, rimmed baking sheet in the oven. Preheat the oven to 450°F(235ºC) with the pan inside. 2. Put the broccoli in a large bowl, and drizzle with 1 tablespoon of the oil. Toss to coat. 3. Carefully remove the hot baking sheet from the oven and spoon the broccoli onto it, leaving some oil in the bottom of the bowl. Add the tomatoes to the same bowl, and toss to coat with the leftover oil (don't add any more oil). Toss the tomatoes with 1 teaspoon of honey, and scrape them onto the baking sheet with the broccoli. 4. Roast for 15 minutes, stirring halfway through. Remove the sheet from the oven, and add the bread cubes. Roast for 3 more minutes. The broccoli is ready when it appears slightly charred on the tips and is tender-crisp when poked with a fork. 5. Spoon the vegetable mixture onto a serving plate or into a large, flat bowl. 6. In a small bowl, whisk the remaining 2 tablespoons of oil together with the vinegar, the remaining ½ teaspoon of honey, and the pepper and salt. Pour over the salad, and toss gently. Sprinkle with cheese and oregano, if desired, and serve.

Per Serving:

calories: 197 | fat: 12g | protein: 7g | carbs: 19g | fiber: 5g | sodium: 296mg

Mediterranean Quinoa and Garbanzo Salad

Prep time: 10 minutes | Cook time: 30 minutes |

Serves 8

4 cups water	garbanzo beans, rinsed and drained
2 cups red or yellow quinoa	
2 teaspoons salt, divided	⅓ cup extra-virgin olive oil
1 cup thinly sliced onions (red or white)	¼ cup lemon juice
1 (16-ounce / 454-g) can	1 teaspoon freshly ground black pepper

1. In a 3-quart pot over medium heat, bring the water to a boil. 2. Add the quinoa and 1 teaspoon of salt to the pot. Stir, cover, and let cook over low heat for 15 to 20 minutes. 3. Turn off the heat, fluff the quinoa with a fork, cover again, and let stand for 5 to 10 more minutes. 4. Put the cooked quinoa, onions, and garbanzo beans in a large bowl. 5. In a separate small bowl, whisk together the olive oil, lemon juice, remaining 1 teaspoon of salt, and black pepper. 6. Add the dressing to the quinoa mixture and gently toss everything together. Serve warm or cold.

Per Serving:

calories: 318 | fat: 13g | protein: 9g | carbs: 43g | fiber: 6g | sodium: 585mg

Endive with Shrimp

Prep time: 15 minutes | Cook time: 2 minutes |

Serves 4

¼ cup olive oil	2 cups salted water
1 small shallot, minced	14 shrimp, peeled and deveined
1 tablespoon Dijon mustard	1 head endive
Juice and zest of 1 lemon	½ cup tart green apple, diced
Sea salt and freshly ground pepper, to taste	2 tablespoons toasted walnuts

1. For the vinaigrette, whisk together the first five ingredients in a small bowl until creamy and emulsified. 2. Refrigerate for at least 2 hours for best flavor. 3. In a small pan, boil salted water. Add the shrimp and cook 1 to 2 minutes, or until the shrimp turns pink. Drain and cool under cold water. 4. To assemble the salad, wash and break the endive. Place on serving plates and top with the shrimp, green apple, and toasted walnuts. 5. Drizzle with the vinaigrette before serving.

Per Serving:

calories: 194 | fat: 16g | protein: 6g | carbs: 8g | fiber: 5g | sodium: 191mg

Cauliflower Tabbouleh Salad

Prep time: 15 minutes | Cook time: 0 minutes |

Serves 4

¼ cup extra-virgin olive oil	⅛ teaspoon ground cinnamon
¼ cup lemon juice	1 pound (454 g) riced cauliflower
Zest of 1 lemon	
¾ teaspoon kosher salt	1 English cucumber, diced
½ teaspoon ground turmeric	12 cherry tomatoes, halved
¼ teaspoon ground coriander	1 cup fresh parsley, chopped
¼ teaspoon ground cumin	½ cup fresh mint, chopped
¼ teaspoon black pepper	

1. In a large bowl, whisk together the olive oil, lemon juice, lemon zest, salt, turmeric, coriander, cumin, black pepper, and cinnamon. 2. Add the riced cauliflower to the bowl and mix well. Add in the cucumber, tomatoes, parsley, and mint and gently mix together.

Per Serving:

calories: 180 | fat: 15g | protein: 4g | carbs: 12g | fiber: 5g | sodium:260 mg

Simple Insalata Mista (Mixed Salad) with Honey Balsamic Dressing

Prep time: 15 minutes | Cook time: 0 minutes | Serves 2

For the Dressing:
¼ cup balsamic vinegar
¼ cup olive oil
1 tablespoon honey
1 teaspoon Dijon mustard
¼ teaspoon salt, plus more to taste
¼ teaspoon garlic powder
Pinch freshly ground black pepper
For the Salad:
4 cups chopped red leaf lettuce
½ cup cherry or grape tomatoes, halved
½ English cucumber, sliced in quarters lengthwise and then cut into bite-size pieces
Any combination fresh, torn herbs (parsley, oregano, basil, chives, etc.)
1 tablespoon roasted sunflower seeds

Make the Dressing: Combine the vinegar, olive oil, honey, mustard, salt, garlic powder, and pepper in a jar with a lid. Shake well. Make the Salad: 1. In a large bowl, combine the lettuce, tomatoes, cucumber, and herbs. 2. Toss well to combine. 3. Pour all or as much dressing as desired over the tossed salad and toss again to coat the salad with dressing. 4. Top with the sunflower seeds.

Per Serving:
calories: 339 | fat: 26g | protein: 4g | carbs: 24g | fiber: 3g | sodium: 171mg

Moroccan Chickpea and Green Bean Salad with Ras el Hanout

Prep time: 10 minutes | Cook time: 10 minutes | Serves 6 to 8

1 pound (454 g) green beans, trimmed
2 tablespoons olive oil
2 tablespoons red wine vinegar
1 garlic clove, minced
2 teaspoons ras el hanout
1 (15½-ounce / 439-g) can no-salt-added chickpeas, drained and rinsed
1 shallot, finely chopped
3 tablespoons chopped fresh parsley

1. Bring a large saucepan of water to a boil. Add the green beans and cook just until crisp-tender. Drain the green beans into a colander and rinse under cool running water to stop the cooking. 2. In a large bowl, whisk together the olive oil, vinegar, garlic, and ras el hanout. 3. Add the chickpeas, green beans, shallot, and parsley and toss to combine. Serve.

Per Serving:
1 cup: calories: 68 | fat: 4g | protein: 2g | carbs: 7g | fiber: 3g | sodium: 16mg

Sicilian Salad

Prep time: 5 minutes | Cook time: 0 minutes | Serves 2

2 tablespoons extra virgin olive oil
1 tablespoon red wine vinegar
2 medium tomatoes (preferably beefsteak variety), sliced
½ medium red onion, thinly sliced
2 tablespoons capers, drained
6 green olives, halved
1 teaspoon dried oregano
Pinch of fine sea salt

1. Make the dressing by combining the olive oil and vinegar in a small bowl. Use a fork to whisk until the mixture thickens slightly. Set aside. 2. Arrange the sliced tomatoes on a large plate and then scatter the onions, capers, and olives over the tomatoes. 3. Sprinkle the oregano and sea salt over the top, then drizzle the dressing over the salad. Serve promptly. (This salad is best served fresh, but can be stored covered in the refrigerator for up to 1 day.)

Per Serving:
calories: 169 | fat: 15g | protein: 2g | carbs: 8g | fiber: 3g | sodium: 336mg

French Lentil Salad with Parsley and Mint

Prep time: 20 minutes | Cook time:25 minutes | Serves 6

For the Lentils:
1 cup French lentils
1 garlic clove, smashed
1 dried bay leaf
For the Salad:
2 tablespoons extra-virgin olive oil
2 tablespoons red wine vinegar
½ teaspoon ground cumin
½ teaspoon kosher salt
¼ teaspoon freshly ground black pepper
2 celery stalks, diced small
1 bell pepper, diced small
½ red onion, diced small
¼ cup fresh parsley, chopped
¼ cup fresh mint, chopped

Make the Lentils: 1. Put the lentils, garlic, and bay leaf in a large saucepan. Cover with water by about 3 inches and bring to a boil. Reduce the heat, cover, and simmer until tender, 20 to 30 minutes. 2. Drain the lentils to remove any remaining water after cooking. Remove the garlic and bay leaf. Make the Salad: 3. In a large bowl, whisk together the olive oil, vinegar, cumin, salt, and black pepper. Add the celery, bell pepper, onion, parsley, and mint and toss to combine. 4. Add the lentils and mix well.

Per Serving:
calories: 200 | fat: 8g | protein: 10g | carbs: 26g | fiber: 10g | sodium: 165mg

Pipirrana (Spanish Summer Salad)

Prep time: 15 minutes | Cook time: 0 minutes | Serves 2

1 medium red onion, diced

2 large tomatoes, cut into small cubes

1 large Persian or mini cucumber, cut into small cubes

1 large green bell pepper, seeded and diced

2 garlic cloves, minced

Pinch of ground cumin

½ teaspoon salt plus a pinch for the garlic paste

3 tablespoons extra virgin olive oil plus a few drops for the garlic paste

2 tablespoons red wine vinegar

1. Place the onions in a small bowl filled with water. Set aside to soak. 2. Place the tomatoes, cucumber, and bell pepper in a medium bowl. Drain the onions and then combine them with the rest of the vegetables. Mix well. 3. In a mortar or small bowl, combine the garlic, cumin, a pinch of salt, and a few drops of olive oil, then roll or mash the ingredients until a paste is formed. 4. In another small bowl, combine 3 tablespoons of the olive oil, vinegar, and ½ teaspoon of the salt. Add the garlic paste and mix well. 5. Add the dressing to the salad and mix well. 6. Cover and refrigerate for 30 minutes before serving. Store in the refrigerator for up to 2 days.

Per Serving:

calories: 274 | fat: 21g | protein: 4g | carbs: 20g | fiber: 6g | sodium: 600mg

Spanish Potato Salad

Prep time: 10 minutes | Cook time: 10 minutes | Serves 6 to 8

4 russet potatoes, peeled and chopped

3 large hard-boiled eggs, chopped

1 cup frozen mixed vegetables, thawed

½ cup plain, unsweetened, full-fat Greek yogurt

5 tablespoons pitted Spanish olives

½ teaspoon freshly ground black pepper

½ teaspoon dried mustard seed

½ tablespoon freshly squeezed lemon juice

½ teaspoon dried dill

Salt

Freshly ground black pepper

1. Boil potatoes for 5 to 7 minutes, until just fork-tender, checking periodically for doneness. You don't want to overcook them. 2. While the potatoes are cooking, in a large bowl, mix the eggs, vegetables, yogurt, olives, pepper, mustard, lemon juice, and dill. Season with salt and pepper. Once the potatoes are cooled somewhat, add them to the large bowl, then mix well and serve.

Per Serving:

calories: 192 | fat: 5g | protein: 9g | carbs: 30g | fiber: 2g | sodium: 59mg

Chapter 12 Pasta

Couscous with Crab and Lemon

Prep time: 10 minutes | Cook time: 7 minutes |

Serves 4

1 cup couscous	1 tablespoon minced fresh dill
1 clove garlic, peeled and minced	8 ounces (227 g) jumbo lump crabmeat
2 cups water	3 tablespoons lemon juice
3 tablespoons extra-virgin olive oil, divided	½ teaspoon ground black pepper
¼ cup minced fresh flat-leaf parsley	¼ cup grated Parmesan cheese

1. Place couscous, garlic, water, and 1 tablespoon oil in the Instant Pot® and stir well. Close lid, set steam release to Sealing, press the Manual button, and set time to 7 minutes. When the timer beeps, let pressure release naturally for 10 minutes, then quick-release the remaining pressure and open lid. 2. Fluff couscous with a fork. Add parsley, dill, crabmeat, lemon juice, pepper, and remaining 2 tablespoons oil, and stir until combined. Top with cheese and serve immediately.

Per Serving:

calories: 360 | fat: 15g | protein: 22g | carbs: 34g | fiber: 2g | sodium: 388mg

Toasted Orzo Salad

Prep time: 15 minutes | Cook time: 8 minutes |

Serves 6

2 tablespoons light olive oil	1 medium red bell pepper, seeded and diced
1 clove garlic, peeled and crushed	¼ cup crumbled feta cheese
2 cups orzo	1 tablespoon extra-virgin olive oil
3 cups vegetable broth	1 tablespoon red wine vinegar
½ cup sliced black olives	½ teaspoon ground black pepper
3 scallions, thinly sliced	¼ teaspoon salt
1 medium Roma tomato, seeded and diced	

1. Press the Sauté button on the Instant Pot® and heat light olive oil. Add garlic and orzo and cook, stirring frequently, until orzo is light golden brown, about 5 minutes. Press the Cancel button. 2. Add broth and stir. Close lid, set steam release to Sealing, press the Manual button, and set time to 3 minutes. When the timer beeps, let pressure release naturally for 5 minutes, then quick-release the remaining pressure until the float valve drops and open lid. 3. Transfer orzo to a medium bowl, then set aside to cool to room temperature, about 30 minutes. Add olives, scallions, tomato, bell pepper, feta, extra-virgin olive oil, vinegar, black pepper, and salt, and stir until combined. Serve at room temperature or refrigerate for at least 2 hours.

Per Serving:

calories: 120 | fat: 4g | protein: 4g | carbs: 17g | fiber: 1g | sodium: 586mg

Roasted Asparagus Caprese Pasta

Prep time: 10 minutes |Cook time: 15 minutes|

Serves: 6

8 ounces (227 g) uncooked small pasta, like orecchiette (little ears) or farfalle (bow ties)	oil
	¼ teaspoon freshly ground black pepper
1½ pounds (680 g) fresh asparagus, ends trimmed and stalks chopped into 1-inch pieces (about 3 cups)	¼ teaspoon kosher or sea salt
	2 cups fresh mozzarella, drained and cut into bite-size pieces (about 8 ounces / 227 g)
1 pint grape tomatoes, halved (about 1½ cups)	⅓ cup torn fresh basil leaves
2 tablespoons extra-virgin olive	2 tablespoons balsamic vinegar

1. Preheat the oven to 400°F(205°C). 2. In a large stockpot, cook the pasta according to the package directions. Drain, reserving about ¼ cup of the pasta water. 3. While the pasta is cooking, in a large bowl, toss the asparagus, tomatoes, oil, pepper, and salt together. Spread the mixture onto a large, rimmed baking sheet and bake for 15 minutes, stirring twice as it cooks. 4. Remove the vegetables from the oven, and add the cooked pasta to the baking sheet. Mix with a few tablespoons of pasta water to help the sauce become smoother and the saucy vegetables stick to the pasta. 5. Gently mix in the mozzarella and basil. Drizzle with the balsamic vinegar. Serve from the baking sheet or pour the pasta into a large bowl. 6. If you want to make this dish ahead of time or to serve it cold, follow the recipe up to step 4, then refrigerate the pasta and vegetables. When you are ready to serve, follow step 5 either with the cold pasta or with warm pasta that's been gently reheated in a pot on the stove.

Per Serving:

calories: 317 | fat: 12g | protein: 16g | carbs: 38g | fiber: 7g | sodium: 110mg

Spaghetti with Fresh Mint Pesto and Ricotta Salata

Prep time: 5 minutes | Cook time: 15 minutes |

Serves 4

1 pound (454 g) spaghetti
¼ cup slivered almonds
2 cups packed fresh mint leaves, plus more for garnish
3 medium garlic cloves
1 tablespoon lemon juice and
½ teaspoon lemon zest from 1

lemon
⅓ cup olive oil
¼ teaspoon freshly ground black pepper
½ cup freshly grated ricotta salata, plus more for garnish

1. Set a large pot of salted water over high heat to boil for the pasta. 2. In a food processor, combine the almonds, mint leaves, garlic, lemon juice and zest, olive oil, and pepper and pulse to a smooth paste. Add the cheese and pulse to combine. 3. When the water is boiling, add the pasta and cook according to the package instructions. Drain the pasta and return it to the pot. Add the pesto to the pasta and toss until the pasta is well coated. Serve hot, garnished with additional mint leaves and cheese, if desired.

Per Serving:
calories: 619 | fat: 31g | protein: 21g | carbs: 70g | fiber: 4g | sodium: 113mg

Pasta Salad with Tomato, Arugula, and Feta

Prep time: 10 minutes | Cook time: 4 minutes |

Serves 8

1 pound (454 g) rotini
4 cups water
3 tablespoons extra-virgin olive oil, divided
2 medium Roma tomatoes, diced
2 cloves garlic, peeled and minced
1 medium red bell pepper,

seeded and diced
2 tablespoons white wine vinegar
5 ounces (142 g) baby arugula
1 cup crumbled feta cheese
½ teaspoon salt
½ teaspoon ground black pepper

1. Add pasta, water, and 1 tablespoon oil to the Instant Pot®. Close lid, set steam release to Sealing, press the Manual button, and set time to 4 minutes. When the timer beeps, quick-release the pressure until the float valve drops, open lid, drain pasta, then rinse with cold water. Set aside. 2. In a large bowl, mix remaining 2 tablespoons oil, tomatoes, garlic, bell pepper, vinegar, arugula, and cheese. Stir in pasta and season with salt and pepper. Cover and refrigerate for 2 hours before serving.

Per Serving:
calories: 332 | fat: 12g | protein: 12g | carbs: 44g | fiber: 3g | sodium: 480mg

Rigatoni with Lamb Meatballs

Prep time: 15 minutes | Cook time: 3 to 5 hours |

Serves 4

8 ounces (227 g) dried rigatoni pasta
2 (28-ounce / 794-g) cans no-salt-added crushed tomatoes or no-salt-added diced tomatoes
1 small onion, diced
1 bell pepper, any color, seeded and diced
3 garlic cloves, minced, divided

1 pound (454 g) raw ground lamb
1 large egg
2 tablespoons bread crumbs
1 tablespoon dried parsley
1 teaspoon dried oregano
1 teaspoon sea salt
½ teaspoon freshly ground black pepper

1. In a slow cooker, combine the pasta, tomatoes, onion, bell pepper, and 1 clove of garlic. Stir to mix well. 2. In a large bowl, mix together the ground lamb, egg, bread crumbs, the remaining 2 garlic cloves, parsley, oregano, salt, and black pepper until all of the ingredients are evenly blended. Shape the meat mixture into 6 to 9 large meatballs. Nestle the meatballs into the pasta and tomato sauce. 3. Cover the cooker and cook for 3 to 5 hours on Low heat, or until the pasta is tender.

Per Serving:
calories: 653 | fat: 29g | protein: 32g | carbs: 69g | fiber: 10g | sodium: 847mg

Fresh Tomato Pasta Bowl

Prep time: 10 minutes | Cook time: 15 minutes |

Serves 4

8 ounces (227 g) whole-grain linguine
1 tablespoon extra-virgin olive oil
2 garlic cloves, minced
¼ cup chopped yellow onion
1 teaspoon chopped fresh oregano
½ teaspoon salt

¼ teaspoon freshly ground black pepper
1 teaspoon tomato paste
8 ounces (227 g) cherry tomatoes, halved
½ cup grated Parmesan cheese
1 tablespoon chopped fresh parsley

1. Bring a large saucepan of water to a boil over high heat and cook the linguine according to the package instructions until al dente (still slightly firm). Drain, reserving ½ cup of the pasta water. Do not rinse the pasta. 2. In a large, heavy skillet, heat the olive oil over medium-high heat. Sauté the garlic, onion, and oregano until the onion is just translucent, about 5 minutes. 3. Add the salt, pepper, tomato paste, and ¼ cup of the reserved pasta water. Stir well and allow it to cook for 1 minute. 4. Stir in the tomatoes and cooked pasta, tossing everything well to coat. Add more pasta water if needed. 5. To serve, mound the pasta in shallow bowls and top with Parmesan cheese and parsley.

Per Serving:
calories: 310 | fat: 9g | protein: 10g | carbs: 49g | fiber: 7g | sodium: 305mg

Chilled Pearl Couscous Salad

Prep time: 15 minutes | Cook time: 10 minutes |

Serves 6

3 tablespoons olive oil, divided	¼ cup slivered almonds
1 cup pearl couscous	¼ cup chopped fresh mint
1 cup water	leaves
1 cup orange juice	2 tablespoons lemon juice
1 small cucumber, seeded and diced	1 teaspoon grated lemon zest
	¼ cup crumbled feta cheese
1 small yellow bell pepper, seeded and diced	¼ teaspoon fine sea salt
	1 teaspoon smoked paprika
2 small Roma tomatoes, seeded and diced	1 teaspoon garlic powder

1. Press the Sauté button and heat 1 tablespoon oil. Add couscous and cook for 2–4 minutes until couscous is slightly browned. Add water and orange juice. Press the Cancel button. 2. Close lid, set steam release to Sealing, press the Manual button, and set time to 5 minutes. When the timer beeps, let pressure release naturally for 5 minutes. Quick-release any remaining pressure until the float valve drops and open lid. Drain any liquid and set aside to cool for 20 minutes. 3. Combine remaining 2 tablespoons oil, cucumber, bell pepper, tomatoes, almonds, mint, lemon juice, lemon zest, cheese, salt, paprika, and garlic powder in a medium bowl. Add couscous and toss ingredients together. Cover and refrigerate overnight before serving.

Per Serving:

calories: 177 | fat: 11g | protein: 5g | carbs: 12g | fiber: 1g | sodium: 319mg

Mixed Vegetable Couscous

Prep time: 20 minutes | Cook time: 10 minutes |

Serves 8

1 tablespoon light olive oil	oregano
1 medium zucchini, trimmed and chopped	2 cups Israeli couscous
	3 cups vegetable broth
1 medium yellow squash, chopped	½ cup crumbled feta cheese
	¼ cup red wine vinegar
1 large red bell pepper, seeded and chopped	¼ cup extra-virgin olive oil
	½ teaspoon ground black
1 large orange bell pepper, seeded and chopped	pepper
	¼ cup chopped fresh basil
2 tablespoons chopped fresh	

1. Press the Sauté button on the Instant Pot® and heat light olive oil. Add zucchini, squash, bell peppers, and oregano, and sauté 8 minutes. Press the Cancel button. Transfer to a serving bowl and set aside to cool. 2. Add couscous and broth to the Instant Pot® and stir well. Close lid, set steam release to Sealing, press the Manual button, and set time to 2 minutes. When the timer beeps, let pressure release naturally for 5 minutes, then quick-release the remaining pressure and open lid. 3. Fluff with a fork and stir in

cooked vegetables, cheese, vinegar, extra-virgin olive oil, black pepper, and basil. Serve warm.

Per Serving:

calories: 355 | fat: 9g | protein: 14g | carbs: 61g | fiber: 7g | sodium: 588mg

Quick Shrimp Fettuccine

Prep time: 10 minutes | Cook time: 10 minutes |

Serves 4 to 6

8 ounces (227 g) fettuccine pasta	⅓ cup lemon juice
	1 tablespoon lemon zest
¼ cup extra-virgin olive oil	½ teaspoon salt
3 tablespoons garlic, minced	½ teaspoon freshly ground
1 pound (454 g) large shrimp (21-25), peeled and deveined	black pepper

1. Bring a large pot of salted water to a boil. Add the fettuccine and cook for 8 minutes. 2. In a large saucepan over medium heat, cook the olive oil and garlic for 1 minute. 3. Add the shrimp to the saucepan and cook for 3 minutes on each side. Remove the shrimp from the pan and set aside. 4. Add the lemon juice and lemon zest to the saucepan, along with the salt and pepper. 5. Reserve ½ cup of the pasta water and drain the pasta. 6. Add the pasta water to the saucepan with the lemon juice and zest and stir everything together. Add the pasta and toss together to evenly coat the pasta. Transfer the pasta to a serving dish and top with the cooked shrimp. Serve warm.

Per Serving:

calories: 615 | fat: 17g | protein: 33g | carbs: 89g | fiber: 4g | sodium: 407mg

Tahini Soup

Prep time: 5 minutes | Cook time: 4 minutes | Serves 6

2 cups orzo	½ teaspoon ground black
8 cups water	pepper
1 tablespoon olive oil	½ cup tahini
1 teaspoon salt	¼ cup lemon juice

1. Add pasta, water, oil, salt, and pepper to the Instant Pot®. Close lid, set steam release to Sealing, press the Manual button, and set time to 4 minutes. When the timer beeps, quick-release the pressure until the float valve drops, and open lid. Set aside. 2. Add tahini to a small mixing bowl and slowly add lemon juice while whisking constantly. Once lemon juice has been incorporated, take about ½ cup hot broth from the pot and slowly add to tahini mixture while whisking, until creamy smooth. 3. Pour mixture into the soup and mix well. Serve immediately.

Per Serving:

calories: 338 | fat: 13g | protein: 12g | carbs: 49g | fiber: 5g | sodium: 389mg

Creamy Spring Vegetable Linguine

Prep time: 10 minutes | Cook time: 10 minutes |
Serves 4 to 6

1 pound (454 g) linguine
5 cups water, plus extra as
needed
1 tablespoon extra-virgin olive
oil
1 teaspoon table salt
1 cup jarred whole baby
artichokes packed in water,
quartered

1 cup frozen peas, thawed
4 ounces (113 g) finely grated
Pecorino Romano (2 cups), plus
extra for serving
½ teaspoon pepper
2 teaspoons grated lemon zest
2 tablespoons chopped fresh
tarragon

1. Loosely wrap half of pasta in dish towel, then press bundle against corner of counter to break noodles into 6-inch lengths; repeat with remaining pasta. 2. Add pasta, water, oil, and salt to Instant Pot, making sure pasta is completely submerged. Lock lid in place and close pressure release valve. Select high pressure cook function and cook for 4 minutes. Turn off Instant Pot and quick-release pressure. Carefully remove lid, allowing steam to escape away from you. 3. Stir artichokes and peas into pasta, cover, and let sit until heated through, about 3 minutes. Gently stir in Pecorino and pepper until cheese is melted and fully combined, 1 to 2 minutes. Adjust consistency with extra hot water as needed. Stir in lemon zest and tarragon, and season with salt and pepper to taste. Serve, passing extra Pecorino separately.

Per Serving:

calories: 390 | fat: 8g | protein: 17g | carbs: 59g | fiber: 4g | sodium: 680mg

Penne with Broccoli and Anchovies

Prep time: 10 minutes | Cook time: 10 minutes |
Serves 4

¼ cup olive oil
1 pound (454 g) whole-wheat
pasta
½ pound (227 g) broccoli or
broccoli rabe cut into 1-inch
florets
3 to 4 anchovy fillets, packed in

olive oil
2 cloves garlic, sliced
Pinch red pepper flakes
¼ cup freshly grated, lowfat
Parmesan
Sea salt and freshly ground
pepper, to taste

1. Heat the olive oil in a deep skillet on medium heat. 2. In the meantime, prepare the pasta al dente, according to the package directions. 3. Fry the broccoli, anchovies, and garlic in the oil until the broccoli is almost tender and the garlic is slightly browned, about 5 minutes or so. 4. Rinse and drain the pasta, and add it to the broccoli mixture. Stir to coat the pasta with the garlic oil. Transfer to a serving dish, toss with red pepper flakes and Parmesan, and season.

Per Serving:

calories: 568 | fat: 17g | protein: 21g | carbs: 89g | fiber: 11g | sodium: 203mg

Pasta with Chickpeas and Cabbage

Prep time: 20 minutes | Cook time: 30 minutes |
Serves 8

1 pound (454 g) rotini pasta
8 cups water, divided
2 tablespoons olive oil, divided
1 stalk celery, thinly sliced
1 medium red onion, peeled and
sliced
1 small head savoy cabbage,
cored and shredded
⅔ cup dried chickpeas, soaked

overnight and drained
8 ounces (227 g) button
mushrooms, sliced
½ teaspoon salt
¾ teaspoon ground black
pepper
½ cup grated Pecorino Romano
cheese

1. Add pasta, 4 cups water, and 1 tablespoon oil to the Instant Pot®. Close lid, set steam release to Sealing, press the Manual button, and set time to 4 minutes. When the timer beeps, quick-release the pressure until the float valve drops, open lid, and drain pasta. Press the Cancel button. Set aside. 2. Press the Sauté button and heat remaining 1 tablespoon oil. Add celery and onion, and cook until just tender, about 4 minutes. Stir in cabbage and cook until wilted, about 2 minutes. Add chickpeas, mushrooms, and remaining 4 cups water. Stir well, then press the Cancel button. 3. Close lid, set steam release to Sealing, press the Manual button, and set time to 20 minutes. When the timer beeps, let pressure release naturally, about 25 minutes. 4. Open lid and stir well. Season with salt and pepper. Use a fork to mash some of the chickpeas to thicken sauce. Pour sauce over pasta and top with cheese. Serve hot.

Per Serving:

calories: 301 | fat: 5g | protein: 9g | carbs: 49g | fiber: 3g | sodium: 207mg

Penne with Tuna and Green Olives

Prep time: 5 minutes | Cook time: 5 minutes | Serves 4

2 tablespoons olive oil
3 garlic cloves, minced
½ cup green olives
½ teaspoon salt
¼ teaspoon freshly ground
black pepper
2 (6-ounce / 170-g) cans tuna in

olive oil (don't drain off the oil)
½ teaspoon wine vinegar
12 ounces (340 g) penne pasta,
cooked according to package
directions
2 tablespoons chopped flat-leaf
parsley

1. Heat the olive oil in a medium skillet over medium heat. Add the garlic and cook, stirring, 2 to 3 minutes, just until the garlic begins to brown. Add the olives, salt, pepper, and the tuna along with its oil. Cook, stirring, for a minute or two to heat the ingredients through. Remove from the heat and stir in the vinegar. 2. Add the cooked pasta to the skillet and toss to combine the pasta with the sauce. Serve immediately, garnished with the parsley.

Per Serving:

calories: 511 | fat: 22g | protein: 31g | carbs: 52g | fiber: 1g | sodium: 826mg

Israeli Pasta Salad

Prep time: 15 minutes | Cook time: 4 minutes | Serves 6

½ pound (227 g) whole-wheat penne pasta
4 cups water
1 tablespoon plus ¼ cup extra-virgin olive oil, divided
1 cup quartered cherry tomatoes
½ English cucumber, chopped
½ medium orange bell pepper, seeded and chopped

½ medium red onion, peeled and chopped
½ cup crumbled feta cheese
1 teaspoon fresh thyme leaves
1 teaspoon chopped fresh oregano
½ teaspoon ground black pepper
¼ cup lemon juice

1. Add pasta, water, and 1 tablespoon oil to the Instant Pot®. Close lid, set steam release to Sealing, press the Manual button, and set time to 4 minutes. 2. When the timer beeps, quick-release the pressure until the float valve drops and open lid. Drain and set aside to cool for 30 minutes. Stir in tomatoes, cucumber, bell pepper, onion, feta, thyme, oregano, black pepper, lemon juice, and remaining ¼ cup oil. Refrigerate for 2 hours.

Per Serving:
calories: 243 | fat: 16g | protein: 7g | carbs: 20g | fiber: 3g | sodium: 180mg

Mediterranean Pasta Salad

Prep time: 20 minutes | Cook time: 15 minutes | Serves 4

4 cups dried farfalle (bow-tie) pasta
1 cup canned chickpeas, drained and rinsed
⅔ cup water-packed artichoke hearts, drained and diced
½ red onion, thinly sliced
1 cup packed baby spinach
½ red bell pepper, diced

1 Roma (plum) tomato, diced
½ English cucumber, quartered lengthwise and cut into ½-inch pieces
⅓ cup extra-virgin olive oil
Juice of ½ lemon
Sea salt
Freshly ground black pepper
½ cup crumbled feta cheese

1. Fill a large saucepan three-quarters full with water and bring to a boil over high heat. Add the pasta and cook according to the package directions until al dente, about 15 minutes. Drain the pasta and run it under cold water to stop the cooking process and cool. 2. While the pasta is cooking, in a large bowl, mix the chickpeas, artichoke hearts, onion, spinach, bell pepper, tomato, and cucumber. 3. Add the pasta to the bowl with the vegetables. Add the olive oil and lemon juice and season with salt and black pepper. Mix well. 4. Top the salad with the feta and serve.

Per Serving:
calories: 702 | fat: 25g | protein: 22g | carbs: 99g | fiber: 10g | sodium: 207mg

Linguine with Avocado Pesto

Prep time: 10 minutes | Cook time: 10 minutes | Serves 4

1 pound (454 g) dried linguine
2 avocados, coarsely chopped
½ cup olive oil
½ cup packed fresh basil
½ cup pine nuts
Juice of 1 lemon
3 garlic cloves

1 tablespoon packed sun-dried tomatoes
⅛ teaspoon Italian seasoning
⅛ teaspoon red pepper flakes
Sea salt
Freshly ground black pepper

1. Fill a large stockpot three-quarters full with water and bring to a boil over high heat. Add the pasta and cook according to the package instructions until al dente, about 15 minutes. 2. While the pasta is cooking, in a food processor, combine the avocados, olive oil, basil, pine nuts, lemon juice, garlic, sun-dried tomatoes, Italian seasoning, and red pepper flakes and process until a paste forms. Taste and season with salt and black pepper. 3. When the pasta is done, drain it and return it to the pot. Add half the pesto and mix. Add more pesto as desired and serve.

Per Serving:
calories: 694 | fat: 29g | protein: 17g | carbs: 93g | fiber: 8g | sodium: 11mg

Avgolemono

Prep time: 10 minutes | Cook time: 3 minutes | Serves 6

6 cups chicken stock
½ cup orzo
1 tablespoon olive oil
12 ounces (340 g) cooked chicken breast, shredded
½ teaspoon salt
½ teaspoon ground black

pepper
¼ cup lemon juice
2 large eggs
2 tablespoons chopped fresh dill
1 tablespoon chopped fresh flat-leaf parsley

1. Add stock, orzo, and olive oil to the Instant Pot®. Close lid, set steam release to Sealing, press the Manual button, and set time to 3 minutes. When the timer beeps, quick-release the pressure until the float valve drops. Open lid and stir in chicken, salt, and pepper. 2. In a medium bowl, combine lemon juice and eggs, then slowly whisk in hot cooking liquid from the pot, ¼ cup at a time, until 1 cup of liquid has been added. Immediately add egg mixture to soup and stir well. Let stand on the Keep Warm setting, stirring occasionally, for 10 minutes. Add dill and parsley. Serve immediately.

Per Serving:
calories: 193 | fat: 5g | protein: 21g | carbs: 15g | fiber: 1g | sodium: 552mg

Puglia-Style Pasta with Broccoli Sauce

Prep time: 15 minutes | Cook time: 25 minutes | Serves 3

1 pound (454 g) fresh broccoli, washed and cut into small florets
7 ounces (198 g) uncooked rigatoni pasta
2 tablespoons extra virgin olive oil, plus 1½ tablespoons for serving
3 garlic cloves, thinly sliced
2 tablespoons pine nuts

4 canned packed-in-oil anchovies
½ teaspoon kosher salt
3 teaspoons fresh lemon juice
3 ounces (85 g) grated or shaved Parmesan cheese, divided
½ teaspoon freshly ground black pepper

1. Place the broccoli in a large pot filled with enough water to cover the broccoli. Bring the pot to a boil and cook for 12 minutes or until the stems can be easily pierced with a fork. Use a slotted spoon to transfer the broccoli to a plate, but do not discard the cooking water. Set the broccoli aside. 2. Add the pasta to the pot with the broccoli water and cook according to package instructions. 3. About 3 minutes before the pasta is ready, place a large, deep pan over medium heat and add 2 tablespoons of the olive oil. When the olive oil is shimmering, add the garlic and sauté for 1 minute, stirring continuously, until the garlic is golden, then add the pine nuts and continue sautéing for 1 more minute. 4. Stir in the anchovies, using a wooden spoon to break them into smaller pieces, then add the broccoli. Continue cooking for 1 additional minute, stirring continuously and using the spoon to break the broccoli into smaller pieces. 5. When the pasta is ready, remove the pot from the heat and drain, reserving ¼ cup of the cooking water. 6. Add the pasta and 2 tablespoons of the cooking water to the pan, stirring until all the ingredients are well combined. Cook for 1 minute, then remove the pan from the heat. 7. Promptly divide the pasta among three plates. Top each serving with a pinch of kosher salt, 1 teaspoon of the lemon juice, 1 ounce (28 g) of the Parmesan, 1½ teaspoons of the remaining olive oil, and a pinch of fresh ground pepper. Store covered in the refrigerator for up to 3 days.

Per Serving:

calories: 610 | fat: 31g | protein: 24g | carbs: 66g | fiber: 12g | sodium: 654mg

Rotini with Red Wine Marinara

Prep time: 10 minutes | Cook time: 25 minutes | Serves 6

1 pound (454 g) rotini
4 cups water
1 tablespoon olive oil
½ medium yellow onion, peeled and diced
3 cloves garlic, peeled and minced
1 (15 ounces / 425 g) can crushed tomatoes

½ cup red wine
1 teaspoon sugar
2 tablespoons chopped fresh basil
½ teaspoon salt
¼ teaspoon ground black pepper

1. Add pasta and water to the Instant Pot®. Close lid, set steam release to Sealing, press the Manual button, and set time to 4 minutes. When the timer beeps, quick-release the pressure until the float valve drops and open the lid. Press the Cancel button. Drain pasta and set aside. 2. Clean pot and return to machine. Press the Sauté button and heat oil. Add onion and cook until it begins to caramelize, about 10 minutes. Add garlic and cook 30 seconds. Add tomatoes, red wine, and sugar, and simmer for 10 minutes. Add basil, salt, pepper, and pasta. Serve immediately.

Per Serving:

calories: 320 | fat: 4g | protein: 10g | carbs: 59g | fiber: 4g | sodium: 215mg

Chapter 13 Desserts

Strawberry Ricotta Parfaits

Prep time: 10 minutes | Cook time: 0 minutes | Serves 4

2 cups ricotta cheese
¼ cup honey
2 cups sliced strawberries
1 teaspoon sugar

Toppings such as sliced almonds, fresh mint, and lemon zest (optional)

1. In a medium bowl, whisk together the ricotta and honey until well blended. Place the bowl in the refrigerator for a few minutes to firm up the mixture. 2. In a medium bowl, toss together the strawberries and sugar. 3. In each of four small glasses, layer 1 tablespoon of the ricotta mixture, then top with a layer of the strawberries and finally another layer of the ricotta. 4. Finish with your preferred toppings, if desired, then serve.

Per Serving:
calories: 311 | fat: 16g | protein: 14g | carbs: 29g | fiber: 2g | sodium: 106mg

Chocolate Pudding

Prep time: 10 minutes | Cook time: 0 minutes | Serves 4

2 ripe avocados, halved and pitted
¼ cup unsweetened cocoa powder
¼ cup heavy whipping cream, plus more if needed
2 teaspoons vanilla extract

1 to 2 teaspoons liquid stevia or monk fruit extract (optional)
½ teaspoon ground cinnamon (optional)
¼ teaspoon salt
Whipped cream, for serving (optional)

1. Using a spoon, scoop out the ripe avocado into a blender or large bowl, if using an immersion blender. Mash well with a fork. 2. Add the cocoa powder, heavy whipping cream, vanilla, sweetener (if using), cinnamon (if using), and salt. Blend well until smooth and creamy, adding additional cream, 1 tablespoon at a time, if the mixture is too thick. 3. Cover and refrigerate for at least 1 hour before serving. Serve chilled with additional whipped cream, if desired.

Per Serving:
calories: 205 | fat: 18g | protein: 3g | carbs: 12g | fiber: 9g | sodium: 156mg

Greek Yogurt Ricotta Mousse

Prep time: 1 hour 5 minutes | Cook time: 0 minutes | Serves 4

9 ounces (255 g) full-fat ricotta cheese
4½ ounces (128 g) 2% Greek yogurt

3 teaspoons fresh lemon juice
½ teaspoon pure vanilla extract
2 tablespoons granulated sugar

1. Combine all of the ingredients in a food processor. Blend until smooth, about 1 minute. 2. Divide the mousse between 4 serving glasses. Cover and transfer to the refrigerator to chill for 1 hour before serving. Store covered in the refrigerator for up to 4 days.

Per Serving:
calories: 156 | fat: 8g | protein: 10g | carbs: 10g | fiber: 0g | sodium: 65mg

Blueberry Pomegranate Granita

Prep time: 5 minutes | Cook time: 10 minutes | Serves 2

1 cup frozen wild blueberries
1 cup pomegranate or pomegranate blueberry juice

¼ cup sugar
¼ cup water

1. Combine the frozen blueberries and pomegranate juice in a saucepan and bring to a boil. Reduce the heat and simmer for 5 minutes, or until the blueberries start to break down. 2. While the juice and berries are cooking, combine the sugar and water in a small microwave-safe bowl. Microwave for 60 seconds, or until it comes to a rolling boil. Stir to make sure all of the sugar is dissolved and set the syrup aside. 3. Combine the blueberry mixture and the sugar syrup in a blender and blend for 1 minute, or until the fruit is completely puréed. 4. Pour the mixture into an 8-by-8-inch baking pan or a similar-sized bowl. The liquid should come about ½ inch up the sides. Let the mixture cool for 30 minutes, and then put it into the freezer. 5. Every 30 minutes for the next 2 hours, scrape the granita with a fork to keep it from freezing solid. 6. Serve it after 2 hours, or store it in a covered container in the freezer.

Per Serving:
calories: 214 | fat: 0g | protein: 1g | carbs: 54g | fiber: 2g | sodium: 15mg

Spiced Baked Pears with Mascarpone

Prep time: 10 minutes | Cook time: 20 minutes |

Serves 2

2 ripe pears, peeled
1 tablespoon plus 2 teaspoons honey, divided
1 teaspoon vanilla, divided
¼ teaspoon ginger
¼ teaspoon ground coriander
¼ cup minced walnuts
¼ cup mascarpone cheese
Pinch salt

1. Preheat the oven to 350°F(180°C) and set the rack to the middle position. Grease a small baking dish. 2. Cut the pears in half lengthwise. Using a spoon, scoop out the core from each piece. Place the pears with the cut side up in the baking dish. 3. Combine 1 tablespoon of honey, ½ teaspoon of vanilla, ginger, and coriander in a small bowl. Pour this mixture evenly over the pear halves. 4. Sprinkle walnuts over the pear halves. 5. Bake for 20 minutes, or until the pears are golden and you're able to pierce them easily with a knife. 6. While the pears are baking, mix the mascarpone cheese with the remaining 2 teaspoons honey, ½ teaspoon of vanilla, and a pinch of salt. Stir well to combine. 7. Divide the mascarpone among the warm pear halves and serve.

Per Serving:
calories: 307 | fat: 16g | protein: 4g | carbs: 43g | fiber: 6g | sodium: 89mg

Olive Oil Greek Yogurt Brownies

Prep time: 5 minutes | Cook time: 25 minutes |

Serves 9

¼ cup extra virgin olive oil
¾ cup granulated sugar
1 teaspoon pure vanilla extract
2 eggs
¼ cup 2% Greek yogurt
½ cup all-purpose flour
⅓ cup unsweetened cocoa powder
¼ teaspoon salt
¼ teaspoon baking powder
⅓ cup chopped walnuts

1. Preheat the oven to 350°F (180°C) and line a 9-inch square baking pan with wax paper. 2. In a small bowl, combine the olive oil and sugar. Stir until well combined, then add the vanilla extract and mix well. 3. In another small bowl, beat the eggs and then add them to the olive oil mixture. Mix well. Add the yogurt and mix again. 4. In medium bowl, combine the flour, cocoa powder, salt, and baking powder, then mix well. Add the olive oil mixture to the dry ingredients and mix well, then add the walnuts and mix again. 5. Carefully pour the brownie mixture into the prepared pan and use a spatula to smooth the top. Transfer to the oven and bake for 25 minutes. 6. Set the brownies aside to cool completely. Lift the wax paper to remove the brownies from the pan. Remove the paper and cut the brownies into 9 squares. Store at room temperature in an airtight container for up to 2 days.

Per Serving:
calories: 198 | fat: 10g | protein: 4g | carbs: 25g | fiber: 2g | sodium: 85mg

Roasted Honey-Cinnamon Apples

Prep time: 15 minutes | Cook time: 20 minutes |

Serves 2

1 teaspoon extra-virgin olive oil
4 firm apples, peeled, cored, and sliced
½ teaspoon salt
1½ teaspoons ground cinnamon, divided
2 tablespoons low-fat milk
2 tablespoons honey

1. Preheat the oven to 375°F(190°C). Grease a small casserole dish with the olive oil. 2. In a medium bowl, toss the apple slices with the salt and ½ teaspoon of the cinnamon. Spread the apples in the baking dish and bake for 20 minutes. 3. Meanwhile, in a small saucepan, heat the milk, honey, and remaining 1 teaspoon cinnamon over medium heat, stirring frequently. When it reaches a simmer, remove the pan from the heat and cover to keep warm. 4. Divide the apple slices between 2 dessert plates and pour the sauce over the apples. Serve warm.

Per Serving:
calories: 285 | fat: 3g | protein: 2g | carbs: 70g | fiber: 10g | sodium: 593mg

Cretan Cheese Pancakes

Prep time: 15 minutes | Cook time: 25 minutes |

Serves 4

2 cups all-purpose flour, plus extra for kneading
½ cup water
2 tablespoons olive oil, plus extra for frying
1 tablespoon freshly squeezed lemon juice
1 tablespoon brandy
1 teaspoon sea salt
5 tablespoons crumbled feta cheese
2 tablespoons olive oil
½ cup chopped nuts of your choice
⅛ to ¼ teaspoon ground cinnamon, for topping
1 tablespoon honey, for drizzling

1. In a large bowl, stir together the flour, water, olive oil, lemon juice, brandy, and salt until a ball of dough forms. Turn the dough out onto a lightly floured surface and knead for 10 minutes. If the dough is too wet, add a little more flour. If it's too dry, add some water. 2. Divide the dough into 5 equal pieces and roll each piece into a ball. Place a dough ball on a lightly floured surface and roll it out into a 6-inch-wide circle about ¼ inch thick. Place 1 tablespoon of the feta in the center, fold the dough over, and knead the dough and cheese together. Once the cheese is well incorporated, roll the dough out flat to the same size. Repeat with the remaining balls of dough. 3. In a large skillet, heat the oil over medium-high heat. Place one round of dough in the skillet and cook for 5 to 6 minutes on each side, until golden brown. Transfer the cooked pancake to a paper towel–lined plate to drain. Repeat to cook the remaining dough pancakes. 4. Sprinkle the pancakes evenly with the nuts and cinnamon, drizzle with the honey, and serve.

Per Serving:
calories: 480 | fat: 24g | protein: 11g | carbs: 57g | fiber: 3g | sodium: 396mg

Strawberry Panna Cotta

Prep time: 10 minutes | Cook time: 10 minutes | Serves 4

2 tablespoons warm water
2 teaspoons gelatin powder
2 cups heavy cream
1 cup sliced strawberries, plus more for garnish
1 to 2 tablespoons sugar-free

sweetener of choice (optional)
1½ teaspoons pure vanilla extract
4 to 6 fresh mint leaves, for garnish (optional)

1. Pour the warm water into a small bowl. Sprinkle the gelatin over the water and stir well to dissolve. Allow the mixture to sit for 10 minutes. 2. In a blender or a large bowl, if using an immersion blender, combine the cream, strawberries, sweetener (if using), and vanilla. Blend until the mixture is smooth and the strawberries are well puréed. 3. Transfer the mixture to a saucepan and heat over medium-low heat until just below a simmer. Remove from the heat and cool for 5 minutes. 4. Whisking constantly, add in the gelatin mixture until smooth. Divide the custard between ramekins or small glass bowls, cover and refrigerate until set, 4 to 6 hours. 5. Serve chilled, garnishing with additional sliced strawberries or mint leaves (if using).

Per Serving:
calories: 229 | fat: 22g | protein: 3g | carbs: 5g | fiber: 1g | sodium: 26mg

Lemon Coconut Cake

Prep time: 5 minutes | Cook time: 40 minutes | Serves 9

Base:
6 large eggs, separated
⅓ cup melted ghee or virgin coconut oil
1 tablespoon fresh lemon juice
Zest of 2 lemons
2 cups almond flour
½ cup coconut flour
¼ cup collagen powder
1 teaspoon baking soda
1 teaspoon vanilla powder or 1 tablespoon unsweetened vanilla extract

Optional: low-carb sweetener, to taste
Topping:
½ cup unsweetened large coconut flakes
1 cup heavy whipping cream or coconut cream
¼ cup mascarpone, more heavy whipping cream, or coconut cream
½ teaspoon vanilla powder or 1½ teaspoons unsweetened vanilla extract

1. Preheat the oven to 285°F (140°C) fan assisted or 320°F (160°C) conventional. Line a baking tray with parchment paper (or use a silicone tray). A square 8 × 8-inch (20 × 20 cm) or a rectangular tray of similar size will work best. 2. To make the base: Whisk the egg whites in a bowl until stiff peaks form. In a separate bowl, whisk the egg yolks, melted ghee, lemon juice, and lemon zest. In a third bowl, mix the almond flour, coconut flour, collagen, baking soda, vanilla and optional sweetener. 3. Add the whisked egg yolk–ghee mixture into the dry mixture and combine well. Gently fold in the egg whites, trying not to deflate them. 4. Pour into the baking tray. Bake for 35 to 40 minutes, until lightly golden on top and set inside. Remove from the oven and let cool completely before adding the topping. 5. To make the topping: Preheat the oven to 350°F (175°C) fan assisted or 380°F (195°C) conventional. Place the coconut flakes on a baking tray and bake for 2 to 3 minutes. Remove from the oven and set aside to cool. 6. Once the cake is cool, place the cream, mascarpone, and vanilla in a bowl. Whip until soft peaks form. Spread on top of the cooled cake and top with the toasted coconut flakes. 7. To store, refrigerate for up to 5 days or freeze for up to 3 months. Coconut flakes will soften in the fridge. If you want to keep them crunchy, sprinkle on top of each slice before serving.

Per Serving:
calories: 342 | fat: 31g | protein: 9g | carbs: 10g | fiber: 4g | sodium: 208mg

Minty Cantaloupe Granita

Prep time: 10 minutes | Cook time: 5 minutes | Serves 4

½ cup plus 2 tablespoons honey
¼ cup water
2 tablespoons fresh mint leaves, plus more for garnish

1 medium cantaloupe (about 4 pounds/ 1.8 kg) peeled, seeded, and cut into 1-inch chunks

1. In a small saucepan set over low heat, combine the honey and water and cook, stirring, until the honey has fully dissolved. Stir in the mint and remove from the heat. Set aside to cool. 2. In a food processor, process the cantaloupe until very smooth. Transfer to a medium bowl. Remove the mint leaves from the syrup and discard them. Pour the syrup into the cantaloupe purée and stir to mix. 3. Transfer the mixture into a 7-by-12-inch glass baking dish and freeze, stirring with a fork every 30 minutes, for 3 to 4 hours, until it is frozen, but still grainy. Serve chilled, scooped into glasses and garnished with mint leaves.

Per Serving:
calories: 174 | fat: 0g | protein: 1g | carbs: 47g | fiber: 1g | sodium: 9mg

Banana Cream Pie Parfaits

Prep time: 10 minutes | Cook time: 0 minutes | Serves 2

1 cup nonfat vanilla pudding
2 low-sugar graham crackers, crushed

1 banana, peeled and sliced
¼ cup walnuts, chopped
Honey for drizzling

1. In small parfait dishes or glasses, layer the ingredients, starting with the pudding and ending with chopped walnuts. 2. You can repeat the layers, depending on the size of the glass and your preferences. 3. Drizzle with the honey. Serve chilled.

Per Serving:
calories: 312 | fat: 11g | protein: 7g | carbs: 50g | fiber: 3g | sodium: 273mg

Chocolate Turtle Hummus

Prep time: 15 minutes | Cook time: 0 minutes |

Serves 2

For the Caramel:
2 tablespoons coconut oil
1 tablespoon maple syrup
1 tablespoon almond butter
Pinch salt
For the Hummus:
½ cup chickpeas, drained and rinsed

2 tablespoons unsweetened cocoa powder
1 tablespoon maple syrup, plus more to taste
2 tablespoons almond milk, or more as needed, to thin
Pinch salt
2 tablespoons pecans

Make the caramel 1. put the coconut oil in a small microwave-safe bowl. If it's solid, microwave it for about 15 seconds to melt it. 2. Stir in the maple syrup, almond butter, and salt. 3. Place the caramel in the refrigerator for 5 to 10 minutes to thicken. Make the hummus 1. In a food processor, combine the chickpeas, cocoa powder, maple syrup, almond milk, and pinch of salt, and process until smooth. Scrape down the sides to make sure everything is incorporated. 2. If the hummus seems too thick, add another tablespoon of almond milk. 3. Add the pecans and pulse 6 times to roughly chop them. 4. Transfer the hummus to a serving bowl and when the caramel is thickened, swirl it into the hummus. Gently fold it in, but don't mix it in completely. 5. Serve with fresh fruit or pretzels.

Per Serving:

calories: 321 | fat: 22g | protein: 7g | carbs: 30g | fiber: 6g | sodium: 100mg

Lemon Fool

Prep time: 25minutes |Cook time: 5 minutes|

Serves: 4

1 cup 2% plain Greek yogurt
1 medium lemon
¼ cup cold water
1½ teaspoons cornstarch

3½ tablespoons honey, divided
⅔ cup heavy (whipping) cream
Fresh fruit and mint leaves, for serving (optional)

1. Place a large glass bowl and the metal beaters from your electric mixer in the refrigerator to chill. Add the yogurt to a medium glass bowl, and place that bowl in the refrigerator to chill as well. 2. Using a Microplane or citrus zester, zest the lemon into a medium, microwave-safe bowl. Halve the lemon, and squeeze 1 tablespoon of lemon juice into the bowl. Add the water and cornstarch, and stir well. Whisk in 3 tablespoons of honey. Microwave the lemon mixture on high for 1 minute; stir and microwave for an additional 10 to 30 seconds, until the mixture is thick and bubbling. 3. Remove the bowl of yogurt from the refrigerator, and whisk in the warm lemon mixture. Place the yogurt back in the refrigerator. 4. Remove the large chilled bowl and the beaters from the refrigerator. Assemble your electric mixer with the chilled beaters. Pour the cream into the chilled bowl, and beat until soft peaks form—1 to 3 minutes, depending on the freshness of your cream. 5. Take the chilled yogurt mixture out of the refrigerator. Gently fold it into the whipped cream using a rubber scraper; lift and turn the

mixture to prevent the cream from deflating. Chill until serving, at least 15 minutes but no longer than 1 hour. 6. To serve, spoon the lemon fool into four glasses or dessert dishes and drizzle with the remaining ½ tablespoon of honey. Top with fresh fruit and mint, if desired.

Per Serving:

calories: 172 | fat: 8g | protein: 4g | carbs: 22g | fiber: 1g | sodium: 52mg

Grilled Fruit Kebabs with Honey Labneh

Prep time: 15 minutes | Cook time: 10 minutes |

Serves 2

⅔ cup prepared labneh, or, if making your own, ⅔ cup full-fat plain Greek yogurt
2 tablespoons honey
1 teaspoon vanilla extract

Pinch salt
3 cups fresh fruit cut into 2-inch chunks (pineapple, cantaloupe, nectarines, strawberries, plums, or mango)

1. If making your own labneh, place a colander over a bowl and line it with cheesecloth. Place the Greek yogurt in the cheesecloth and wrap it up. Put the bowl in the refrigerator and let sit for at least 12 to 24 hours, until it's thick like soft cheese. 2. Mix honey, vanilla, and salt into labneh. Stir well to combine and set it aside. 3. Heat the grill to medium (about 300°F/ 150ºC) and oil the grill grate. Alternatively, you can cook these on the stovetop in a heavy grill pan (cast iron works well). 4. Thread the fruit onto skewers and grill for 4 minutes on each side, or until fruit is softened and has grill marks on each side. 5. Serve the fruit with labneh to dip.

Per Serving:

calories: 292 | fat: 6g | protein: 5g | carbs: 60g | fiber: 4g | sodium: 131mg

Grilled Peaches with Greek Yogurt

Prep time: 5 minutes | Cook time: 30 minutes |

Serves 4

4 ripe peaches, halved and pitted
2 tablespoons olive oil
1 teaspoon ground cinnamon,

plus extra for topping
2 cups plain full-fat Greek yogurt
¼ cup honey, for drizzling

1. Preheat the oven to 350°F (180ºC). 2. Place the peaches in a baking dish, cut-side up. 3. In a small bowl, stir together the olive oil and cinnamon, then brush the mixture over the peach halves. 4. Bake the peaches for about 30 minutes, until they are soft. 5. Top the peaches with the yogurt and drizzle them with the honey, then serve.

Per Serving:

calories: 259 | fat: 11g | protein: 6g | carbs: 38g | fiber: 3g | sodium: 57mg

Dried Fruit Compote

Prep time: 15 minutes | Cook time: 8 minutes |

Serves 6

8 ounces (227 g) dried apricots, quartered	1 cup golden raisins
8 ounces (227 g) dried peaches, quartered	1½ cups orange juice
	1 cinnamon stick
	4 whole cloves

1. Place all ingredients in the Instant Pot®. Stir to combine. Close lid, set steam release to Sealing, press the Manual button, and set time to 3 minutes. When the timer beeps, let pressure release naturally, about 20 minutes. Press the Cancel button and open lid. 2. Remove and discard cinnamon stick and cloves. Press the Sauté button and simmer for 5–6 minutes. Serve warm or allow to cool, and then cover and refrigerate for up to a week.

Per Serving:

calories: 258 | fat: 0g | protein: 4g | carbs: 63g | fiber: 5g | sodium: 7mg

Avocado-Orange Fruit Salad

Prep time: 10 minutes | Cook time: 0 minutes |

Serves 5 to 6

2 large Gala apples, chopped	1 tablespoon extra-virgin olive oil
2 oranges, segmented and chopped	½ teaspoon grated orange zest
⅓ cup sliced almonds	1 large avocado, semi-ripened, medium diced
½ cup honey	

1. In a large bowl, combine the apples, oranges, and almonds. Mix gently. 2. In a small bowl, whisk the honey, oil, and orange zest. Set aside. 3. Drizzle the orange zest mix over the fruit salad and toss. Add the avocado and toss gently one more time.

Per Serving:

calories: 296 | fat: 12g | protein: 3g | carbs: 51g | fiber: 7g | sodium: 4mg

Mediterranean Orange Yogurt Cake

Prep time: 10 minutes | Cook time: 3 to 5 hours |

Serves 4 to 6

Nonstick cooking spray	½ cup mild-flavored, extra-virgin olive oil
¾ cup all-purpose flour	
¾ cup whole-wheat flour	3 large eggs
2 teaspoons baking powder	2 teaspoons vanilla extract
¼ teaspoon salt	Grated zest of 1 orange
1 cup coconut palm sugar	Juice of 1 orange
½ cup plain Greek yogurt	

1. Generously coat a slow cooker with cooking spray, or line the bottom and sides with parchment paper or aluminum foil. 2. In a large bowl, whisk together the all-purpose and whole-wheat flours, baking powder, and salt. 3. In another large bowl, whisk together the sugar, yogurt, olive oil, eggs, vanilla, orange zest, and orange juice until smooth. 4. Add the dry ingredients to the wet ingredients and mix together until well-blended. Pour the batter into the prepared slow cooker. 5. Cover the cooker and cook for 3 to 5 hours on Low heat, or until the middle has set and a knife inserted into it comes out clean.

Per Serving:

calories: 544 | fat: 33g | protein: 11g | carbs: 53g | fiber: 4g | sodium: 482mg

Creamy Rice Pudding

Prep time: 5 minutes | Cook time: 45 minutes |

Serves 6

1¼ cups long-grain rice	1 tablespoon rose water or orange blossom water
5 cups whole milk	
1 cup sugar	1 teaspoon cinnamon

1. Rinse the rice under cold water for 30 seconds. 2. Put the rice, milk, and sugar in a large pot. Bring to a gentle boil while continually stirring. 3. Turn the heat down to low and let simmer for 40 to 45 minutes, stirring every 3 to 4 minutes so that the rice does not stick to the bottom of the pot. 4. Add the rose water at the end and simmer for 5 minutes. 5. Divide the pudding into 6 bowls. Sprinkle the top with cinnamon. Cool for at least 1 hour before serving. Store in the fridge.

Per Serving:

calories: 394 | fat: 7g | protein: 9g | carbs: 75g | fiber: 1g | sodium: 102mg

Grilled Pineapple Dessert

Prep time: 5 minutes | Cook time: 12 minutes |

Serves 4

Oil for misting or cooking spray	2 tablespoons slivered almonds, toasted
4½-inch-thick slices fresh pineapple, core removed	Vanilla frozen yogurt or coconut sorbet
1 tablespoon honey	
¼ teaspoon brandy	

1. Spray both sides of pineapple slices with oil or cooking spray. Place into air fryer basket. 2. Air fry at 390°F (199°C) for 6 minutes. Turn slices over and cook for an additional 6 minutes. 3. Mix together the honey and brandy. 4. Remove cooked pineapple slices from air fryer, sprinkle with toasted almonds, and drizzle with honey mixture. 5. Serve with a scoop of frozen yogurt or sorbet on the side.

Per Serving:

calories: 65 | fat: 2g | protein: 1g | carbs: 11g | fiber: 1g | sodium: 1mg

Ricotta Cheesecake

Prep time: 2 minutes | Cook time: 45 to 50 minutes | Serves 12

2 cups skim or fat-free ricotta cheese (one 15 ounces / 425 g container)
1¼ cups sugar

1 teaspoon vanilla extract
6 eggs
Zest of 1 orange

1. Preheat the oven to 375ºF (190ºC). Grease an 8-inch square baking pan with butter or cooking spray. 2. In a medium bowl, stir together the ricotta and sugar. Add the eggs one at a time until well incorporated. Stir in the vanilla and orange zest. 3. Pour the batter into the prepared pan. Bake for 45 to 50 minutes, until set. Let cool in the pan for 20 minutes. Serve warm.

Per Serving:

calories: 160 | fat: 5g | protein: 12g | carbs: 15g | fiber: 0g | sodium: 388mg

Cinnamon-Stewed Dried Plums with Greek Yogurt

Prep time: 5 minutes | Cook time: 3 minutes | Serves 6

3 cups dried plums
2 cups water
2 tablespoons sugar

2 cinnamon sticks
3 cups low-fat plain Greek yogurt

1. Add dried plums, water, sugar, and cinnamon to the Instant Pot®. Close lid, set steam release to Sealing, press the Manual button, and set time to 3 minutes. 2. When the timer beeps, quick-release the pressure until the float valve drops. Press the Cancel button and open lid. Remove and discard cinnamon sticks. Serve warm over Greek yogurt.

Per Serving:

calories: 301 | fat: 2g | protein: 14g | carbs: 61g | fiber: 4g | sodium: 50mg

Fresh Figs with Chocolate Sauce

Prep time: 5 minutes | Cook time: 0 minutes | Serves 4

¼ cup honey
2 tablespoons cocoa powder

8 fresh figs

1. Combine the honey and cocoa powder in a small bowl, and mix well to form a syrup. 2. Cut the figs in half and place cut side up. Drizzle with the syrup and serve.

Per Serving:

calories: 112 | fat: 1g | protein: 1g | carbs: 30g | fiber: 3g | sodium: 3mg

Honey-Vanilla Apple Pie with Olive Oil Crust

Prep time: 10 minutes | Cook time: 45 minutes | Serves 8

For the crust:
¼ cup olive oil
1½ cups whole-wheat flour
½ teaspoon sea salt
2 tablespoons ice water
For the filling:
4 large apples of your choice,

peeled, cored, and sliced
Juice of 1 lemon
1 tablespoon pure vanilla extract
1 tablespoon honey
½ teaspoon sea salt
Olive oil

Make the crust: 1. Put the olive oil, flour, and sea salt in a food processor and process until dough forms. 2. Slowly add the water and pulse until you have a stiff dough. 3. Form the dough into 2 equal-sized balls, wrap in plastic wrap, and put in the refrigerator while you make the filling. Make the filling: 1. Combine the apples, lemon juice, vanilla, honey, and sea salt in a large bowl. 2. Stir and allow to sit for at least 10 minutes. Preheat oven to 400ºF (205ºC). 3. Roll 1 crust out on a lightly floured surface. Transfer to a 9-inch pie plate and top with filling. 4. Roll the other ball of dough out and put on top of the pie. Cut a few slices in the top to vent the pie, and lightly brush the top of the pie with olive oil. 5. Bake for 45 minutes, or until top is browned and apples are bubbly. 6. Allow to cool completely before slicing and serving with your favorite frozen yogurt.

Per Serving:

calories: 208 | fat: 8g | protein: 3g | carbs: 34g | fiber: 5g | sodium: 293mg

Honey Ricotta with Espresso and Chocolate Chips

Prep time: 5 minutes | Cook time: 0 minutes | Serves 2

8 ounces (227 g) ricotta cheese
2 tablespoons honey
2 tablespoons espresso, chilled

or room temperature
1 teaspoon dark chocolate chips or chocolate shavings

1. In a medium bowl, whip together the ricotta cheese and honey until light and smooth, 4 to 5 minutes. 2. Spoon the ricotta cheese-honey mixture evenly into 2 dessert bowls. Drizzle 1 tablespoon espresso into each dish and sprinkle with chocolate chips or shavings.

Per Serving:

calories: 235 | fat: 10g | protein: 13g | carbs: 25g | fiber: 0g | sodium: 115mg

S'mores

Prep time: 5 minutes | Cook time: 30 seconds |
Makes 8 s'mores

Oil, for spraying
8 graham cracker squares
2 (1½-ounce / 43-g) chocolate

bars
4 large marshmallows

1. Line the air fryer basket with parchment and spray lightly with oil. 2. Place 4 graham cracker squares in the prepared basket. 3. Break the chocolate bars in half and place 1 piece on top of each graham cracker. Top with 1 marshmallow. 4. Air fry at 370°F (188°C) for 30 seconds, or until the marshmallows are puffed and golden brown and slightly melted. 5. Top with the remaining graham cracker squares and serve.

Per Serving:

calories: 154 | fat: 7g | protein: 2g | carbs: 22g | fiber: 2g | sodium: 75mg

Baklava and Honey

Prep time: 40 minutes | Cook time: 1 hour | Serves 6
to 8

2 cups very finely chopped
walnuts or pecans
1 teaspoon cinnamon
1 cup (2 sticks) of unsalted

butter, melted
1 (16-ounce / 454-g) package
phyllo dough, thawed
1 (12-ounce / 340-g) jar honey

1. Preheat the oven to 350°F(180°C). 2. In a bowl, combine the chopped nuts and cinnamon. 3. Using a brush, butter the sides and bottom of a 9-by-13-inch inch baking dish. 4. Remove the phyllo dough from the package and cut it to the size of the baking dish using a sharp knife. 5. Place one sheet of phyllo dough on the bottom of the dish, brush with butter, and repeat until you have 8 layers. 6. Sprinkle ⅓ cup of the nut mixture over the phyllo layers. Top with a sheet of phyllo dough, butter that sheet, and repeat until you have 4 sheets of buttered phyllo dough. 7. Sprinkle ⅓ cup of the nut mixture for another layer of nuts. Repeat the layering of nuts and 4 sheets of buttered phyllo until all the nut mixture is gone. The last layer should be 8 buttered sheets of phyllo. 8. Before you bake, cut the baklava into desired shapes; traditionally this is diamonds, triangles, or squares. 9. Bake the baklava for 1 hour or until the top layer is golden brown. 10. While the baklava is baking, heat the honey in a pan just until it is warm and easy to pour. 11. Once the baklava is done baking, immediately pour the honey evenly over the baklava and let it absorb it, about 20 minutes. Serve warm or at room temperature.

Per Serving:

calories: 1235 | fat: 89g | protein: 18g | carbs: 109g | fiber: 7g | sodium: 588mg

Steamed Dessert Bread

Prep time: 5 minutes | Cook time: 1 hour | Serves 8

½ cup all-purpose flour
½ cup stone-ground cornmeal
½ cup whole-wheat flour
½ teaspoon baking powder
¼ teaspoon salt

¼ teaspoon baking soda
½ cup maple syrup
½ cup buttermilk
1 large egg
1 cup water

1. Grease the inside of a 6-cup heatproof pudding mold or baking pan. 2. Add flour, cornmeal, whole-wheat flour, baking powder, salt, and baking soda to a medium mixing bowl. Stir to combine. Add maple syrup, buttermilk, and egg to another mixing bowl or measuring cup. Whisk to mix and then pour into the flour mixture. Mix until a thick batter is formed. 3. Pour enough batter into prepared baking pan to fill it three-quarters full. 4. Butter one side of a piece of heavy-duty aluminum foil large enough to cover the top of the baking dish. Place the foil butter side down over the pan and crimp the edges to seal. 5. Add water to the Instant Pot® and place the rack inside. Fold a long piece of aluminum foil in half lengthwise. Lay foil over rack to form a sling. Place pan on rack so it rests on the sling. 6. Close lid, set steam release to Sealing, press the Manual button, set time to 1 hour, and press the Adjust button and set pressure to Low. When the timer beeps, let pressure release naturally, about 25 minutes. 7. Open lid, lift pan from Instant Pot® using the sling, and place on a cooling rack. Remove foil. Test bread with a toothpick. If the toothpick comes out wet, place the foil over the pan and return it to the Instant Pot® to cook for 10 additional minutes. If the bread is done, use a knife to loosen it and invert it onto the cooling rack. Serve warm.

Per Serving:

calories: 175 | fat: 1g | protein: 4g | carbs: 37g | fiber: 2g | sodium: 102mg

Chapter 14 Snacks and Appetizers

Savory Lentil Dip

Prep time: 10 minutes | Cook time: 32 minutes | Serves 16

2 tablespoons olive oil
½ medium yellow onion, peeled and diced
3 cloves garlic, peeled and minced
2 cups dried red lentils, rinsed and drained

4 cups water
1 teaspoon salt
¼ teaspoon ground black pepper
2 tablespoons minced fresh flat-leaf parsley

1. Press the Sauté button on the Instant Pot® and heat oil. Add onion and cook 2–3 minutes, or until translucent. Add garlic and cook until fragrant, about 30 seconds. Add lentils, water, and salt to pot, and stir to combine. Close lid, set steam release to Sealing, press the Bean button, and cook for the default time of 30 minutes. 2. When the timer beeps, let pressure release naturally for 10 minutes. Quick-release any remaining pressure until the float valve drops, then open lid. Transfer lentil mixture to a food processor and blend until smooth. Season with pepper and garnish with parsley. Serve warm.

Per Serving:
calories: 76 | fat: 2g | protein: 5g | carbs: 11g | fiber: 2g | sodium: 145mg

Spiced Maple Nuts

Prep time: 5 minutes | Cook time:10 minutes | Makes about 2 cups

2 cups raw walnuts or pecans (or a mix of nuts)
1 teaspoon extra-virgin olive oil
1 teaspoon ground sumac

½ teaspoon pure maple syrup
¼ teaspoon kosher salt
¼ teaspoon ground ginger
2 to 4 rosemary sprigs

1. Preheat the oven to 350ºF (180ºC). Line a baking sheet with parchment paper or foil. 2. In a large bowl, combine the nuts, olive oil, sumac, maple syrup, salt, and ginger; mix together. Spread in a single layer on the prepared baking sheet. Add the rosemary. Roast for 8 to 10 minutes, or until golden and fragrant. 3. Remove the rosemary leaves from the stems and place in a serving bowl. Add the nuts and toss to combine before serving.

Per Serving:
¼ cup: calories: 175 | fat: 18g | protein: 3g | carbs: 4g | fiber: 2g | sodium: 35mg

Garlic-Mint Yogurt Dip

Prep time: 5 minutes | Cook time: 0 minutes | Serves 4 to 6

1 cup plain Greek yogurt
Zest and juice of 1 lemon
1 garlic clove, minced
3 tablespoons chopped fresh mint

¼ teaspoon Aleppo pepper or cayenne pepper
¼ teaspoon salt
Freshly ground black pepper (optional)

1. In a small bowl, stir together all the ingredients until well combined. Season with black pepper, if desired. Refrigerate until ready to serve.

Per Serving:
1 cup: calories: 52 | fat: 2g | protein: 2g | carbs: 7g | fiber: 0g | sodium: 139mg

Charred Eggplant Dip with Feta and Mint

Prep time: 5 minutes | Cook time: 20 minutes | Makes about 1½ cups

1 medium eggplant (about 1 pound / 454 g)
2 tablespoons lemon juice
¼ cup olive oil
½ cup crumbled feta cheese
½ cup finely diced red onion

3 tablespoons chopped fresh mint leaves
1 tablespoon finely chopped flat-leaf parsley
¼ teaspoon cayenne pepper
¾ teaspoon salt

1. Preheat the broiler to high. 2. Line a baking sheet with aluminum foil. 3. Put the whole eggplant on the prepared baking sheet and poke it in several places with the tines of a fork. Cook under the broiler, turning about every 5 minutes, until the eggplant is charred on all sides and very soft in the center, about 15 to 20 minutes total. Remove from the oven and set aside until cool enough to handle. 4. When the eggplant is cool enough to handle, cut it in half lengthwise and scoop out the flesh, discarding the charred skin. 5. Add the lemon juice and olive oil and mash to a chunky purée with a fork. Add the cheese, onion, mint, parsley, cayenne, and salt. 6. Serve at room temperature.

Per Serving:
½ cup: calories: 71 | fat: 6g | protein: 2g | carbs: 3g | fiber: 2g | sodium: 237mg

Steamed Artichokes with Herbs and Olive Oil

Prep time: 10 minutes | Cook time: 10 minutes | Serves 6

3 medium artichokes with stems cut off
1 medium lemon, halved
1 cup water
¼ cup lemon juice
⅓ cup extra-virgin olive oil
1 clove garlic, peeled and minced

¼ teaspoon salt
1 teaspoon chopped fresh oregano
1 teaspoon chopped fresh rosemary
1 teaspoon chopped fresh flat-leaf parsley
1 teaspoon fresh thyme leaves

1. Run artichokes under running water, making sure water runs between leaves to flush out any debris. Slice off top ⅓ of artichoke and pull away any tough outer leaves. Rub all cut surfaces with lemon. 2. Add water and lemon juice to the Instant Pot®, then add rack. Place artichokes upside down on rack. Close lid, set steam release to Sealing, press the Manual button, and set time to 10 minutes. When the timer beeps, let pressure release naturally, about 20 minutes. 3. Press the Cancel button and open lid. Remove artichokes, transfer to a cutting board, and slice in half. Place halves on a serving platter. 4. In a small bowl, combine oil, garlic, salt, oregano, rosemary, parsley, and thyme. Drizzle half of mixture over artichokes, then serve remaining mixture in a small bowl for dipping. Serve warm.

Per Serving:

calories: 137 | fat: 13g | protein: 2g | carbs: 7g | fiber: 4g | sodium: 158mg

Baked Eggplant Baba Ganoush

Prep time: 10 minutes | Cook time: 1 hour | Makes about 4 cups

2 pounds (907 g, about 2 medium to large) eggplant
3 tablespoons tahini
Zest of 1 lemon
2 tablespoons lemon juice
¾ teaspoon kosher salt

½ teaspoon ground sumac, plus more for sprinkling (optional)
⅓ cup fresh parsley, chopped
1 tablespoon extra-virgin olive oil

1. Preheat the oven to 350ºF (180ºC). Place the eggplants directly on the rack and bake for 60 minutes, or until the skin is wrinkly. 2. In a food processor add the tahini, lemon zest, lemon juice, salt, and sumac. Carefully cut open the baked eggplant and scoop the flesh into the food processor. Process until the ingredients are well blended. 3. Place in a serving dish and mix in the parsley. Drizzle with the olive oil and sprinkle with sumac, if desired.

Per Serving:

calories: 50 | fat: 16g | protein: 4g | carbs: 2g | fiber: 1g | sodium: 110mg

Stuffed Fried Mushrooms

Prep time: 20 minutes | Cook time: 10 to 11 minutes | Serves 10

½ cup panko bread crumbs
½ teaspoon freshly ground black pepper
½ teaspoon onion powder
½ teaspoon cayenne pepper
1 (8-ounce / 227-g) package

cream cheese, at room temperature
20 cremini or button mushrooms, stemmed
1 to 2 tablespoons oil

1. In a medium bowl, whisk the bread crumbs, black pepper, onion powder, and cayenne until blended. 2. Add the cream cheese and mix until well blended. Fill each mushroom top with 1 teaspoon of the cream cheese mixture 3. Preheat the air fryer to 360ºF (182ºC). Line the air fryer basket with a piece of parchment paper. 4. Place the mushrooms on the parchment and spritz with oil. 5. Cook for 5 minutes. Shake the basket and cook for 5 to 6 minutes more until the filling is firm and the mushrooms are soft.

Per Serving:

calories: 120 | fat: 9g | protein: 3g | carbs: 7g | fiber: 1g | sodium: 125mg

Lebanese Muhammara

Prep time: 15 minutes | Cook time: 15 minutes | Serves 6

2 large red bell peppers
¼ cup plus 2 tablespoons extra-virgin olive oil
1 cup walnut halves
1 tablespoon agave nectar or honey
1 teaspoon fresh lemon juice

1 teaspoon ground cumin
1 teaspoon kosher salt
1 teaspoon red pepper flakes
Raw vegetables (such as cucumber, carrots, zucchini slices, or cauliflower) or toasted pita chips, for serving

1. Drizzle the peppers with 2 tablespoons of the olive oil and place in the air fryer basket. Set the air fryer to 400ºF (204ºC) for 10 minutes. 2. Add the walnuts to the basket, arranging them around the peppers. Set the air fryer to 400ºF (204ºC) for 5 minutes. 3. Remove the peppers, seal in a resealable plastic bag, and let rest for 5 to 10 minutes. Transfer the walnuts to a plate and set aside to cool. 4. Place the softened peppers, walnuts, agave, lemon juice, cumin, salt, and ½ teaspoon of the pepper flakes in a food processor and purée until smooth. 5. Transfer the dip to a serving bowl and make an indentation in the middle. Pour the remaining ¼ cup olive oil into the indentation. Garnish the dip with the remaining ½ teaspoon pepper flakes. 6. Serve with vegetables or toasted pita chips.

Per Serving:

calories: 219 | fat: 20g | protein: 3g | carbs: 9g | fiber: 2g | sodium: 391mg

Turmeric-Spiced Crunchy Chickpeas

Prep time: 15 minutes | Cook time: 30 minutes |

Serves 4

2 (15 ounces / 425 g) cans organic chickpeas, drained and rinsed	2 teaspoons turmeric
	½ teaspoon dried oregano
	½ teaspoon salt
3 tablespoons extra-virgin olive oil	¼ teaspoon ground ginger
	⅛ teaspoon ground white pepper (optional)
2 teaspoons Turkish or smoked paprika	

1. Preheat the oven to 400°F(205°C). Line a baking sheet with parchment paper and set aside. 2. Completely dry the chickpeas. Lay the chickpeas out on a baking sheet, roll them around with paper towels, and allow them to air-dry. I usually let them dry for at least 2½ hours, but can also be left to dry overnight. 3. In a medium bowl, combine the olive oil, paprika, turmeric, oregano, salt, ginger, and white pepper (if using). 4. Add the dry chickpeas to the bowl and toss to combine. 5. Put the chickpeas on the prepared baking sheet and cook for 30 minutes, or until the chickpeas turn golden brown. At 15 minutes, move the chickpeas around on the baking sheet to avoid burning. Check every 10 minutes in case the chickpeas begin to crisp up before the full cooking time has elapsed. 6. Remove from the oven and set them aside to cool.

Per Serving:

½ cup: calories: 308 | fat: 13g | protein: 11g | carbs: 40g | fiber: 11g | sodium: 292mg

Baked Italian Spinach and Ricotta Balls

Prep time: 15 minutes | Cook time: 2 minutes |

Serves 4

1½ tablespoons extra virgin olive oil	2 tablespoons chopped fresh basil
1 garlic clove	¾ teaspoon salt, divided
9 ounces (255 g) fresh baby leaf spinach, washed	¼ teaspoon plus a pinch of freshly ground black pepper, divided
3 spring onions (white parts only), thinly sliced	4½ tablespoons plus ⅓ cup unseasoned breadcrumbs, divided
9 ounces (255 g) ricotta, drained	1 egg
1¾ ounces (50 g) grated Parmesan cheese	

1. Preheat the oven to 400°F (205°C). Line a large baking pan with parchment paper. 2. Add the olive oil and garlic clove to a large pan over medium heat. When the oil begins to shimmer, add the spinach and sauté, tossing continuously, until the spinach starts to wilt, then add the spring onions. Continue tossing and sautéing until most of the liquid has evaporated, about 6 minutes, then transfer the spinach and onion mixture to a colander to drain and cool for 10 minutes. 3. When the spinach mixture has cooled, discard the garlic clove and squeeze the spinach to remove as much of the liquid as possible. Transfer the spinach mixture to a cutting board and finely chop. 4. Combine the ricotta, Parmesan, basil, ½ teaspoon of the salt, and ¼ teaspoon of the black pepper in a large bowl. Use a fork to mash the ingredients together, then add the spinach and continue mixing until the ingredients are combined. Add 4½ tablespoons of the breadcrumbs and mix until all ingredients are well combined. 5. In a small bowl, whisk the egg with the remaining ¼ teaspoon salt and a pinch of the black pepper. Place the remaining ⅓ cup of breadcrumbs on a small plate. Scoop out 1 tablespoon of the spinach mixture and roll it into a smooth ball, then dip it in the egg mixture and then roll it in the breadcrumbs. Place the ball on the prepared baking pan and continue the process with the remaining spinach mixture. 6. Bake for 16–20 minutes or until the balls turn a light golden brown. Remove the balls from the oven and serve promptly. Store covered in the refrigerator for up to 1 day. (Reheat before serving.)

Per Serving:

calories: 311 | fat: 19g | protein: 18g | carbs: 18g | fiber: 3g | sodium: 684mg

Loaded Vegetable Pita Pizzas with Tahini Sauce

Prep time: 5 minutes | Cook time: 12 minutes |

Serves 2

2 (6-inch) pita breads	2 teaspoons extra virgin olive oil
4 canned artichoke hearts, chopped	Pinch of kosher salt
¼ cup chopped tomato (any variety)	Juice of 1 lemon
	Tahini Sauce:
¼ cup chopped onion (any variety)	2 tablespoons tahini
	2 tablespoons fresh lemon juice
4 Kalamata olives, pitted and sliced	1 tablespoon water
	1 garlic clove, minced
4 green olives, pitted and sliced	Pinch of freshly ground black pepper
2 teaspoons pine nuts	

1. Preheat the oven to 400°F (205°C) and line a large baking sheet with wax paper. 2. Make the tahini sauce by combining the tahini and lemon juice in a small bowl. While stirring rapidly, begin adding the water, garlic, and black pepper. Continue stirring rapidly until the ingredients are well combined and smooth. 3. Place the pita breads on the prepared baking sheet. Spread about 1 tablespoon of the tahini sauce over the top of each pita and then top each pita with the chopped artichoke hearts, 2 tablespoons of the tomatoes, 2 tablespoons of the onions, half of the sliced Kalamata olives, half of the green olives, and 1 teaspoon of the pine nuts. 4. Transfer the pizzas to the oven and bake for 12 minutes or until the edges of the pita breads turn golden and crunchy. 5. Drizzle 1 teaspoon of the olive oil over each pizza, then sprinkle a pinch of kosher salt over the top followed by a squeeze of lemon. Cut the pizzas into quarters. Store covered in the refrigerator for up to 2 days.

Per Serving:

calories: 381 | fat: 17g | protein: 15g | carbs: 52g | fiber: 19g | sodium: 553mg

Cream Cheese Wontons

Prep time: 15 minutes | Cook time: 6 minutes |

Makes 20 wontons

Oil, for spraying
20 wonton wrappers

4 ounces (113 g) cream cheese

1. Line the air fryer basket with parchment and spray lightly with oil. 2. Pour some water in a small bowl. 3. Lay out a wonton wrapper and place 1 teaspoon of cream cheese in the center. 4. Dip your finger in the water and moisten the edge of the wonton wrapper. Fold over the opposite corners to make a triangle and press the edges together. 5. Pinch the corners of the triangle together to form a classic wonton shape. Place the wonton in the prepared basket. Repeat with the remaining wrappers and cream cheese. You may need to work in batches, depending on the size of your air fryer. 6. Air fry at 400°F (204°C) for 6 minutes, or until golden brown around the edges.

Per Serving:

1 wonton: calories: 43 | fat: 2g | protein: 1g | carbs: 5g | fiber: 0g | sodium: 66mg

Asiago Shishito Peppers

Prep time: 5 minutes | Cook time: 10 minutes |

Serves 4

Oil, for spraying
6 ounces (170 g) shishito peppers
1 tablespoon olive oil

½ teaspoon salt
½ teaspoon lemon pepper
⅓ cup grated Asiago cheese, divided

1. Line the air fryer basket with parchment and spray lightly with oil. 2. Rinse the shishitos and pat dry with paper towels. 3. In a large bowl, mix together the shishitos, olive oil, salt, and lemon pepper. Place the shishitos in the prepared basket. 4. Roast at 350°F (177°C) for 10 minutes, or until blistered but not burned. 5. Sprinkle with half of the cheese and cook for 1 more minute. 6. Transfer to a serving plate. Immediately sprinkle with the remaining cheese and serve.

Per Serving:

calories: 81 | fat: 6g | protein: 3g | carbs: 5g | fiber: 1g | sodium: 443mg

Smoky Baba Ghanoush

Prep time: 50 minutes | Cook time: 40 minutes |

Serves 6

2 large eggplants, washed
¼ cup lemon juice
1 teaspoon garlic, minced
1 teaspoon salt

½ cup tahini paste
3 tablespoons extra-virgin olive oil

1. Grill the whole eggplants over a low flame using a gas stovetop or grill. Rotate the eggplant every 5 minutes to make sure that all sides are cooked evenly. Continue to do this for 40 minutes. 2. Remove the eggplants from the stove or grill and put them onto a plate or into a bowl; cover with plastic wrap. Let sit for 5 to 10 minutes. 3. Using your fingers, peel away and discard the charred skin of the eggplants. Cut off the stem. 4. Put the eggplants into a food processor fitted with a chopping blade. Add the lemon juice, garlic, salt, and tahini paste, and pulse the mixture 5 to 7 times. 5. Pour the eggplant mixture onto a serving plate. Drizzle with the olive oil. Serve chilled or at room temperature.

Per Serving:

calories: 230 | fat: 18g | protein: 5g | carbs: 16g | fiber: 7g | sodium: 416mg

Roasted Chickpeas

Prep time: 5 minutes | Cook time: 15 minutes |

Makes about 1 cup

1 (15 ounces / 425 g) can chickpeas, drained
2 teaspoons curry powder

¼ teaspoon salt
1 tablespoon olive oil

1. Drain chickpeas thoroughly and spread in a single layer on paper towels. Cover with another paper towel and press gently to remove extra moisture. Don't press too hard or you'll crush the chickpeas. 2. Mix curry powder and salt together. 3. Place chickpeas in a medium bowl and sprinkle with seasonings. Stir well to coat. 4. Add olive oil and stir again to distribute oil. 5. Air fry at 390°F (199°C) for 15 minutes, stopping to shake basket about halfway through cooking time. 6. Cool completely and store in airtight container.

Per Serving:

¼ cup: calories: 181 | fat: 6g | protein: 8g | carbs: 24g | fiber: 7g | sodium: 407mg

Roasted Mushrooms with Garlic

Prep time: 3 minutes | Cook time: 22 to 27 minutes |

Serves 4

16 garlic cloves, peeled
2 teaspoons olive oil, divided
16 button mushrooms
½ teaspoon dried marjoram

⅛ teaspoon freshly ground black pepper
1 tablespoon white wine or low-sodium vegetable broth

1. In a baking pan, mix the garlic with 1 teaspoon of olive oil. Roast in the air fryer at 350°F (177°C) for 12 minutes. 2. Add the mushrooms, marjoram, and pepper. Stir to coat. Drizzle with the remaining 1 teaspoon of olive oil and the white wine. 3. Return to the air fryer and roast for 10 to 15 minutes more, or until the mushrooms and garlic cloves are tender. Serve.

Per Serving:

calories: 57 | fat: 3g | protein: 3g | carbs: 7g | fiber: 1g | sodium: 6mg

Black Bean Corn Dip

Prep time: 10 minutes | Cook time: 10 minutes |
Serves 4

½ (15 ounces / 425 g) can black beans, drained and rinsed
½ (15 ounces / 425 g) can corn, drained and rinsed
¼ cup chunky salsa
2 ounces (57 g) reduced-fat cream cheese, softened

¼ cup shredded reduced-fat Cheddar cheese
½ teaspoon ground cumin
½ teaspoon paprika
Salt and freshly ground black pepper, to taste

1. Preheat the air fryer to 325ºF (163ºC). 2. In a medium bowl, mix together the black beans, corn, salsa, cream cheese, Cheddar cheese, cumin, and paprika. Season with salt and pepper and stir until well combined. 3. Spoon the mixture into a baking dish. 4. Place baking dish in the air fryer basket and bake until heated through, about 10 minutes. 5. Serve hot.

Per Serving:

calories: 119 | fat: 2g | protein: 8g | carbs: 19g | fiber: 6g | sodium: 469mg

Goat'S Cheese & Hazelnut Dip

Prep time: 10 minutes | Cook time: 0 minutes |
Serves 8

2 heads yellow chicory or endive
Enough ice water to cover the leaves
Pinch of salt
Dip:
12 ounces (340 g) soft goat's cheese
3 tablespoons extra-virgin olive oil
1 tablespoon fresh lemon juice
1 teaspoon lemon zest (about ½ lemon)

1 clove garlic, minced
Freshly ground black pepper, to taste
Salt, if needed, to taste
Topping:
2 tablespoons chopped fresh chives
¼ cup crushed hazelnuts, pecans, or walnuts
1 tablespoon extra-virgin olive oil
Chile flakes or black pepper, to taste

1. Cut off the bottom of the chicory and trim the leaves to get rid of any that are limp or brown. Place the leaves in salted ice water for 10 minutes. This will help the chicory leaves to become crisp. Drain and leave in the strainer. 2. To make the dip: Place the dip ingredients in a bowl and use a fork or spatula to mix until smooth and creamy. 3. Stir in the chives. Transfer to a serving bowl and top with the crushed hazelnuts, olive oil, and chile flakes. Serve with the crisp chicory leaves. Store in a sealed jar in the fridge for up to 5 days.

Per Serving:

calories: 219 | fat: 18g | protein: 10g | carbs: 5g | fiber: 4g | sodium: 224mg

Crispy Spiced Chickpeas

Prep time: 5 minutes | Cook time: 25 minutes |
Serves 6

3 cans (15 ounces / 425 g each) chickpeas, drained and rinsed
1 cup olive oil
1 teaspoon paprika
½ teaspoon ground cumin

½ teaspoon kosher salt
¼ teaspoon ground cinnamon
¼ teaspoon ground black pepper

1. Spread the chickpeas on paper towels and pat dry. 2. In a large saucepan over medium-high heat, warm the oil until shimmering. Add 1 chickpea; if it sizzles right away, the oil is hot enough to proceed. 3. Add enough chickpeas to form a single layer in the saucepan. Cook, occasionally gently shaking the saucepan until golden brown, about 8 minutes. With a slotted spoon, transfer to a paper towel–lined plate to drain. Repeat with the remaining chickpeas until all the chickpeas are fried. Transfer to a large bowl. 4. In a small bowl, combine the paprika, cumin, salt, cinnamon, and pepper. Sprinkle all over the fried chickpeas and toss to coat. The chickpeas will crisp as they cool.

Per Serving:

calories: 175 | fat: 9g | protein: 6g | carbs: 20g | fiber: 5g | sodium: 509mg

Cheesy Dates

Prep time: 15 minutes | Cook time: 10 minutes |
Serves 12 to 15

1 cup pecans, shells removed
1 (8-ounce / 227-g) container

mascarpone cheese
20 Medjool dates

1. Preheat the oven to 350°F(180ºC). Put the pecans on a baking sheet and bake for 5 to 6 minutes, until lightly toasted and aromatic. Take the pecans out of the oven and let cool for 5 minutes. 2. Once cooled, put the pecans in a food processor fitted with a chopping blade and chop until they resemble the texture of bulgur wheat or coarse sugar. 3. Reserve ¼ cup of ground pecans in a small bowl. Pour the remaining chopped pecans into a larger bowl and add the mascarpone cheese. 4. Using a spatula, mix the cheese with the pecans until evenly combined. 5. Spoon the cheese mixture into a piping bag. 6. Using a knife, cut one side of the date lengthwise, from the stem to the bottom. Gently open and remove the pit. 7. Using the piping bag, squeeze a generous amount of the cheese mixture into the date where the pit used to be. Close up the date and repeat with the remaining dates. 8. Dip any exposed cheese from the stuffed dates into the reserved chopped pecans to cover it up. 9. Set the dates on a serving plate; serve immediately or chill in the fridge until you are ready to serve.

Per Serving:

calories: 253 | fat: 4g | protein: 2g | carbs: 31g | fiber: 4g | sodium: 7mg

Bravas-Style Potatoes

Prep time: 15 minutes | Cook time: 50 minutes | Serves 8

4 large russet potatoes (about 2½ pounds / 1.1 kg), scrubbed and cut into 1' cubes
1 teaspoon kosher salt, divided
½ teaspoon ground black pepper
¼ teaspoon red-pepper flakes
½ small yellow onion, chopped
1 large tomato, chopped
1 tablespoon sherry vinegar
1 teaspoon hot paprika
1 tablespoon chopped fresh flat-leaf parsley Hot sauce (optional)

1. Preheat the oven to 450°F(235°C). Bring a large pot of well-salted water to a boil. 2. Boil the potatoes until just barely tender, 5 to 8 minutes. Drain and transfer the potatoes to a large rimmed baking sheet. Add 1 tablespoon of the oil, ½ teaspoon of the salt, the black pepper, and pepper flakes. With 2 large spoons, toss very well to coat the potatoes in the oil. Spread the potatoes out on the baking sheet. Roast until the bottoms are starting to brown and crisp, 20 minutes. Carefully flip the potatoes and roast until the other side is golden and crisp, 15 to 20 minutes. 3. Meanwhile, in a small skillet over medium heat, warm the remaining 1 teaspoon oil. Cook the onion until softened, 3 to 4 minutes. Add the tomato and cook until it's broken down and saucy, 5 minutes. Stir in the vinegar, paprika, and the remaining ½ teaspoon salt. Cook for 30 seconds, remove from the heat, and cover to keep warm. 4. Transfer the potatoes to a large serving bowl. Drizzle the tomato mixture over the potatoes. Sprinkle with the parsley. Serve with hot sauce, if using.

Per Serving:
calories: 173 | fat: 2g | protein: 4g | carbs: 35g | fiber: 3g | sodium: 251mg

Vegetable Pot Stickers

Prep time: 12 minutes | Cook time: 11 to 18 minutes | Makes 12 pot stickers

1 cup shredded red cabbage
¼ cup chopped button mushrooms
¼ cup grated carrot
2 tablespoons minced onion
2 garlic cloves, minced
2 teaspoons grated fresh ginger
12 gyoza/pot sticker wrappers
2½ teaspoons olive oil, divided

1. In a baking pan, combine the red cabbage, mushrooms, carrot, onion, garlic, and ginger. Add 1 tablespoon of water. Place in the air fryer and air fry at 370°F (188°C) for 3 to 6 minutes, until the vegetables are crisp-tender. Drain and set aside. 2. Working one at a time, place the pot sticker wrappers on a work surface. Top each wrapper with a scant 1 tablespoon of the filling. Fold half of the wrapper over the other half to form a half circle. Dab one edge with water and press both edges together. 3. To another pan, add 1¼ teaspoons of olive oil. Put half of the pot stickers, seam-side up, in the pan. Air fry for 5 minutes, or until the bottoms are light golden brown. Add 1 tablespoon of water and return the pan to the air fryer. 4. Air fry for 4 to 6 minutes more, or until hot. Repeat with the remaining pot stickers, remaining 1¼ teaspoons of oil, and another tablespoon of water. Serve immediately.

Per Serving:
1 pot stickers: calories: 36 | fat: 1g | protein: 1g | carbs: 6g | fiber: 0g | sodium: 49mg

Lemony Olives and Feta Medley

Prep time: 10 minutes | Cook time: 0 minutes | Serves 8

1 (1-pound / 454-g) block of Greek feta cheese
3 cups mixed olives (Kalamata and green), drained from brine; pitted preferred
¼ cup extra-virgin olive oil
3 tablespoons lemon juice
1 teaspoon grated lemon zest
1 teaspoon dried oregano
Pita bread, for serving

1. Cut the feta cheese into ½-inch squares and put them into a large bowl. 2. Add the olives to the feta and set aside. 3. In a small bowl, whisk together the olive oil, lemon juice, lemon zest, and oregano. 4. Pour the dressing over the feta cheese and olives and gently toss together to evenly coat everything. 5. Serve with pita bread.

Per Serving:
calories: 269 | fat: 24g | protein: 9g | carbs: 6g | fiber: 2g | sodium: 891mg

Shrimp and Chickpea Fritters

Prep time: 5 minutes | Cook time: 10 minutes | Serves 6

2 tablespoons olive oil, plus ¼ cup, divided
½ small yellow onion, finely chopped
12 ounces (340 g) raw medium shrimp, peeled, deveined, and finely chopped
¼ cup chickpea flour
2 tablespoon all-purpose flour
2 tablespoons roughly chopped parsley
1 teaspoon baking powder
½ teaspoon hot or sweet paprika
¾ teaspoon salt, plus additional to sprinkle over finished dish
½ lemon

1. Heat 2 tablespoons of the olive oil in a large skillet over medium-high heat. Add the onion and cook, stirring frequently, until softened, about 5 minutes. Using a slotted spoon, transfer the cooked onions to a medium bowl. Add the shrimp, chickpea flour, all-purpose flour, parsley, baking powder, paprika, and salt and mix well. Let sit for 10 minutes. 2. Heat the remaining ¼ cup olive oil in the same skillet set over medium-high heat. When the oil is very hot, add the batter, about 2 tablespoons at a time. Cook for about 2 minutes, until the bottom turns golden and the edges are crisp. Flip over and cook for another minute or two until the second side is golden and crisp. Drain on paper towels. Serve hot, with lemon squeezed over the top. Season with salt just before serving.

Per Serving:
calories: 148 | fat: 6g | protein: 15g | carbs: 9g | fiber: 3g | sodium: 435mg

Tirokafteri (Spicy Feta and Yogurt Dip)

Prep time: 10 minutes | Cook time: 0 minutes | Serves 8

1 teaspoon red wine vinegar
1 small green chili, seeded and sliced
2 teaspoons extra virgin olive

oil
9 ounces (255 g) full-fat feta
¾ cup full-fat Greek yogurt

1. Combine the vinegar, chili, and olive oil in a food processor. Blend until smooth. 2. In a small bowl, combine the feta and Greek yogurt, and use a fork to mash the ingredients until a paste is formed. Add the pepper mixture and stir until blended. 3. Cover and transfer to the refrigerator to chill for at least 1 hour before serving. Store covered in the refrigerator for up to 3 days.

Per Serving:

calories: 109 | fat: 8g | protein: 6g | carbs: 4g | fiber: 0g | sodium: 311mg

Mediterranean Trail Mix

Prep time: 5 minutes | Cook time: 0 minutes | Serves 6

1 cup roughly chopped unsalted walnuts
½ cup roughly chopped salted almonds

½ cup shelled salted pistachios
½ cup roughly chopped apricots
½ cup roughly chopped dates
⅓ cup dried figs, sliced in half

1. In a large zip-top bag, combine the walnuts, almonds, pistachios, apricots, dates, and figs and mix well.

Per Serving:

calories: 348 | fat: 24g | protein: 9g | carbs: 33g | fiber: 7g | sodium: 95mg

Marinated Olives and Mushrooms

Prep time: 10 minutes | Cook time: 0 minutes | Serves 8

1 pound (454 g) white button mushrooms
1 pound (454 g) mixed, high-quality olives
2 tablespoons fresh thyme leaves
1 tablespoon white wine

vinegar
½ tablespoon crushed fennel seeds
Pinch chili flakes
Olive oil, to cover
Sea salt and freshly ground pepper, to taste

1. Clean and rinse mushrooms under cold water and pat dry. 2. Combine all ingredients in a glass jar or other airtight container. Cover with olive oil and season with sea salt and freshly ground pepper. 3. Shake to distribute the ingredients. Allow to marinate for at least 1 hour. Serve at room temperature.

Per Serving:

calories: 61 | fat: 4g | protein: 2g | carbs: 5g | fiber: 2g | sodium: 420mg

Flatbread with Ricotta and Orange-Raisin Relish

Prep time: 5 minutes | Cook time: 8 minutes | Serves 4 to 6

¾ cup golden raisins, roughly chopped
1 shallot, finely diced
1 tablespoon olive oil
1 tablespoon red wine vinegar
1 tablespoon honey
1 tablespoon chopped flat-leaf parsley
1 tablespoon fresh orange zest

strips
Pinch of salt
1 oval prebaked whole-wheat flatbread, such as naan or pocketless pita
8 ounces (227 g) whole-milk ricotta cheese
½ cup baby arugula

1. Preheat the oven to 450°F(235°C). 2. In a small bowl, stir together the raisins, shallot, olive oil, vinegar, honey, parsley, orange zest, and salt. 3. Place the flatbread on a large baking sheet and toast in the preheated oven until the edges are lightly browned, about 8 minutes. 4. Spoon the ricotta cheese onto the flatbread, spreading with the back of the spoon. Scatter the arugula over the cheese. Cut the flatbread into triangles and top each piece with a dollop of the relish. Serve immediately.

Per Serving:

calories: 195 | fat: 9g | protein: 6g | carbs: 25g | fiber: 1g | sodium: 135mg

Warm Olives with Rosemary and Garlic

Prep time: 5 minutes | Cook time: 3 minutes | Serves 4

1 tablespoon olive oil
1 clove garlic, chopped
2 sprigs fresh rosemary

¼ teaspoon salt
1 cup whole cured black olives, such as Kalamata

1. Heat the olive oil in a medium saucepan over medium heat. Add the garlic, rosemary, and salt. Reduce the heat to low and cook, stirring, for 1 minute. 2. Add the olives and cook, stirring occasionally, for about 2 minutes, until the olives are warm. 3. To serve, scoop the olives from the pan using a slotted spoon into a serving bowl. Pour the rosemary and garlic over the olives and serve warm.

Per Serving:

calories: 71 | fat: 7g | protein: 1g | carbs: 3g | fiber: 1g | sodium: 441mg

Savory Mediterranean Popcorn

Prep time: 5 minutes | Cook time: 2 minutes | Serves 4 to 6

3 tablespoons extra-virgin olive oil
¼ teaspoon garlic powder
¼ teaspoon freshly ground black pepper
¼ teaspoon sea salt

⅛ teaspoon dried thyme
⅛ teaspoon dried oregano
12 cups plain popped popcorn

1. In a large sauté pan or skillet, heat the oil over medium heat, until shimmering, and then add the garlic powder, pepper, salt, thyme, and oregano until fragrant. 2. In a large bowl, drizzle the oil over the popcorn, toss, and serve.

Per Serving:

calories: 183 | fat: 12g | protein: 3g | carbs: 19g | fiber: 4g | sodium: 146mg

Chapter 15 Staples, Sauces, Dips, and Dressings

Kidney Bean Dip with Cilantro, Cumin, and Lime

Prep time: 10 minutes | Cook time: 30 minutes | Serves 16

1 cup dried kidney beans, soaked overnight and drained
4 cups water
3 cloves garlic, peeled and crushed
¼ cup roughly chopped

cilantro, divided
¼ cup extra-virgin olive oil
1 tablespoon lime juice
2 teaspoons grated lime zest
1 teaspoon ground cumin
½ teaspoon salt

1. Place beans, water, garlic, and 2 tablespoons cilantro in the Instant Pot®. Close the lid, set steam release to Sealing, press the Bean button, and cook for the default time of 30 minutes. 2. When the timer beeps, let pressure release naturally, about 20 minutes. Press the Cancel button, open lid, and check that beans are tender. Drain off excess water and transfer beans to a medium bowl. Gently mash beans with potato masher or fork until beans are mashed but chunky. Add oil, lime juice, lime zest, cumin, salt, and remaining 2 tablespoons cilantro and stir to combine. Serve warm or at room temperature.

Per Serving:
calories: 65 | fat: 3g | protein: 2g | carbs: 7g | fiber: 2g | sodium: 75mg

Roasted Harissa

Prep time: 5 minutes | Cook time: 15 minutes | Makes ¾ cup

1 red bell pepper
2 small fresh red chiles, or more to taste
4 garlic cloves, unpeeled
½ teaspoon ground coriander

½ teaspoon ground cumin
½ teaspoon ground caraway
1 tablespoon fresh lemon juice
½ teaspoon salt

1. Preheat the broiler to high. 2. Put the bell pepper, chiles, and garlic on a baking sheet and broil for 6 to 8 minutes. Turn the vegetables over and broil for 5 to 6 minutes more, until the pepper and chiles are softened and blackened. Remove from the broiler and set aside until cool enough to handle. Remove and discard the stems, skin, and seeds from the pepper and chiles. Remove and discard the papery skin from the garlic. 3. Put the flesh of the pepper and chiles with the garlic cloves in a blender or food processor. Add the coriander, cumin, caraway, lemon juice, and salt and blend until smooth. 4. This may be stored refrigerated for up to 3 days. Store in an airtight container, and cover the sauce with a ¼-inch layer of oil.

Per Serving:
calories: 28 | fat: 0g | protein: 1g | carbs: 6g | fiber: 1g | sodium: 393mg

Chickpea, Parsley, and Dill Dip

Prep time: 5 minutes | Cook time: 21 minutes | Makes 2 cups

8 cups plus 2 tablespoons water, divided
1 cup dried chickpeas
3 tablespoons olive oil, divided
2 garlic cloves, peeled and minced

2 tablespoons chopped fresh parsley
2 tablespoons chopped fresh dill
1 tablespoon lemon juice
¼ teaspoon salt

1. Add 4 cups water and chickpeas to the Instant Pot®. Close lid, set steam release to Sealing, press the Manual button, and set time to 1 minute. When the timer beeps, quick-release the pressure until the float valve drops, press the Cancel button, and open lid. 2. Drain water, rinse chickpeas, and return to pot with 4 cups fresh water. Set aside to soak for 1 hour. 3. Add 1 tablespoon oil to pot. Close lid, set steam release to Sealing, press the Manual button, and set time to 20 minutes. When the timer beeps, let pressure release naturally, about 20 minutes. Press the Cancel button, open lid, and drain chickpeas. 4. Transfer chickpeas to a food processor or blender, and add garlic, parsley, dill, lemon juice, and remaining 2 tablespoons water. Blend for about 30 seconds. 5. With the processor or blender lid still in place, slowly add remaining 2 tablespoons oil while still blending, then add salt. Serve warm or at room temperature.

Per Serving:
2 tablespoons: calories: 76 | fat: 4g | protein: 2g | carbs: 8g | fiber: 2g | sodium: 44mg

Cider Yogurt Dressing

Prep time: 5 minutes | Cook time: 0 minutes | Serves 2

1 cup plain, unsweetened, full-fat Greek yogurt
½ cup extra-virgin olive oil
1 tablespoon apple cider vinegar
½ lemon, juiced
1 tablespoon chopped fresh

oregano
½ teaspoon dried parsley
½ teaspoon kosher salt
¼ teaspoon garlic powder
¼ teaspoon freshly ground black pepper

1. In a large bowl, combine the yogurt, olive oil, vinegar, lemon juice, oregano, parsley, salt, garlic powder, and pepper and whisk well.

Per Serving:

calories: 402 | fat: 40g | protein: 8g | carbs: 4g | fiber: 1g | sodium: 417mg

Herbed Oil

Prep time: 5 minutes | Cook time: 0 minutes | Serves 2

½ cup extra-virgin olive oil
1 teaspoon dried basil
1 teaspoon dried parsley
1 teaspoon fresh rosemary

leaves
2 teaspoons dried oregano
⅛ teaspoon salt

1. Pour the oil into a small bowl and stir in the basil, parsley, rosemary, oregano, and salt while whisking the oil with a fork.

Per Serving:

calories: 486 | fat: 54g | protein: 1g | carbs: 2g | fiber: 1g | sodium: 78mg

Pepper Sauce

Prep time: 10 minutes | Cook time: 20 minutes | Makes 4 cups

2 red hot fresh chiles, seeded
2 dried chiles
½ small yellow onion, roughly chopped

2 garlic cloves, peeled
2 cups water
2 cups white vinegar

1. In a medium saucepan, combine the fresh and dried chiles, onion, garlic, and water. Bring to a simmer and cook for 20 minutes, or until tender. Transfer to a food processor or blender. 2. Add the vinegar and blend until smooth.

Per Serving:

1 cup: calories: 41 | fat: 0g | protein: 1g | carbs: 5g | fiber: 1g | sodium: 11mg

Tahini Sauce

Prep time: 5 minutes | Cook time: 0 minutes | Makes about 1 cup

½ cup tahini
½ cup water

¼ cup lemon juice (2 lemons)
2 garlic cloves, minced

1. Whisk all ingredients in bowl until smooth (mixture will appear broken at first). Season with salt and pepper to taste. Let sit at room temperature for at least 30 minutes to allow flavors to meld. (Sauce can be refrigerated for up to 4 days; bring to room temperature before serving.)

Per Serving:

¼ cup: calories: 184 | fat: 16g | protein: 5g | carbs: 8g | fiber: 3g | sodium: 36mg

Pickled Turnips

Prep time: 5 minutes | Cook time: 0 minutes | Serves 2

1 pound (454 g) turnips, washed well, peeled, and cut into 1-inch batons
1 small beet, roasted, peeled, and cut into 1-inch batons
2 garlic cloves, smashed

1 teaspoon dried Turkish oregano
3 cups warm water
½ cup red wine vinegar
½ cup white vinegar

1. In a jar, combine the turnips, beet, garlic, and oregano. Pour the water and vinegars over the vegetables, cover, then shake well and put it in the refrigerator. The turnips will be pickled after 1 hour.

Per Serving:

calories: 3 | fat: 0g | protein: 1g | carbs: 0g | fiber: 0g | sodium: 6mg

Piri Piri Sauce

Prep time: 5 minutes | Cook time: 0 minutes | Makes about 1 cup

4 to 8 fresh hot, red chiles, stemmed and coarsely chopped
2 cloves garlic, minced

Juice of 1 lemon
Pinch of salt
½ to 1 cup olive oil

1. In a food processor, combine the chiles (with their seeds), garlic, lemon juice, salt, and ½ cup of olive oil. Process to a smooth purée. Add additional oil as needed to reach the desired consistency. 2. Pour the mixture into a glass jar or non-reactive bowl, cover, and refrigerate for at least 3 days before using. Store in the refrigerator for up to a month.

Per Serving:

calories:84 | fat: 10g | protein: 0g | carbs: 0g | fiber: 0g | sodium: 13mg

Green Olive Tapenade with Harissa

Prep time: 5 minutes | Cook time: 0 minutes | Makes about 1½ cups

1 cup pitted, cured green olives
1 clove garlic, minced
1 tablespoon harissa
1 tablespoon lemon juice
1 tablespoon chopped fresh parsley
¼ cup olive oil, or more to taste

1. Finely chop the olives (or pulse them in a food processor until they resemble a chunky paste). 2. Add the garlic, harissa, lemon juice, parsley, and olive oil and stir or pulse to combine well.

Per Serving:

¼ cup: calories: 215 | fat: 23g | protein: 1g | carbs: 5g | fiber: 2g | sodium: 453mg

Herbed Butter

Prep time: 10 minutes | Cook time: 0 minutes | Makes ½ cup

½ cup (1 stick) butter, at room temperature
1 garlic clove, finely minced
2 teaspoons finely chopped
fresh rosemary
1 teaspoon finely chopped fresh oregano
½ teaspoon salt

1. In a food processor, combine the butter, garlic, rosemary, oregano, and salt and pulse until the mixture is well combined, smooth, and creamy, scraping down the sides as necessary. Alternatively, you can whip the ingredients together with an electric mixer. 2. Using a spatula, scrape the butter mixture into a small bowl or glass container and cover. Store in the refrigerator for up to 1 month.

Per Serving:

⅛ cup: calories: 206 | fat: 23g | protein: 0g | carbs: 206g | fiber: 0g | sodium: 294mg

Red Pepper Hummus

Prep time: 5 minutes | Cook time: 30 minutes | Makes 2 cups

1 cup dried chickpeas
4 cups water
1 tablespoon plus ¼ cup extra-virgin olive oil, divided
½ cup chopped roasted red pepper, divided
⅓ cup tahini
1 teaspoon ground cumin
¾ teaspoon salt
½ teaspoon ground black pepper
¼ teaspoon smoked paprika
⅓ cup lemon juice
½ teaspoon minced garlic

1. Place chickpeas, water, and 1 tablespoon oil in the Instant Pot®. Close the lid, set steam release to Sealing, press the Manual button, and set time to 30 minutes. 2. When the timer beeps, quick-release the pressure until the float valve drops. Press the Cancel button and open lid. Drain, reserving the cooking liquid. 3. Place chickpeas, ⅓ cup roasted red pepper, remaining ¼ cup oil, tahini, cumin, salt, black pepper, paprika, lemon juice, and garlic in a food processor and process until creamy. If hummus is too thick, add reserved cooking liquid 1 tablespoon at a time until it reaches desired consistency. Serve at room temperature, garnished with reserved roasted red pepper on top.

Per Serving:

2 tablespoons: calories: 96 | fat: 8g | protein: 2g | carbs: 10g | fiber: 4g | sodium: 122mg

White Bean Dip with Garlic and Herbs

Prep time: 10 minutes | Cook time: 30 minutes | Serves 16

1 cup dried white beans, rinsed and drained
3 cloves garlic, peeled and crushed
8 cups water
¼ cup extra-virgin olive oil
¼ cup chopped fresh flat-leaf parsley
1 tablespoon chopped fresh
oregano
1 tablespoon chopped fresh tarragon
1 teaspoon chopped fresh thyme leaves
1 teaspoon grated lemon zest
¼ teaspoon salt
¼ teaspoon ground black pepper

1. Place beans and garlic in the Instant Pot® and stir well. Add water, close lid, set steam release to Sealing, press the Manual button, and set time to 30 minutes. 2. When the timer beeps, let pressure release naturally, about 20 minutes. Open lid and check that beans are tender. Press the Cancel button, drain off excess water, and transfer beans and garlic to a food processor with olive oil. Pulse until mixture is smooth with some small chunks. Add parsley, oregano, tarragon, thyme, lemon zest, salt, and pepper, and pulse 3 to 5 times to mix. Transfer to a storage container and refrigerate for 4.hours or overnight. Serve cold or at room temperature.

Per Serving:

calories: 47 | fat: 3g | protein: 1g | carbs: 3g | fiber: 1g | sodium: 38mg

Apple Cider Dressing

Prep time: 5 minutes | Cook time: 0 minutes | Serves 2

2 tablespoons apple cider vinegar
⅓ lemon, juiced
⅓ lemon, zested
Salt and freshly ground black pepper, to taste

1. In a jar, combine the vinegar, lemon juice, and zest. Season with salt and pepper, cover, and shake well.

Per Serving:

calories: 7 | fat: 0g | protein: 0g | carbs: 1g | fiber: 0g | sodium: 1mg

Spicy Cucumber Dressing

Prep time: 5 minutes | Cook time: 0 minutes | Serves 2

1½ cups plain, unsweetened, full-fat Greek yogurt
1 cucumber, seeded and peeled
½ lemon, juiced and zested
1 tablespoon dried, minced garlic
½ tablespoon dried dill
2 teaspoons dried oregano
Salt

1. In a food processor, combine the yogurt, cucumber, lemon juice, garlic, dill, oregano, and a pinch of salt and process until smooth. Adjust the seasonings as needed and transfer to a serving bowl.

Per Serving:
calories: 209 | fat: 10g | protein: 18g | carbs: 14g | fiber: 2g | sodium: 69mg

Garlic-Rosemary Infused Olive Oil

Prep time: 5 minutes | Cook time: 45 minutes | Makes 1 cup

1 cup extra-virgin olive oil
4 large garlic cloves, smashed
4 (4- to 5-inch) sprigs rosemary

1. In a medium skillet, heat the olive oil, garlic, and rosemary sprigs over low heat. Cook until fragrant and garlic is very tender, 30 to 45 minutes, stirring occasionally. Don't let the oil get too hot or the garlic will burn and become bitter. 2. Remove from the heat and allow to cool slightly. Remove the garlic and rosemary with a slotted spoon and pour the oil into a glass container. Allow to cool completely before covering. Store covered at room temperature for up to 3 months.

Per Serving:
⅛ cup: calories: 241 | fat: 27g | protein: 0g | carbs: 1g | fiber: 0g | sodium: 1mg

Melitzanosalata (Greek Eggplant Dip)

Prep time: 10 minutes | Cook time: 3 minutes | Serves 8

1 cup water
1 large eggplant, peeled and chopped
1 clove garlic, peeled
½ teaspoon salt
1 tablespoon red wine vinegar
½ cup extra-virgin olive oil
2 tablespoons minced fresh parsley

1. Add water to the Instant Pot®, add the rack to the pot, and place the steamer basket on the rack. 2. Place eggplant in steamer basket. Close lid, set steam release to Sealing, press the Manual button, and set time to 3 minutes. When the timer beeps, quick-release the pressure until the float valve drops. Press the Cancel button and open lid. 3. Transfer eggplant to a food processor and add garlic, salt, and vinegar. Pulse until smooth, about 20 pulses. 4. Slowly add oil to the eggplant mixture while the food processor runs continuously until oil is completely incorporated. Stir in parsley. Serve at room temperature.

Per Serving:
calories: 134 | fat: 14g | protein: 1g | carbs: 3g | fiber: 2g | sodium: 149mg

White Bean Hummus

Prep time: 10 minutes | Cook time: 30 minutes | Serves 12

⅔ cup dried white beans, rinsed and drained
3 cloves garlic, peeled and crushed
¼ cup olive oil
1 tablespoon lemon juice
½ teaspoon salt

1. Place beans and garlic in the Instant Pot® and stir well. Add enough cold water to cover ingredients. Close lid, set steam release to Sealing, press the Manual button, and set time to 30 minutes. 2. When the timer beeps, let pressure release naturally, about 20 minutes. Press the Cancel button and open lid. Use a fork to check that beans are tender. Drain off excess water and transfer beans to a food processor. 3. Add oil, lemon juice, and salt to the processor and pulse until mixture is smooth with some small chunks. Transfer to a storage container and refrigerate for at least 4 hours. Serve cold or at room temperature. Store in the refrigerator for up to one week.

Per Serving:
calories: 57 | fat: 5g | protein: 1g | carbs: 3g | fiber: 1g | sodium: 99mg

Riced Cauliflower

Prep time: 5 minutes | Cook time: 10 minutes | Serves 6 to 8

1 small head cauliflower, broken into florets
¼ cup extra-virgin olive oil
2 garlic cloves, finely minced
1½ teaspoons salt
½ teaspoon freshly ground black pepper

1. Place the florets in a food processor and pulse several times, until the cauliflower is the consistency of rice or couscous. 2. In a large skillet, heat the olive oil over medium-high heat. Add the cauliflower, garlic, salt, and pepper and sauté for 5 minutes, just to take the crunch out but not enough to let the cauliflower become soggy. 3. Remove the cauliflower from the skillet and place in a bowl until ready to use. Toss with chopped herbs and additional olive oil for a simple side, top with sautéed veggies and protein, or use in your favorite recipe.

Per Serving:
calories: 69 | fat: 7g | protein: 1g | carbs: 2g | fiber: 1g | sodium: 446mg

Crunchy Yogurt Dip

Prep time: 5 minutes | Cook time: 0 minutes | Serves 2 to 3

1 cup plain, unsweetened, full-fat Greek yogurt
½ cup cucumber, peeled, seeded, and diced
1 tablespoon freshly squeezed lemon juice
1 tablespoon chopped fresh mint

1 small garlic clove, minced
Salt
Freshly ground black pepper

1. In a food processor, combine the yogurt, cucumber, lemon juice, mint, and garlic. Pulse several times to combine, leaving noticeable cucumber chunks. 2. Taste and season with salt and pepper.

Per Serving:

calories: 128 | fat: 6g | protein: 11g | carbs: 7g | fiber: 0g | sodium: 47mg

Appendix 1: Measurement Conversion Chart

MEASUREMENT CONVERSION CHART

VOLUME EQUIVALENTS(DRY)

US STANDARD	METRIC (APPROXIMATE)
1/8 teaspoon	0.5 mL
1/4 teaspoon	1 mL
1/2 teaspoon	2 mL
3/4 teaspoon	4 mL
1 teaspoon	5 mL
1 tablespoon	15 mL
1/4 cup	59 mL
1/2 cup	118 mL
3/4 cup	177 mL
1 cup	235 mL
2 cups	475 mL
3 cups	700 mL
4 cups	1 L

VOLUME EQUIVALENTS(LIQUID)

US STANDARD	US STANDARD (OUNCES)	METRIC (APPROXIMATE)
2 tablespoons	1 fl.oz.	30 mL
1/4 cup	2 fl.oz.	60 mL
1/2 cup	4 fl.oz.	120 mL
1 cup	8 fl.oz.	240 mL
1 1/2 cup	12 fl.oz.	355 mL
2 cups or 1 pint	16 fl.oz.	475 mL
4 cups or 1 quart	32 fl.oz.	1 L
1 gallon	128 fl.oz.	4 L

TEMPERATURES EQUIVALENTS

FAHRENHEIT(F)	CELSIUS(C) (APPROXIMATE)
225 °F	107 °C
250 °F	120 °C
275 °F	135 °C
300 °F	150 °C
325 °F	160 °C
350 °F	180 °C
375 °F	190 °C
400 °F	205 °C
425 °F	220 °C
450 °F	235 °C
475 °F	245 °C
500 °F	260 °C

WEIGHT EQUIVALENTS

US STANDARD	METRIC (APPROXIMATE)
1 ounce	28 g
2 ounces	57 g
5 ounces	142 g
10 ounces	284 g
15 ounces	425 g
16 ounces (1 pound)	455 g
1.5 pounds	680 g
2 pounds	907 g

Appendix 2: The Dirty Dozen and Clean Fifteen

The Dirty Dozen and Clean Fifteen

The Environmental Working Group (EWG) is a nonprofit, nonpartisan organization dedicated to protecting human health and the environment Its mission is to empower people to live healthier lives in a healthier environment. This organization publishes an annual list of the twelve kinds of produce, in sequence, that have the highest amount of pesticide residue-the Dirty Dozen-as well as a list of the fifteen kinds ofproduce that have the least amount of pesticide residue-the Clean Fifteen.

THE DIRTY DOZEN	THE CLEAN FIFTEEN
• The 2016 Dirty Dozen includes the following produce. These are considered among the year's most important produce to buy organic:	• The least critical to buy organically are the Clean Fifteen list. The following are on the 2016 list:

THE DIRTY DOZEN		THE CLEAN FIFTEEN	
Strawberries	Spinach	Avocados	Papayas
Apples	Tomatoes	Corn	Kiw
Nectarines	Bell peppers	Pineapples	Eggplant
Peaches	Cherry tomatoes	Cabbage	Honeydew
Celery	Cucumbers	Sweet peas	Grapefruit
Grapes	Kale/collard greens	Onions	Cantaloupe
Cherries	Hot peppers	Asparagus	Cauliflower
		Mangos	

• *The Dirty Dozen list contains two additional itemskale/collard greens and hot peppers-because they tend to contain trace levels of highly hazardous pesticides.*

• *Some of the sweet corn sold in the United States are made from genetically engineered (GE) seedstock. Buy organic varieties of these crops to avoid GE produce.*

Printed in Great Britain
by Amazon

27605951R00066